Understanding and Supporting
Children with Literacy Difficulties

Understanding and Supporting Children with Literacy Difficulties

An Evidence-Based Guide for Practitioners

Dr Valerie Muter

Foreword by Professor Margaret Snowling

Jessica Kingsley Publishers
London and Philadelphia

First published in Great Britain in 2021 by Jessica Kingsley Publishers
An Hachette Company

1

Copyright © Dr Valerie Muter 2021
Foreword copyright © Professor Margaret Snowling 2021

Front cover image sources: Shutterstock®.

A CIP catalogue record for this title is available from
the British Library and the Library of Congress

ISBN 978 1 78775 057 9
eISBN 978 1 78775 058 6

Printed and bound in Great Britain by TJ Books Ltd

Jessica Kingsley Publishers' policy is to use papers that are natural,
renewable and recyclable products and made from wood grown in
sustainable forests. The logging and manufacturing processes are expected
to conform to the environmental regulations of the country of origin.

Jessica Kingsley Publishers
Carmelite House
50 Victoria Embankment
London EC4Y 0DZ

www.jkp.com

MIX
Paper from
responsible sources
FSC® C013056

Dedicated to my brother

Brian Muter

Without his full-time care for our mother during her final years this book could not have been written.

Contents

Acknowledgements

I have for a number of years wanted to write a 'swan song' book in which I hoped to share with practitioners what I have learned from more than 30 years of clinical practice and research experience. This was made possible when at a conference in 2018, Amy Lankester-Owen of Jessica Kingsley Publishers, having attended a workshop I had given, approached me to ask if I would consider writing such a book. I very much wanted this book to reflect both my academic and practitioner interests within the field of literacy disorders. Indeed, it has long been my view that that the academic and practitioner strands in this field can and should inform each other's development.

I would first like to thank Professor Margaret Snowling who made invaluable suggestions when I was first planning the format and content of my book. Amy Lankester-Owen offered helpful guidance as I worked my way through the first few chapters. On the book's completion, Dr Jasmin Aquan Assee, a clinical psychologist colleague, and Dr Kevin Smith, an experienced literacy teacher and Professional Development Co-ordinator of the Professional Association of Teachers of Specific Learning Difficulties, PATOSS, read through the entire text; I am very grateful for their many helpful suggestions which informed a revision that I feel greatly improved the book. Special thanks are extended to Dr Susan Harrison who was able to guide me through practitioner issues within the field of educational psychology. Finally, the recommendations made by an anonymous external reviewer were much appreciated as I made the final refinements.

I am grateful to David Chamberlain who, as well as drawing

Figure 3.1, provided much morale-boosting support over the 18 months it took me to write the book.

I should like to thank my research and writing collaborators including Professor Margaret Snowling, Professor Charles Hulme and Dr Helen Likierman. And lastly, a special thanks must go to the many hundreds (possibly thousands) of children I have worked with clinically or who have participated in my research studies and who have informed my knowledge of literacy disorders.

Foreword

In this book, Valerie Muter provides an up-to-date, accessible overview of current research on the development of reading and uses this to frame advice on the assessment and management of children with disorders of language and literacy. Drawing on her many years of clinical experience, she provides valuable insights into how research can shape practice and how it needs to be adapted for the individual child and their family, whether in the clinic or school setting. The book begins by explaining our current understanding of the reading process and how children learn to read for meaning.

Valerie Muter then proceeds to consider how reading (and spelling) development may fail and what the obstacles are to successful acquisition. Emphasizing the importance of longitudinal evidence, she discusses the multiple risk factors that can accumulate to lead to a diagnosis of reading disorder (dyslexia) as well as the hypothesized protective factors that promote successful compensation for underlying weaknesses. These may be biological, cognitive, environmental and/or temperamental. In so doing, she does not shy away from the complexity of the interaction of reading deficits with symptoms associated with co-occurring disorders, such as mathematics disorder (dyscalculia) or attention deficit hyperactivity disorder (ADHD). Nor does she shy away from issues that surround terminology in this field – SpLD, dyslexia or reading disorder – the name is less important than an understanding that we are talking of 'dimensional disorders' that occur on a continuum. It is for the clinician to formulate not a 'diagnosis' but a diagnostic profile which can only be achieved after careful hypothesis-led assessment that, in turn, will have implications for treatment.

It is with regard to assessment that Valerie Muter's experience, not only in the clinic but in training professionals, comes to the fore in what is a clear exposition of not only the core components of an assessment but also how to decide on the tests to be used to probe a possible weakness. She illustrates this process through a series of carefully crafted case studies which take the reader well beyond the traditional 'classic' dyslexic child to embrace children with a range of language learning difficulties and co-occurring disorders. Finally, Muter provides an overview of current interventions, emphasizing the need for an evidence-based approach to the choice of treatments and, where evidence is lacking, the need to follow best practice. The book closes by addressing the important contemporary issues of children learning in a second language and prematurity.

The ability to translate theory into practice is a rare skill that shines through the pages of this excellent guide. It is highly recommended to professionals, practitioners and interested parents who wish to understand how best to prevent, ameliorate and compensate for the difficulties associated with language and literacy disorders in the school-age child and it has much to say that is relevant to other learning disorders as well.

Professor Margaret Snowling CBE, FBA, FMed Sci., Oxford

Introduction

Why is learning to read so important? Arguably, it is the single most important educational challenge a child faces during their first two to three years of school life. The child who experiences early success in learning to read will usually develop a positive attitude to reading and academic learning that stretches well into adulthood. Conversely, children who struggle to learn to read are at risk of educational failure that can have lifelong consequences in terms of restricting their job opportunities and even impacting their behavioural and social adjustment. With substantial numbers of children experiencing literacy difficulties, it is not surprising that there is wide interest, and indeed concern, as to how best to support and manage these children.

Having had a career of more than 30 years spent in the field of cognitive developmental neuropsychology, I wanted to share with other professionals what I have learned from both my research and my clinical practice. My research has explored the early stages of typical literacy development and I have also carried out studies that have addressed the core learning difficulties experienced by children with literacy disorders. Fifteen years of working as a consultant neuropsychologist at Great Ormond St Hospital for Children has provided me with a unique opportunity to work with children whose literacy difficulties arise from a range of underlying conditions, some developmental (like dyslexia and language disorders) and others of neurological origin (such as focal brain injury and extreme prematurity).

This book is intended as a practical guide for those working with children who have literacy problems, in particular practising educational psychologists, clinical psychologists and cognitive developmental neuropsychologists, speech and language therapists, special needs teachers, literacy tutors, and classroom teachers with a special interest in literacy. While the intention is for the book to be strongly grounded in theory and research, there is no attempt to provide an exhaustive review of academic papers in reading development and literacy disorder, but rather to focus on key studies whose findings have direct relevance for a practitioner readership.

A main feature of the book is a series of six case studies that illustrate key concepts, and which also provide examples of good practice in assessment and intervention. I have drawn on my many years' experience as a practising child psychologist to create cases which are an amalgam of children that I have personally assessed. The cases are introduced in the early chapters of the book when key concepts and issues are described and then revisited in the later chapters that address assessment, diagnostic formulation and intervention/management. This book focuses only on children with literacy disorders, not older adolescents or adults. I will address issues that are of relevance to older children only up to the age of 16 years, but not beyond; consequently, higher order study skills that are relevant to tertiary level education, disability student allowance and so on will not be covered other than in passing – the reader will need to source information relating to these domains elsewhere.

The first chapter describes how the typical child learns to read. It is hard to appreciate the underlying difficulties facing the child with a literacy disorder unless we have a good understanding of the skills that are needed for reading to progress normally. A strong emphasis will be placed on my own research into the cognitive (i.e. learning) processes that contribute to the development of word level reading skills (in particular the early stages), and especially the important role played by language skills and phonology. Non-cognitive factors that impact reading development (including cultural influences such as socioeconomic status and parental input) will also be considered. The specific language in which the child learns to read is relevant in its own right and in relation to the later chapter on multilingualism and literacy disorders. We will look at a simplified explanation of computer-based connectionist models that explain the process of learning to read. Finally, the skills needed to develop reading comprehension will be described.

Chapter 2 shifts to addressing what happens when literacy development fails to proceed normally, that is, the difficulties faced by children who have either word level reading and spelling problems (dyslexia) or reading comprehension disorders. We will start with an appraisal of definitions of dyslexia, including controversies around terminology, and in particular the recent challenge posed by Julian Elliott and Elena Grigorenko in their book *The Dyslexia Debate* (2014). This is followed by a brief look at dyslexia's genetic and neurological bases. A major focus will be on evidence that demonstrates that phonological deficits are causally related to dyslexia, and specifically on how these impair children's ability to decode print (the phonological deficit model of dyslexia). Literacy disorders may present differently at different ages, hence the importance of taking a longitudinal perspective and charting the development of reading skills over the course of childhood. A long-term 'at risk' study of dyslexia will be described and its implications for practice discussed in this and subsequent chapters. Finally, there is an analysis of the nature of reading comprehension difficulties, and in particular how these relate to underlying language problems.

Chapter 3 begins with an explanation of why the phonological deficit model of dyslexia described in the previous chapter does not on its own adequately explain the dimensional nature of this disorder and the considerable individual variation that we see. Rather, we recognize the need for a shift from this single deficit perspective to what is termed a multiple deficit model in which a range of 'risk' and protective factors influence presentation and outcome (including environmental influences that moderate risk). The first in the series of six case studies is introduced, specifically one which provides a longitudinal perspective of a child with early language delay who goes on to experience significant word level reading and also comprehension difficulties. Chapter 4 continues the risk theme, looking at 'shared' and 'non-shared' (biological and cognitive) risk factors that explain why dyslexia commonly co-occurs alongside other learning disorders. Three further case studies are introduced that illustrate dyslexia co-occurring with maths problems (dyscalculia), attention problems and visual motor difficulties.

Chapters 5 and 6 address the important practitioner theme of assessing children presenting with literacy disorders. Chapter 5 begins by providing a framework for assessing the child with literacy difficulties within the context of multi-dimensional causal models. Specific issues will be addressed, including the relevance (or not) of IQ/ability testing; the importance of assessing at both the cognitive (phonological/language) and educational (reading/spelling) levels; a description of tests that are available to teachers as well as psychologists; and how to interpret test results and develop diagnostic formulations. Predicting outcome in a meaningful way is a challenge for assessors; we look at 'moderator variables', some of which are inherent in the child and some environmentally based, that influence outcome. Case Study 1 will be revisited as an example of assessing a literacy disorder in the context of early language delay. Chapter 6 begins by re-emphasizing that the majority of children presenting with a literacy problem will have at least one co-occurring (or accompanying) learning difficulty. This highlights the likely need for 'hypothesis driven testing' in which the assessor draws on existing test results, concerns of parents and teachers, and behavioural observations to determine whether further testing is needed to identify the presence of additional learning problems. Specific tests to assess maths, attention, and visual motor problems are described, which might include checklists and questionnaires for when testing time and resources are limited. The interpretation of the test results and the resultant formulation for what is often a 'tricky' diagnostic profile follows. Case Studies 2 to 4 are revisited within this assessment context, and formulations provided.

Chapters 7 and 8 address intervention and beyond for children with literacy disorders. Chapter 7 emphasizes the importance of interventions that are both theoretically motivated and scientifically proven through randomized controlled trials (RCTs). Following a discussion of the RCT criteria that need to be employed to guarantee that an intervention does what it claims, an example of a strong cognitive/behavioural based reading intervention study is described in some depth. Interventions that target cognitive and educational levels are discussed; these include phonological awareness training, phonic decoding programmes, and morphemic approaches to teaching spelling. Literacy and language programmes that can be delivered effectively by supervised teaching assistants demonstrate that children's literacy difficulties can be addressed even when financial and specialist resources are limited. Alternative (biologically based) interventions such as dietary approaches, motor-based therapies and tinted lenses are also (critically) evaluated. Finally, interventions for addressing reading comprehension difficulties are described. Case Study 1 is revisited as an example of employing language-, phonological- and phonic-based approaches to literacy intervention when both word level and reading comprehension difficulties need to be addressed. Chapter 8 revisits the multi-dimensional theme by looking at interventions for children who have co-occurring difficulties, including treatment approaches that address attention problems, maths difficulties and visual motor problems. We will return to Case Studies 2 to 4 to provide examples of additional interventions that target co-occurring difficulties. Broader school- and home-based management strategies are also addressed; these include accommodations within the classroom and for written tests and examinations, how parents can support their child, the use of technology (including laptops and Dictaphones), and accessing specialist assessment routes such as education, health and care (EHC) plans for children who have severe and complex difficulties.

Multilingualism, the topic of Chapter 9, is an example of a sociocultural (environmental) risk factor that is experienced by large numbers of children and which can provide challenges for practitioners assessing and teaching children who have more than one language. This chapter begins by looking at cross-linguistic studies which have compared predictor measures of literacy in different languages. We then see if using already available measures of phonological processing can predict ease of learning to read in children who have exposure to multiple languages. The research studies of Esther Geva with immigrant children in

Canada have enabled a better understanding of how children from non-English language backgrounds learn to read in their second language; this work has important implications for how and when teachers should assess multilingual poor readers and how these children should be taught. Case Study 5 describes a child with exposure to two languages who experiences literacy difficulties.

Chapter 10 highlights a further risk factor, specifically the neurologically based risk of being born very premature. This is becoming an increasingly prevalent phenomenon, given that many children born at under 32 weeks are now surviving due to medical advances. Research has shown that two-thirds of these will develop learning difficulties, many of them exhibiting multiple problems across a wide range of learning domains. Problems of attention, processing, visual motor skill and language, as well as educational difficulties, are well documented in the literature. Case Study 6 is a child born at 28 weeks with neonatal cerebral haemorrhage who goes on to have multiple specific learning, including literacy, difficulties.

By the end of this book, I hope that the reader will have recognized the need for the shift from single to multiple deficit models of literacy disorder and developed an appreciation of how these better explain dimensionality, individual variation and the high rates of co-occurrence with other disorders. Most importantly, I would want the reader to understand how important the multiple deficit model has proved in influencing how we assess, teach and manage children with literacy disorders.

Chapter 1

The Development of Literacy Skills

Most modern societies recognize that reading is the key route to learning and acquiring knowledge. It follows that achieving good reading skills is a fundamental goal for all children entering education. Indeed, Amanda Spielman, chief of Ofsted, commented (Spielman 2018):

> It is impossible to overstate the importance of early literacy. I'd describe reading as the linchpin of a good education. Children who can read learn through their own reading. If they can't read, they can't grasp other subjects properly. And reading empowers children, giving them independence to discover what most interests them. So, when you make a reader you give them the world.

In evolutionary terms, reading is a skill that has appeared relatively recently in human development, far later than spoken language communication. Indeed, learning to read is not the same as learning to talk. Most pre-school children acquire spoken language simply by being exposed to speech at home and in their broader environment, including at nursery. They do not need to be explicitly taught how to speak. They rapidly acquire vocabulary knowledge and they learn about the structure and rules of spoken language without apparent conscious effort and with no explicit teaching – as long as they are raised in an environment where speech is used in a meaningful and appropriate way. As Steven Pinker has pointed out, the learning of a spoken language is 'instinctual'

(Pinker 1994). This is not the case for written language; children need to be explicitly taught how to read, write and spell.

Gerry Altman in his book *The Ascent of Babel* (1997) rates the development of the written word as one of mankind's greatest achievements, ranking alongside the uses of fire and the invention of the wheel. As Altman points out, 'science and technology would hardly have progressed beyond the dark ages were it not for the written word – science simply relies on too much information for it to be passed down through the generations by word of mouth alone' (p.160). Not all knowledge can be committed to memory; we need a permanent record to refer back to and to pass on to others. Altman goes on to say, 'it is only through writing that almost all that is known today is known at all' (p.179).

Although achieving literacy skills presents few difficulties for the majority of children (who by the age of seven will be able to access a remarkable range of reading materials), there are substantial numbers of children who have enormous problems acquiring these fundamental skills of reading and writing. Indeed, as many as one in six children fail to read at a level that enables them to access their school curriculum meaningfully. Such failure has serious implications not only for their educational development, but also their long-term emotional and behavioural adjustment. Conversely, children who experience early success in learning to read appear to have positive attitudes to reading experiences that can stretch well into adulthood. Cunningham and Stanovich (1997, p.934) claim that 'rapid acquisition of reading abilities might well help the development of the life-time habit of reading'. In support of their argument, these authors report the findings of their study that initially assessed children's first-grade reading skills when they were six years old. They then followed this same group of children longitudinally over a ten-year period to see how much reading for pleasure they did and how well they understood and recalled what they had read. The children who made a good start in reading in grade 1 read significantly more books and had a far better understanding and recall of what they read in grade 11 than those who had made a slow start. There are two implications that follow from these findings. First, making a successful early start in reading clearly has a positive effect on later literacy development and outcome. Second, this study explodes the myth that children who make a slow start in learning to read 'catch up and are ok in the end'.

In this chapter, we will look in some depth at research which has furthered our knowledge of how children learn to read. Principles of research methodology and of statistical terminology will be defined as they arise, but also included is a Glossary of Terms box which provides an additional reference source of definitions that some readers may find useful.

It is hard to appreciate the underlying difficulties facing the child with a literacy disorder unless we have a good understanding of the skills that are needed for reading to progress normally. What we understand about how children learn to read and why this can go wrong stems largely from research that employs what might be termed a 'predictor approach', both in typical (normally developing) and high-risk samples of children (the latter are usually children born into families in which several members are known to have literacy problems). The most commonly studied predictors are cognitive skills or abilities that have been demonstrated to contribute to literacy development, and which are definable, measurable and potentially modifiable through teaching. However, there are also non-cognitive factors that impact literacy development (including socioeconomic and parental influences) and which also predict educational progress and outcome. In the case of very young children, cognitive predictors indicate what underlying skills or knowledge need to be in place to enable them to begin to learn to read. Cognitive measures also enable us to predict (albeit with some degree of error) which children will find reading easy and which will find it difficult. Arguably, the most studied of the cognitive predictors of reading are phonological skills: the child's sensitivity to speech sounds in words and their ability to analyse and process them. The nature of the connection between phonological abilities and literacy will be a main focus of this chapter.

Glossary of terms

Orthography: The writing systems of the world are known as 'orthographies'. In alphabetic languages, 'graphemes' record phonemes (sounds) in written form. In English, there are 26 letters but 44 phonemes; combinations of letters are used to represent some of the phonemes, for example *chimpanzee, bring.*

Correlational research: Most predictor research takes the form of correlational studies which examine the relationship between predictor factors (such as phonological ability) and reading (outcome) skills. A correlation provides a measure of the strength of the relationship between two variables or measures. Correlational research can be concurrent which means that we study the relationship between predictor and reading skills at the same time point. However, a concurrent correlation merely means that two skills or behaviours are occurring simultaneously and have some consistent relationship with each other. These correlations do not tell us about the direction of the relationship, nor can they make claims about prediction over time. Consequently, much predictor research is now conducted longitudinally.

Longitudinal research: In longitudinal research, children are assessed at a given point in time on tasks that are thought to measure predictor skills in reading. Their reading (outcome) skills are then assessed some time later to see if how they performed on a given predictor measure (e.g. phonological ability) affects, or contributes to, their subsequent progress in learning to read. Longitudinal studies establish not only the presence and strength of a relationship between two measures but even more importantly the *direction* of that relationship. Most studies also include other potential predictor variables that might provide alternative explanations for the relationship under study (e.g. IQ, environmental experiences and their possible impact on reading); this means that we can compare and contrast the relative contributions made by several predictors and so determine which are the most relevant and powerful.

Statistical significance: The correlation between two measures whether studied concurrently or longitudinally may be described as 'statistically significant' or not. This term is used to determine if a null hypothesis should be rejected or retained. The null hypothesis is the default assumption that nothing happened or nothing changed. If a correlation is significant it means that there is a real and consistent relationship between the two measures that is not occurring by chance. Many research studies also report 'effect size' which reflects practical significance by providing a quantitative measure of the magnitude of the correlation.

Per cent contribution: In predictor research, we frequently reflect effect size in the form of a per cent contribution statistic. For instance, in the studies of cognitive predictors of reading, a phonological awareness measure and a letter knowledge measure might jointly account for say 80 per cent of the variance in learning to read. This means that these two measures together explain 80 per cent of individual differences in a reading score, which is a huge amount. It implies that there is little room for any other factors to play a role in determining the development of reading skill. In contrast, in the studies of parental influences on reading, shared story book reading accounts for only 8 per cent of the variance in children's later reading scores which means that it makes a relatively small (though very likely still statistically significant) contribution to children's learning to read.

Beginning to read

The first two to three years of learning to read are especially critical, for two reasons. First, it is during this time that the child 'cracks the alphabetic code' which forms the foundation of literacy skill and which enables them to forge ahead to become independent readers; this means that that they come to understand how letters that they see in text represent corresponding speech sounds. Second, there is substantial evidence to show that reading skills stabilize from about the age of eight onwards, with little change in reading patterns thereafter. Consequently, most research into reading development has focused on these critical early years.

Children's awareness of the phonological (or sound) structure of words becomes increasingly fine grained as they move through pre-school into the early years of school. Awareness of whole words is of course evident first, followed by an understanding of the *syllabic* structure of words. As children enter school, they begin to be aware of what is termed the *onset-rime* structure of spoken words. The onset of a word is its initial consonant or consonant cluster while the rime is the following vowel sound and any succeeding consonants; in the word 'dog', the onset is the consonant /d/ and the rime is the vowel-consonant cluster /og/. Rhyming tasks are thought to tap into children's appreciation of the onset-rime structure of words. It is not until children begin to learn to read that they are able to process and analyze *phonemes* in words. The phoneme is the smallest pronounceable unit of sound in a word; 'p', 'e', 'sh', 'th' are examples of phonemes.

The powerful influence of phonological awareness

Phonological awareness refers to children's ability to reflect upon and manipulate the speech sounds in words; it can be tapped by a range of speech sound tasks, some being more challenging than others. At the simplest level, children can be asked to identify, segment or blend syllables within multisyllabic words; for instance, by asking them to identify the beginning syllable (or 'beat') in the word 'carpet' (answer: 'car'), or by asking them to say 'carpet' without the first syllable 'car' (answer: 'pet'). Many children can process syllables even before they start school. They also usually have a basic understanding of rhyme, for instance being able to recite simple nursery rhymes. More advanced rhyming skills become evident after the child begins school; these include being able to detect rhyme, which can be identified by asking them to say which of the words 'play, sat, dog' rhymes with 'cat'? (answer: 'sat'), or to produce rhymes ('how many words can you say that rhyme with 'cat'? to which the child could respond 'sat, fat, mat', etc.). As children begin to develop a basic sight-reading vocabulary and acquire alphabet knowledge, they are able to process words at the level of the phoneme. Children aged five to six years should be able to identify and blend phonemes in words, and they should also be able to segment at least beginning and end sounds within words, for example 'cat' without the 'c' says 'at', 'keep' without the 'p' says 'kee'. More advanced skills, like deleting middle sounds from words ('stick' without the 't' says 'sick') or transposing phonemes in words (transposing the initial and final phonemes within the word 'pat' makes the word 'tap') are evident in many six- to seven-year-olds.

Phonological awareness is strongly related to reading and spelling. This has been demonstrated in studies that have shown a high correlation between a child's score on a phonological aware-ness task and their score on a reading test. Phonological awareness is also a predictor measure of learning to read. There are countless longitudinal studies that have found that a child's score on a phonological awareness task at one point in time predicts their reading level one to two years later – which suggests that there is a *causal relationship* between early phonological awareness and later reading ability.

Figure 1.1 shows the development of specific phonological awareness skills with increasing age and relates this to the stage the child is at in learning to read. This figure also points to there being a two-way interactive process between phonological skills and learning to read. So, phonological awareness promotes reading development, but reading also helps develop phonological skills. Indeed, the ability to carry out more advanced phonolog-ical analyses depends to a significant degree on the experience of learning to read; certainly, the ability to delete, substitute and transpose phonemes in spoken words is rarely seen in children who have not had exposure to letters and printed words.

How do we characterize the process through which phonological awareness influences learning to read during the first two years of school? To answer this question, Margaret Snowling, Charles Hulme and I conducted two longitudinal studies of typically developing children attending North London state primary schools during their first two years of learning to read (Muter *et al.* 2004; Muter *et al.* 1998). In the first study, we recruited four-year-olds in their last term at nursery school; we selected 38 children who were all screened as 'non-readers'. They were administered a wide range of standardized cognitive and educational tests, including measures of phonological awareness, letter knowledge, short-term verbal working memory, vocabulary and grammatical awareness, and reading accuracy and comprehension. The children were then reassessed the following year at age five (end of their Reception Year), and finally again one year later at age six (end of Year 1).

Age	Progression of phonological skills	Print experience		
4 years	Nursery rhymes	L		
	Recognizing rhymes	E		
	Blending syllables	T		
	Segmenting syllables	T		
5 years	Alliteration	E	S	
	Sound matching beginning letters	R	I	
	Segmenting onsets and rhymes	S	G	
	Producing rhymes		H	D
5 years 6 months	Manipulating syllables		T	E
	Identifying beginning and end sounds			C
	Blending phonemes		W	O
	Segmenting phonemes		O	D
6 years	Deleting phonemes		R	I
	Adding phonemes		D	N
	Substituting phonemes		S	G

Figure 1.1 The development of phonological awareness skills

The first question we asked was: are there different types of phonological awareness? We had three measures of what we termed phonological segmentation. The first was a measure of phoneme identification. Specifically, the child had to supply the final sound of a single syllable word accompanied by a picture, for example: 'Here is a picture of a dog; I'll say the first bit of the word – can you finish it off for me?'; so the adult would say 'Here is a do' to which the child responded /g/. The second was a measure of phoneme manipulation: deleting the initial sound of a single syllable word. So, 'cat' without the /c/ sound says 'at'. The final measure was a phoneme blending test in which the child had to 'join together' a series of slowly presented phonemes, for example 'c-a-t' blends to make the word 'cat'. We also had two measures of rhyming skill. The first was a rhyme detection task in which the child had to say which of three words rhymed with a presented target word (presented pictorially as well as orally), for example: 'Which of "mouse, horse, window" rhymes with the word "house"?' (answer: 'mouse'). The second was a rhyme production task in which the child was asked to produce as many words as they could in 30 seconds that rhymed with one of two target words, 'day' and 'bell'. The three segmentation measures correlated well with each other while the two rhyming measures correlated highly with each other. However, the phoneme segmentation measures did not correlate with the rhyming measures, which suggests that rhyming and segmentation are two separate and independent types of skill within the phonological awareness domain. We then carried out a further analysis called *principal components analysis* which allowed us to identify two distinct and relatively independent factors or subskills within this domain: rhyming (tapped by the measures of rhyme detection and rhyme production) and phonological segmentation (tapped by the measures of phoneme identification, phoneme deletion and phoneme blending). Because these two subskills did not correlate highly, it is possible for a young child to be good at rhyming and weak at segmentation and conversely for another child to be weak at rhyming and good at segmentation.

This leads to our second question. Which of the two phonological awareness skills, rhyming or segmentation, is the more influential in the process of learning to read, or put another way, which is the better predictor? To answer this question, we carried out a statistical procedure called *path analysis* which generated path diagrams that showed the relationship between verbal IQ (especially vocabulary), phonological segmentation, rhyming and reading. Figure 1.2 charts the relationship between verbal IQ measured at Time 1 when the children were aged four, rhyming and segmentation skills assessed at both Times 1 and 2 (ages four and five years) and reading measured at Time 3 when the children were aged six (using a standardized single word reading test). The arrows in the path diagram indicate causal connections between the variables. The model moves from left to right, with the left-indicated measures being causally related to those on the right. The arrows indicate significant predictive relationships whereas the absence of arrows indicates non-significant relationships. It is clear from this path diagram that rhyming has no impact on the first two years of learning to read whereas segmentation at age four predicts this same skill a year later, which in turn then influences reading after two years of formal schooling. Interestingly, verbal IQ assessed at Time 1 predicted both rhyming and segmentation skills a year later. However, its effect on reading ability is indirect; its impact is mediated by segmentation ability which means that more verbally able children find segmenting words into phonemes easier than less able children, and it is this segmentation ability that drives early reading development. Indeed, there is good evidence that the development of increasingly refined phonological skill is driven by vocabulary growth. This is because the more words a child knows the more likely these are to overlap in their sound properties. As a result, the child becomes increasingly aware of these sound consistencies amongst the words they know and this helps to promote phonological development.

Ages 4/5 (Times 1 and 2)   Age 6 (Time 3)

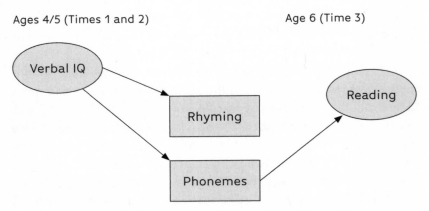

Figure 1.2 Rhymes or phonemes as predictors of reading

Our second reading study (Muter *et al.* 2004) confirmed the findings of our earlier study, this time with a larger sample of 90 children. Again, rhyming and phonological segmentation were found to be relatively independent of one another and it was segmentation ability (not rhyming) that drove learning to read during the first two years at school. This is a far from trivial finding. Earlier studies by Peter Bryant and Usha Goswami (Goswami 1990; Goswami and Bryant 1990) had suggested that rhyming ability and its impact on the awareness of onset-rime structures in words had the greater impact on early reading progress, with phoneme awareness playing a greater role later on (and then primarily in relation to spelling). The Bryant and Goswami model played a significant role in influencing how reading was taught in primary schools during the 1990s and early 2000s when there was considerable emphasis on promoting children's rhyming skills and their onset-rime awareness. Following on from this, it was recommended that children be taught reading and spelling through word families or analogies, that is words that rhymed and shared a common onset-rime structure e.g. 'fight, sight, might' and so on. In contrast, our findings suggest that promoting children's phoneme awareness (and indeed phonic-based teaching) has a more important role to play than rhyming during children's first two years at school. That is not to say that teaching by analogy might not be useful for older children when they are learning to spell seemingly irregular words that have complex rime spellings (like 'ight').

The role of letter knowledge

Phonological awareness is not the only critical determiner of learning to read during the first two years at school. Indeed, it is not the strongest predictor of early years reading. In both our longitudinal studies, letter knowledge acquisition – the speed at which children learned to identify the individual letters of the alphabet – was the best single predictor of learning to read during the first two years at school. It is self-evident that knowledge of letter names or sounds is an important prerequisite for children learning to read in an alphabetic orthography like English (and indeed other European languages). Knowledge of letter names or sounds is necessary for children to come to appreciate that there is a systematic relationship between how words are spelled and their pronunciations. In our 1998 study, not only did phonological segmentation and letter knowledge make separate and significant contributions to the first two years of learning to read, but there was also an additional significant contribution from what we termed the 'letter knowledge x segmentation' product term. This was a statistical measure obtained by multiplying the children's phonological segmentation and letter knowledge scores which aimed to reflect the interaction of these two component skills. This product term exerted a small but significant influence on reading, *additional to* that provided by segmentation and letter knowledge as separate skills. For children to make optimal progress in learning to read they need to forge a meaningful connection between their appreciation of the sound structure of words and their knowledge of the alphabet. Hatcher, Hulme and Ellis (1994) refer to this as 'phonological linkage'. It is not enough for children to know the letters of the alphabet and have an awareness of the sound structure of words; these skills need to work interactively with one another to promote reading development. Figure 1.3 shows in path diagram format the relationship between phonological awareness, letter knowledge and their joint and indeed interactive impact on beginning reading. While segmentation and letter knowledge each make a separate and significant contribution to reading development, it is the third path – letter knowledge x segmentation – that describes children's ability to form explicit links between their emerging phonological skills and their experience of print.

Although letter knowledge is a far more powerful predictor of reading success in the first year or so at school than even phonological awareness, its role diminishes as children achieve full knowledge of all 26 letters of the alphabet; in other words they hit 'ceiling' for this measure which means that it then no longer has the ability to reflect individual differences between children that are needed to make predictions. In our later large-scale longitudinal study, the impact of letter knowledge on reading ability in the second year at school was far smaller than in the first year. Thus, letter knowledge has a temporary, though nonetheless powerful, effect on young readers' progress in reading. This is in contrast to phonological awareness which, as we shall shortly see, continues to play a significant role in reading throughout the primary school years.

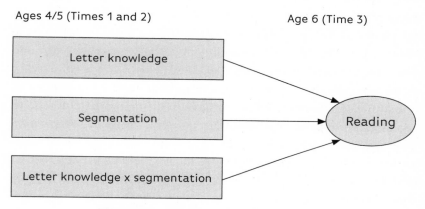

Figure 1.3 Role of letter knowledge in reading

Phonological linkage and the alphabetic principle

When young children make a connection between their ability to analyze phonemes in words and their knowledge of the alphabet, they acquire what Brian Byrne termed the *alphabetic principle*. In a classic book written in 1998, Byrne defined the alphabetic principle as children's understanding that 'the letters that comprise our printed language stand for the individual sounds that comprise our spoken language' (Byrne 1998, p.1). In an earlier paper, based on an experimental study, he states that the alphabetic principle 'provides the useable knowledge of the fact that phonemes can be represented by letters, such that whenever a particular phoneme occurs in a word, and in whatever position, it can be represented by the same letter' (Byrne and Fielding-Barnsley 1989, p.313). While this seems both simple and obvious, achieving the alphabetic principle is no mean feat for children encountering print for the first time. Byrne believes that the acquisition of the alphabetic principle forms the foundation upon which all subsequent literacy development is built. Most children achieve this understanding by the time they have completed their first two years at school, and they use this as a building block to broaden and expand their reading vocabularies. It is thus not surprising that reading patterns stabilize thereafter: their trajectories of reading progress change relatively little from the age of eight onwards.

Given the importance of the alphabetic principle in children's early reading development, we need to look at the prerequisites for its acquisition, in other words the skills children need to have in place for them to make the connection between phonology and print. Byrne and Fielding-Barnsley (1989) used what is referred to as an experimental transfer task to determine the specific skills and knowledge children need to have in place in order to acquire the alphabetic principle. They first taught a group of pre-reading children how to read the words *mat* and *sat*. They then asked them to decide whether the printed word *mow* should be pronounced as *mow* or *sow*. Success on this transfer task was achieved only by those children who could phonemically segment the speech items, who identified the initial sound segments, and who had learned the letter symbols for the sounds 'm' and 's'. This suggests that both phoneme awareness and printed letter knowledge are needed in combination for the successful acquisition of the alphabetic principle. This is a virtually identical conclusion to that drawn in our first longitudinal study that highlighted the additional contribution made by the letter knowledge x segmentation factor in predicting reading ability (that was beyond the separate roles played by letter knowledge and phoneme segmentation). For children to achieve phonological linkage or to acquire the alphabetic principle they need, first, to have a minimal level of phonological awareness that enables them to break spoken words into their constituent sounds, second, to have learned most of the letters of the alphabet, and finally, to be able to forge a connection between their phonological awareness and their experience of print.

Phonological processing skills

We have looked in some depth at phonological awareness and its role in the development of reading skills. There are two further subskills within the broader phonological domain which also have an influence on literacy, albeit not quite as strongly or as consistently as phonological awareness; these are automatically engaged *processing* skills.

The first of these phonological processing skills is *phonological memory* which refers to the coding of information as a speech sound representation for temporary storage in short-term working memory. The part of memory most involved in storing phonological information is the phonological loop; this provides very brief storage of auditory information, though this can be lengthened by a rehearsal process which refreshes information in the loop. Phonological memory has been shown to influence an individual's ability to learn new written and spoken vocabulary (Gathercole, Baddeley and Willis 1991). Although phonological memory correlates quite highly with phonological awareness, it is nonetheless regarded as distinct from it. Examples of phonological memory tasks include recalling sequences of digits forwards or backwards, and repeating increasingly lengthy nonsense words (like 'nolcrid, perplisteronk'). Phonological memory correlates moderately with reading ability (0.34 in the normative sample from the Comprehensive Test of Phonological Processing 2; Wagner *et al.* 2013); this is, however, a lower correlation than that demonstrated between phonological awareness (measured by phoneme deletion and blending tasks) and reading in the same sample of children (0.48).

The second phonological processing subskill is *naming speed* (sometimes referred to as rapid automatized naming). Children are asked to name as rapidly as they can sequences of colours, objects, numbers or letters while their speed to completion is recorded. The general consensus is that rapid naming tasks assess the speed and efficiency with which children retrieve phonological representations from long-term memory. The mixed modality of this task (scanning a visual array while producing an auditory response) captures what is happening when a child is pronouncing a written word out loud. Wagner *et al.* (1997) found that individual differences in naming speed predicted word level reading ability, though the association between naming speed and reading is not as consistent or as robust as the association between phonological awareness and reading. Nor are processing measures especially stable predictors in that their influence over literacy skill may wax and wane according to the stage of development a child is at. Some recent evidence has suggested that there is an especially strong and persisting relationship between naming speed and spelling (especially of irregularly constructed words) and between naming speed and speed of reading (Stainthorp, Powell and Stuart 2013).

What happens in the later stages of reading development?

The first two years of learning to read are critical for children to develop the necessary skills that enable them to forge ahead to become independent readers. Thereafter, reading patterns appear to stabilize; nonetheless, phonological awareness (though not letter knowledge) continues to play a role in children's later reading development. Moreover, longitudinal studies by Wagner and his colleagues (Wagner, Torgesen and Rashotte 1994; Wagner *et al.* 1997) have demonstrated that phonological skills are highly stable and robust predictors of progress in learning to read – and this pattern is consistent throughout and beyond middle childhood.

Margaret Snowling and I had the opportunity to follow up the phonological and reading development of 34 of the original 38 children from the Muter *et al.* 1998 study nearly three years later, when they were in their penultimate year at primary school (Muter and Snowling 1998). At this follow-up, they were administered a similar, though more difficult, phoneme deletion task to the one they were given at ages four to six years. This involved deleting a specified phoneme from a nonsense word in order to produce a real word; not only were they required to delete initial or final phonemes – for example, 'bice' without the /b/ says 'ice', 'bloot' without the /t/ says 'blue' respectively – but for some items they were asked to delete medial phonemes, for example 'hift' without the /f/ says 'hit'. The children's performance on the simple initial phoneme deletion task administered at ages five or six predicted significantly the children's performance on the more difficult phoneme deletion task given at age nine, a finding that demonstrates clearly the stability of phonological skills over time. The relative contribution of rhyming and segmentation abilities to reading skills that we demonstrated in our two earlier studies was evident also in the long-term follow-up study. We found that the phoneme deletion scores obtained by the children at ages five and six were significantly predictive of reading ability at age nine, while the earlier rhyming scores were not. Indeed, we found that the best long-term predictors of reading accuracy skill at age nine were phoneme deletion at ages five and six, together with nonword repetition (a phonological processing task which had also been administered at ages five and six). We then went on to carry out a statistical analysis called *discriminant function analysis* which allows the prediction of group membership; we found that knowledge of the children's scores on the phoneme deletion and nonword repetition tests at ages five and six predicted with 80 per cent accuracy whether they were designated 'good' or 'poor' readers at age nine. This suggests that administering simple tests of phonological awareness and processing might form the basis of a screening instrument that could be used to predict whether children as young as five or six might be 'at risk' for developing literacy problems. Interestingly, we found that neither the phoneme deletion test nor the nonword repetition test administered at age four predicted reading ability at age nine; clearly, screening for reading failure prior to age five is likely to be unreliable.

Phonological awareness, letter knowledge and the acquisition of the alphabetic principle are essential to children learning how to read at the single word level. However, as children proceed through school, they are exposed to increasingly complex texts which raises the question as to whether broader based language skills begin to play an increasingly important role as children progress beyond single word reading. In our follow-up study, we found that an important concurrent predictor of reading accuracy at age nine was grammatical awareness. The task we used to assess this tapped children's knowledge of grammatical rules, mainly inflection endings of words; specifically, they had to supply the final word of a sentence given orally by the examiner, for instance, 'The girl plants a tree... Here is the tree she...' (planted). We found that this grammatical awareness task predicted the children's scores on a prose reading accuracy test but did not predict their performance on a single word reading test. Thus, as text becomes increasingly complex and context driven, grammatical (and presumably also other linguistic) knowledge comes to play an increasingly important role in improving reading accuracy through the appreciation of context and content clues that can help inform word pronunciation.

Can computers model how children learn to read?

In our technology-driven age, we tend to turn a lot to computers to simulate how the human brain works in relation to developing specific skills – and reading is no exception. Computer simulations are based on the idea that the brain is a large neural network whose function can be simulated by computers. If we can replicate the way humans read by studying how a computer acquires a reading vocabulary, we might come to understand not only the processes involved in typical reading development but also arrive at an explanation of how this process fails if the network is in some way damaged – as it is presumed to be in children who have a literacy disorder. What are termed connectionist models of reading are based on complex mathematical learning algorithms, the description of which is well beyond the scope of this book. So, what I will attempt is a brief and simplified explanation of connectionism and how it explains normal reading development. In the next chapter, we will revisit this to look at how damage to a component of the reading neural network can offer an explanation of literacy disorders.

The first premise of a connectionist model is that the representation of a word in the neural network is not holistic but is distributed across many simple processing elements or units in what are termed input and output systems. The input system encodes the printed letters we see in a page of text and also their position in the word; these are the orthographic units. The output system encodes the phonological features of the pronunciation of letters and words; these are the phonological units. The computer 'trains' the neural network over many trials to learn how to read a given word, by enabling it to develop patterns of associations or 'mappings' between the orthographic and the phonological units. The strength of these connections is measured as 'weights' which gradually become greater with more learning trials. Before training has commenced, the model has either no, or at best weak and random, connection weights between the units. For each training trial, the computer presents the neural network with input sets of letters that generate a pattern of activity across the network. This process is achieved through a learning algorithm which works by altering the weights on the connections in such a direction as to reduce error. As training progresses, partial mappings emerge between the orthographic and phonological units which gradually increase in their weights over trials so that the word may be partly, though not wholly, correctly read. By the end of training, full mappings between the orthographic and phonological units are in place, and what is termed the *phonological pathway* to reading is established. Over the course of training, the error is reduced to zero so that a perfect match appears between the spoken word and its printed representation; the word can then be fully and correctly read. This training process eventually forms a knowledge base which can be drawn upon when the network is presented with a new word to read. The model seems to exhibit human rule-like behaviour though this learning does not take place in a conscious way. Figure 1.4 shows the development of the mappings between the orthographic and phonological units during training that create the phonological pathway.

While the phonological pathway is of great importance in the beginning stages of learning to read, later reading comes to rely increasingly on what is termed the *semantic pathway*. This pathway maps orthography onto phonology via semantics (word meanings). Essentially, a written word as input produces direct activation of the word's meaning which then in turn activates pronunciation of the word. The semantic pathway seems to be especially important for the reading of exception (irregularly constructed) words that the phonological pathway does not handle easily or efficiently.

Before training: no mappings evident so the word cannot be read

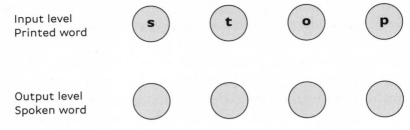

Midway through training: partial mappings emerge so the word may be partly read

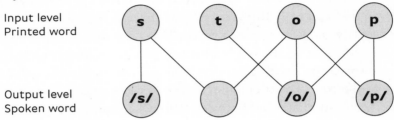

End of training: full mappings emerge so word is read accurately

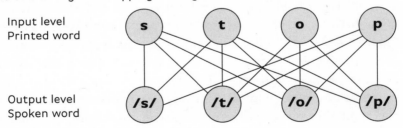

Figure 1.4 The creation of the phonological pathway

Learning to read: does the orthography matter?

Much of the research into reading and its relation to phonology has been conducted in the English language. English is, however, a much harder language in which to learn to read, write and spell than is for instance Spanish, Italian or German. Languages such as Spanish and Italian are termed *phonologically transparent* which means that there is greater consistency in their spelling patterns; when you hear a specific sound in Spanish, for instance, it is usually spelled with the same letter sequence irrespective of the word in which it appears. English has a *complex morpho-phonological* structure which means that it is structurally based on both morphemes (units of meaning) as well as phonemes (units of sound). When spelling in English, it is not unusual for morphemic structures to be preserved even at the expense of phonology. For instance, when asked to spell the word 'healthy', the young child might be tempted to spell the word phonically, thus writing 'helthy'. However, the root word of 'healthy' is 'health' and it is this morphemic root that is preserved when spelling 'healthy', making it seemingly irregular in its spelling. There are many English spellings like this which can present a significant challenge for young children. Also, many of the commonest words in the English language do not obviously conform to standard phonological based pronunciations – words like 'was, because, one, are, said'. Moreover, the same sound in English may be represented in print by a number of different letter combinations; for instance, the sound /ee/ can be written as 'ee' as in 'meet', 'ea' as in 'seat', or 'ei' as in 'receipt'.

Thus, the language in which a child is taught to read is a factor that can affect ease of reading acquisition, in particular for children who might be predisposed to reading problems in the first place. This is well illustrated in a study carried out by Philip Seymour (2005) who traced early literacy development over three years in English-speaking and Finnish-speaking children. He wanted to determine how much easier it is to learn to read in a highly phonologically transparent language like Finnish than in a 'deep' (non-phonologically transparent) language, of which English is perhaps the best European example. He found that it took the English-speaking children two years to learn to read to an agreed criterion of reading proficiency, in contrast to the Finnish-speaking children who took only one year to reach the same standard (even after taking into account – controlling for – the different ages at which children start to learn to read in these countries).

A more recent study of learning to read in different languages was conducted by Marketa Caravolas (Caravolas *et al.* 2012) who co-ordinated a longitudinal study which aimed to chart reading development in five- to eight-year-olds learning to read in a range of different European languages, varying in transparency from deep (e.g. English) through to largely transparent (e.g. Croatian). This was a cross-linguistic study in that the same tasks were used for all the languages, thus enabling direct comparisons across the different orthographies. Caravolas and her colleagues found that, first, phoneme awareness developed more rapidly in children learning to read in transparent orthographies than those learning in a deep orthography. The main aim of this study, however, was to determine whether the same measures were independent unique predictors of reading development irrespective of transparency of orthography. The authors did indeed find that early phonological awareness, emerging letter knowledge and rapid automatized naming predicted later reading development in *all* of the languages, accounting for a high 62 per cent of the variance in learning to read. This clearly demonstrates that alphabetic reading systems are built on the same early foundations regardless of the extent of orthographic consistency.

Learning to read: non-cognitive factors

Phonological skill and alphabetic learning are cognitive predictors of learning to read. However, there are also non-cognitive determinants of children's progress in learning to read that enable us to put together a more complete picture of how children learn to read in an environmental or cultural context. Of course, culture influences the values that families place on reading and writing. Middle-class professional families value literacy skills highly because of the important role they play in enabling their child to achieve academic success. In contrast, traveller communities have oral traditions that are stronger than written. In essence, the language in which a given child learns to read is a cultural factor that predicts ease of reading acquisition, though it is not one that can be easily controlled or modified. Other non-cognitive, essentially cultural, factors we will consider in this chapter are socioeconomic status and the home literacy environment (including parents reading to their children).

Additionally, in Chapter 9 we will evaluate the sociocultural impact of bilingualism and learning to read in a language that is not the child's mother tongue.

It has been well established for many years that children's early language proficiency and also their reading skills are correlated with their parent's socioeconomic status. Studies such as those conducted by Bowey (1995) and Hecht *et al.* (2000) have found that the lower levels of reading skill reported in children from disadvantaged backgrounds are largely explained by their weaker vocabulary skills, their less well-developed phonological awareness and their reduced print knowledge (which would include letter knowledge). This raises the concern that many young children from socially disadvantaged homes are arriving at school with limited vocabulary knowledge, underdeveloped phonological abilities and having had little exposure to print experiences – which of course then negatively impacts their ease of learning to read. This suggests that it is especially important to target these children during their nursery years and the first year at school so that they can have exposure to activities that foster the development of improved language, phonological and letter knowledge skills.

A further non-cognitive factor beyond that of social class relates to the role that parents play in promoting their children's reading development; this is sometimes referred to as the 'home literacy environment'. Most early studies concentrated on the extent to which parents read story books to their children and the impact this had on their subsequent ease of learning to read. Scarborough and Dobrich (1994) reviewed 31 studies that looked at the effect of parents' reading to their pre-school children on the children's oral language and early literacy development. Twenty of these studies examined the relationship between measures such as amount of time spent reading to children or frequency of story book reading with outcome measures like oral language proficiency, phonological awareness and emerging literacy skill. The remaining 11 studies were intervention programmes that compared the reading skills of children whose parents were given instruction and guidance on how to read to their children with those children in a control group whose parents had not benefited from specific instruction and support. Scarborough and Dobrovich found that the results from one study to another varied a great deal even when similar measures were used. However, they were able to draw some general conclusions. First, it appeared that frequency of reading was an important factor; quality of shared reading, which was a measure in some studies, proved too difficult to quantify meaningfully. Second, the correlational studies showed that frequency of story book reading was most strongly associated with oral language proficiency, growth in spoken vocabulary knowledge and emergent literacy skills (which would include print awareness and letter knowledge). For the intervention studies, positive results emerged for the oral language (but not the literacy) outcome measures. Third, although there appears to be a significant association between parent reading frequency and their children's language/literacy outcome, this was of modest proportions; most correlations were at or less than 0.28, accounting for no more than 8 per cent of the overall variance in language or literacy achievement. This contrasts sharply with the variance in reading outcome predicted by a combination of cognitive factors like phonological awareness and letter knowledge which in some studies (including Muter *et al.* 1998) is as high as 90 per cent.

A classic study by Senechal *et al.* (1998) made a more explicit comparison of the impact of parent's frequency of story book reading on children's oral versus written language outcome over a one-year period while they were in kindergarten and grade 1. These authors found that story book exposure contributed to the children's oral language skills but not their written language. However, when parents drew their children's attention to printed words, letters and sounds while reading to them, that is they specifically targeted their pre-literacy skills, this resulted in their children achieving higher reading scores. So, reading stories per se to children seems to foster mostly their oral language development but less so their reading outcome, unless parents make a specific effort to incorporate pre-literacy work into these story book experiences; this might be done by, for instance, pointing to and pronouncing high frequency words, drawing children's attention to initial letters in printed words and then supplying them with its corresponding sound, asking the child to come up with other words that begin with the same letter and so on. Further evidence for the importance of targeting pre-literacy skills in story book reading comes from a recent study by Bierman *et al.* (2015). They found that providing parents with guided story book reading combined with letter-sound activities resulted in improvements in children's emergent literacy skills.

While story book reading seems to improve primarily oral language development, it may have an indirect impact on reading via the role played by story book reading on vocabulary growth. We have seen that children's vocabulary development is an important precursor of emerging phonological awareness. Arguably, story book reading might have an indirect impact on phonological skills (and therefore ultimately reading), through being mediated by the role played by story books in enhancing children's spoken vocabulary. This point is very much reinforced in a study of a parent-delivered language enrichment programme, with two- to three-year-old children from socially diverse backgrounds (Burgoyne *et al.* 2018). These authors found that children's oral language skills could be significantly enhanced through a programme that involved parents engaging in interactive story book reading with their children, together with direct teaching of vocabulary and oral narrative skills. In the vocabulary enrichment component, one new word was targeted for each story reading session, its meaning explained and its use demonstrated in a range of different contexts. The oral narrative work targeted picture-based story sequencing, summarizing stories and/or retelling them. Children who had experience of the parent-delivered oral language programme made significantly larger gains in language and oral narrative skill than control children who received a motor skills programme. The effects on language were maintained six months later and at this point, the language programme group also scored higher on tests of early literacy. The authors concluded that 'while the language programme evaluated here did not explicitly target literacy, we speculate that the shared book reading experiences fostered an awareness of the relationship between sounds and printed letters and words' (p.553).

Bookstart is a UK-based government funded national scheme that aims to foster reading- and book-related experiences in the pre-school years via the Health Visitor Service. Books and related materials are supplied free of charge to all families when their children are aged eight months, eighteen months, three years and four to five years. The children's books are accompanied by parent/carer guidelines which recommend how parents should use these books to optimize their role in promoting children's enjoyment of stories, their awareness of print conventions, their vocabulary knowledge and their familiarity with letters and numbers. It is hoped that the Bookstart scheme will help to 'even the playing field' for those children from disadvantaged backgrounds who do not automatically have the same access to books and related materials enjoyed by children from more advantaged homes. Despite the wide availability of Bookstart materials, the charity BookTrust estimated in a recent survey that only 28 per cent of parents find the time to regularly read their child a bedtime story – a disappointing statistic, given we have seen that shared book reading promotes children's oral language development and (albeit possibly less directly) their emerging literacy skills.

Developing reading comprehension skills

Children's reading comprehension refers to their ability to understand, retain and recall what they have read. Arguably, children's ability to read for meaning is the most important reading skill of all. Children's reading comprehension can be measured by asking them to, for instance, retell a story they have read or to answer specific questions that assess their understanding and recall of the content of the text.

The Simple View of Reading model proposed by Gough and Tunmer (1986) has been the most studied and indeed the most influential of models of reading comprehension. It views reading comprehension as the product of word recognition and listening comprehension. Word recognition can be measured by a single word reading test, a test of prose reading accuracy or even a nonword reading test. (Nonword reading tests require the child to attempt to read nonsense words, such as 'fug, tweep, nolcrid', which can only be read by applying a phonic decoding or 'sounding out' strategy.) Listening comprehension is a term used to denote children's ability to understand language in spoken form; obviously, this is dependent on the child's development of oral language skills. The listening comprehension component of the Simple View of Reading model has been measured in many different ways in a wide range of studies, including asking children to recall orally a story that has been read to them, and also through standardized tests of verbal intelligence, vocabulary knowledge and grammar. The consensus of opinion is that, irrespective of what specific word recognition and listening comprehension measures are taken, these together usually account for around 90 per cent of the variance in reading comprehension.

Our 2004 longitudinal study provided clear evidence for the Simple View of Reading model (Muter *et al.* 2004). When the children were aged five, they were administered tests not only of phonological awareness, word recognition and letter knowledge but also tests of vocabulary knowledge, syntactic awareness and morphological generation. These latter tests tapped into the children's language skills which would constitute the listening comprehension component of the simple model. The vocabulary task required the children to give spoken definitions of individual words. Syntactic awareness was assessed by a word order correction task (Tunmer 1989). Specifically, the children heard a sequence of words presented in incorrect order and were asked to rearrange these to make a meaningful sentence; so, 'Ben throwing was stones' was corrected to 'Ben was throwing stones'. The morphological generation task required the children to demonstrate their knowledge of word inflections (the same task used in the Muter and Snowling 1998 study). One year later, when the child were aged six, they completed a prose reading test (Neale Analysis of Reading Ability II; Neale 1997) which provided measures of prose reading accuracy and reading comprehension (the child answered questions about the content of the story they had read). We then carried out a path analysis which showed that children's vocabulary knowledge, syntactic awareness and morphological knowledge assessed at age five significantly contributed to their reading comprehension scores at age six. This was additional to the significant contribution made by reading accuracy at age five to reading comprehension a year later. These findings are summarized in the path diagram shown in Figure 1.5. Together, reading accuracy, vocabulary and grammatical awareness assessed at age five accounted for 86 per cent of the individual variation in reading comprehension skill at age six. These results are exactly in line with the predictions made by the Simple View of Reading model and provide good support for a causal theory that views children's reading comprehension as depending on their ability to read accurately, their knowledge of word meanings and their ability to draw on grammatical information (syntax and morphology) to generate meaning from text. In contrast, reading accuracy skills at age 6 are predicted by phoneme awareness and letter knowledge skills from the previous year, but not by grammatical awareness.

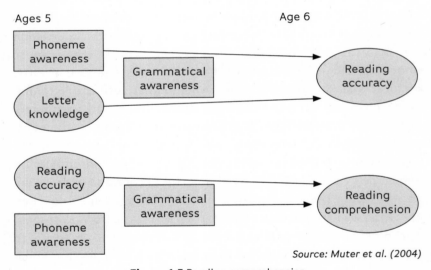

Source: Muter et al. (2004)

Figure 1.5 Reading comprehension

The Simple View of Reading model is very robust. Spencer, Quinn and Wagner (2014) were able to demonstrate that of 425,000 poor reader comprehenders – children who could read print accurately but failed to understand what they were reading – less than 1 per cent were adequate in both decoding and vocabulary (the authors measures of word recognition and listening comprehension respectively). What this means is that reading comprehension difficulties that are not associated with either poor word recognition or listening comprehension (the two components of the Simple View of Reading model) are very rare indeed. Two recent research studies have refined the model. The first refinement is that vocabulary knowledge has an especially important role to play in reading comprehension that goes beyond the contributions made by word recognition and listening comprehension (Tunmer and Chapman 2012). Indeed, even infant vocabulary knowledge is a predictor of later reading comprehension. Duff *et al.* (2015) studied the vocabularies of 300 infants aged between 16 and 24 months and related this to their vocabulary, phonological and reading skills five years later. They found that infant vocabulary accounted for 18 per cent of the variance in reading comprehension five years on, while for later reading accuracy this was a smaller 11 per cent. The authors argued for a strong longitudinal relationship between early vocabulary and the more semantic-laden aspects of later reading. The second refinement is that, while word recognition and listening comprehension both contribute to reading comprehension in the early years, the impact of word recognition lessens over the course of development; indeed, by the time the child reaches the latter stages of primary school, it is listening comprehension that assumes the greater role in predicting reading comprehension (Lonigan, Burgess and Schatschneider 2018). Thus, linguistic competence becomes the driving factor in the development of children's reading comprehension skills during their senior school years. It seems that, as most children achieve a sufficient level of reading accuracy by the end of primary school, it is only variations in linguistic competence that can explain individual differences in their reading comprehension skills.

Summary

- Phonological awareness refers to children's appreciation of, and their ability to process and analyze, the speech sound segments of spoken words; it is a powerful, stable and robust predictor of reading achievement.

- Letter knowledge acquisition is an even stronger determiner of early reading ability, though its role is largely restricted to the first two years of learning to read.
- When children combine their phoneme awareness with their knowledge of sound-to-letter relationships, they acquire the *alphabetic principle*: the understanding that the sounds in spoken language are systematically represented by (and indeed are mapped onto) letters in printed language. It is the acquisition of the alphabetic principle that forms the foundation for children's subsequent rapid expansion of their reading vocabulary.
- Tasks of phonological processing (auditory working memory, nonword repetition and naming speed) are thought to tap into the ease with which children can access phonological representations in their long-term memory store; this skill also has an influence on literacy development, albeit not quite as strongly or as consistently as phonological awareness.
- Other (non-cognitive) factors that influence children's ease of learning to read include the orthography in which they are learning to read, how much they are read to as pre-schoolers and the quality of this 'print exposure'.
- Reading comprehension is the product of word recognition and listening comprehension, with the latter playing an increasingly important role in reading for meaning as children get older.
- Given that oral language, especially vocabulary, influences both the development of phonological skills needed for progress in word level reading and also reading comprehension, it follows that language forms the foundation for acquiring literacy skills.

Chapter 2

When Literacy Development Goes Wrong
Literacy Disorders

The previous chapter highlighted the importance of phonological and language abilities in learning to read and understand print. If children fail to develop these underpinning abilities we would expect them to find it hard to acquire literacy skills; indeed, many of these children will go on to be described as having a *literacy disorder*. In this chapter, we will begin by focusing on disorders of word level reading or reading accuracy (commonly referred to as dyslexia) before turning our attention to disorders of reading comprehension.

Defining dyslexia

In the previous chapter, we saw that children who have well developed phonological skills from an early age appear to find it easy to learn to read print. Does it therefore follow that children who struggle to acquire word level reading skills are likely to have compromised phonological systems? A primary focus of this chapter is to look at the evidence for phonological deficits in children who are described as having dyslexia.

Before reviewing the evidence of a phonological weakness being the primary deficit in dyslexia, we should look at definitions of dyslexia which have in themselves been a source of controversy. In classifications of psychiatric and related disorders, such as the DSM (Diagnostic and Statistical Manual of Mental Disorders), definitions have changed dramatically over the last 20 years. In previous incarnations of DSM, it was usual to define dyslexia as reading achievement that is substantially below expectation given the person's chronological age, measured intelligence (IQ) and age appropriate education. This is essentially a *discrepancy* definition; while definitions of this sort are still widely used in research and in epidemiological (population) studies, they have fallen out of favour in clinical and educational contexts. The latest version (5th edition) of the *Diagnostic and Statistical Manual of Mental Disorders* (DSM-5) (American Psychiatric Association 2013) advocates against the adoption of discrepancy definitions for developmental disorders, including dyslexia. There are a number of reasons for this. First, IQ and reading do not correlate as highly as we might expect for there to be strong justification in using a discrepancy definition (though to be fair, the correlation between verbal IQ and reading is higher than for nonverbal IQ and reading). Second, poor readers often show a decline in their verbal IQ as a consequence of their limited reading experiences; thus, a low verbal IQ could mask the specificity of the child's reading problem. Finally, there is no evidence that children who have word level reading problems vary in their responsiveness to intervention according to their ability level; from a theoretical perspective, this means that there is no reason to believe that the causes of reading difficulties are different in children who have low rather than high IQs. DSM-5 groups together reading disorders, mathematics disorders and disorders of written expression under a single over-riding diagnosis of specific learning disorders within the broader category of neurodevelopmental disorders. An admittedly rather old, but nonetheless still widely accepted, definition of dyslexia that holds up well is that proposed by Margaret Snowling in 2000 (pp.213–14):

> Dyslexia is a specific form of language impairment that affects the way in which the brain encodes phonological features of spoken words. The core deficit is in phonological processing and stems from poorly specified phonological processing. Dyslexia specifically affects the development of reading and spelling skills but its effects can be modified through development leading to a variety of behavioural manifestations.

There has been a recent debate in the scientific literature which has not only whipped up controversy in respect of definitions of dyslexia, but has also challenged whether indeed such a disorder actually exists. Julian Elliott and Elena Grigorenko in their book *The Dyslexia Debate* (2014) challenge the validity of what they term the 'dyslexia construct'. They begin by (quite rightly) dismissing the discrepancy definition of dyslexia before looking at the many differing ways in which dyslexia has been conceptualized within the research and clinical literature. They argue that at the current time, it is not possible to separate poor readers into clear causal groups based upon either biological or cognitive phenomena. Nor, they continue, can we identify a biologically- or cognitively-(presumably phonologically-) based dyslexic subgroup within a larger pool of poor readers. (In fact, it does need to be borne in mind that environmental factors such as poor school attendance or inadequate teaching may be a sufficient explanation for some children's poor reading skills.) Elliott and Grigorenko also claim that there is an erroneous belief that a diagnosis of dyslexia can result in appropriately tailored forms of intervention that address the child's underlying deficit and which will therefore improve their reading capabilities. They appear to particularly object to the so-called vast dyslexia industry which provides assessments and interventions that are accessible to middle-class families but are denied to disadvantaged families. The authors conclude by calling for an end to the dyslexia label and for it to be replaced by more detailed descriptors of the deficits that underpin reading difficulties in a given child. Following on from this, they highlight the need for assessment for intervention (as opposed to diagnosis) which will give children access to the most effective evidence-based interventions at as early an age as possible.

While not disagreeing with these authors' conclusions in relation to assessment for intervention, I would argue that their view of dyslexia is based on an outmoded model of dyslexia as first, being 'all or none' (i.e. the view that you have dyslexia or you don't), and second, that dyslexia must have a single biological and cognitive causal basis. In this and the next two chapters, we will review evidence for dyslexia being a *dimensional* not an 'all or none' disorder; there are no clear cut-off criteria and having a phonological deficit is in itself not sufficient to cause dyslexia. Indeed, its expression may vary in individual children and over the course of development, dependent on factors such as the severity of the phonological deficit, the presence of additional learning difficulties and of course environmental (including teaching) experiences. Viewed from this perspective, it is possible to agree with Elliott and Grigorenko's broad pedagogic recommendations while at the same time disagreeing with the arguments that inform these. Personally, I do not think it matters whether we describe an individual child's reading difficulty as dyslexia or a specific reading problem or a literacy disorder, as long as we recognize that it is important to arrive at an understanding of the nature of their difficulties and how they might be addressed so as to improve their overall educational outcome. On a more positive note, this recent debate has resulted in the consensus of opinion that the term dyslexia or reading disorder (if the latter is preferred) should be most appropriately reserved for those individuals with persisting literacy difficulties who have not responded to robust and intensive intervention. Indeed, it has been suggested that the slow response to intervention typically seen in many dyslexic children might be a better way of identifying these children than measured reading skills.

A causal model of dyslexia

A very useful framework for studying the causal basis for dyslexia is one that was proposed by Uta Frith in 1997 (see Figure 2.1). This model describes three different levels of study in a causal chain: the biological, the cognitive and the behavioural. It also shows how environmental factors can influence the causal pathway.

At the uppermost level of the Frith Model is the *biological* basis of dyslexia. Indeed, there is good evidence for dyslexia having a genetic basis that in turn impacts brain function. At the next level, is the *cognitive* dysfunction, specifically a phonological deficit, which causally influences the *behavioural* expression of dyslexia, namely that of difficulty in learning to read and spell. *Environmental* factors that affect the causal pathway might include social and family factors, the writing system (transparent versus deep) in which the child is learning to read, and quality of teaching.

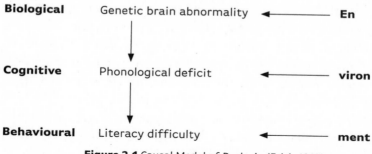

Biological	Genetic brain abnormality	⟵	En
Cognitive	Phonological deficit	⟵	viron
Behavioural	Literacy difficulty	⟵	ment

Figure 2.1 Causal Model of Dyslexia (Frith 1997)

The biological basis of dyslexia

It is well documented that dyslexia 'runs in families' which suggests that it is a strongly inherited disorder. To demonstrate this in quantitative terms, Snowling and Melby-Lervåg (2016) carried out a meta-analysis of family at-risk studies. A meta-analysis involves combining the results of a number of different studies to increase the power of the statistical analyses and to draw out generalized findings which might not be evident from looking at each study individually. Family at-risk studies examine the learning profiles of young children who have a first degree relative (typically a parent) who is known to have dyslexia. The findings from this meta-analysis indicate that there is a 45 per cent risk of a child developing dyslexia if a parent is found to have this disorder. This is much higher than the population incidence of dyslexia which is of the order 3–6 per cent (Snowling 2009).

Twin studies have played an important role in understanding the important contribution of genes to developmental disorders like dyslexia. Comparisons of identical twins who share 100 per cent of their genes and fraternal twins who share 50 per cent of their genes have shown that where one twin is dyslexic the probability that the other will be too is 90 per cent in identical twins, while for fraternal twins it is much lower (40%). Estimates of the genetic contribution to reading are usually expressed as *heritability* values that range from 0 to 1; a value of 1 would indicate that all of the variance on a given reading measure in the twins is due to genetic factors whereas 0 would indicate that the trait under study is not at all influenced by genetic factors. Heritabilities can vary from study to study in dyslexia research but are generally in the region between 0.4 and 0.5, indicating that reading skills are moderately strongly inherited (DeFries, Alarcon and Olson 1997). There is some evidence that the relative contribution of genetic versus environmental influence on reading varies according to age; environmental factors seem to be more important in the pre-school years when the home literacy environment plays an important role and again in the later schooling years when teaching influences make a large contribution (Stevenson *et al.* 1987). There is also evidence for some subcomponents of reading skill being more strongly inherited than others. Gayan and Olson (1999) found that the heritability of phonological awareness, at 0.89, was much higher than for other subcomponents of the reading process like word recognition (0.68) and phonic decoding (0.77); this is because these latter subcomponents are more likely than phonological awareness to be influenced by environmental factors such as print exposure and specific teaching strategies.

In parallel with the genetic studies of dyslexia, there are increasing numbers of studies that relate the difficulties experienced by people with dyslexia to specific aspects of brain function. We have seen that language abilities (in particular phonological processes) have a substantial effect on children's ease of learning to read and spell. It is likely therefore that the brain regions responsible for language and related processes will be impaired in individuals presenting with dyslexia. Over the course of early development, language skills become increasingly lateralized to the left hemisphere of the brain, broadly to the frontal-temporo-parietal regions of this hemisphere. Elena Grigorenko carried out a review of brain studies in dyslexia, most of which pointed to structural differences and reduced activity in some regions of the brain in dyslexic individuals (Grigorenko 2001). Many studies use functional magnetic resonance imaging (MRI) technology which measures the metabolic activity in nerve cells that reflects patterns of brain activation. These have shown that there is decreased activation in the left temporal areas when dyslexic participants carry out phonological and reading tasks (in contrast to non-dyslexics who show increased activation in this region), which in turn very likely reflects inefficient phonological processing in the dyslexic brain. However, this reduced activity is not infrequently accompanied by enhancement of activity in other brain regions in dyslexic participants, either other regions of the left hemisphere or even within the right hemisphere. It may be that environmental influences and even self-reorganization of cognitive systems can result in these other brain regions being 'pulled in'. These *recruited* regions might attempt to take over the phonological processing usually carried out by the specialized left hemisphere regions though they may do this far less well because they have not been specifically designed to carry out these tasks. Alternatively, newly recruited areas might be involved in a compensatory process that involves using non-phonological skills to access print; for instance, visual routes to word recognition or the adoption of other verbal mechanisms to aid word identification, such as verbal memorization or forming links between word and meaning.

How can we demonstrate that there is a causal role of brain impairments in the development of dyslexia? Most of the brain-behaviours studies described in the Grigorenko review are correlational, which means that they indicate that there is a relationship between brain function and reading proficiency but the causal direction is not clear; it could be that brain activation differences in individuals with dyslexia is a consequence not a cause of their reading problems. To get around this problem, we need to look at studies that demonstrate a longitudinal relationship between early recorded patterns of brain activation during phonological processing tasks and later recorded reading skills. One such study by Hoeft *et al.* (2007) with 64 poor readers demonstrated that patterns of brain activation were longitudinal predictors of later reading ability. Interestingly, their brain activation measures proved better predictors of reading skill than behavioural measures like IQ and phonological awareness. Thus, patterns of brain activation reflect differences in brain function that are causally related to children's ability to learn to read.

Another promising approach is to look at neural correlates of dyslexia in infants and toddlers, focusing particularly on children born to families with a high risk of dyslexia. The challenge is then to see if measures of brain activity in the earliest stage of development are predictive of later reading skill. Some studies have indeed done this. Van Zuijen *et al.* (2013) used magnitude of evoked response potentials (ERPs) to measure auditory processing in two-month-old infants from dyslexia at-risk families compared to controls from non at-risk families. The babies in the at-risk group showed reduced ERP responses, reflecting an auditory processing deficit, which was predictive of their reading scores years later after they had started school.

In summary, dyslexia is a developmental disorder that is strongly inherited. Genetic variations seen in individuals with dyslexia act to influence the development of brain regions that underlie children's ability to learn to read. In dyslexia, there is evidence of structural and functional differences in the left hemisphere brain regions that are specific to the development of language and literacy skills. Deficits in pre-school auditory and phonological processing and reduced brain activation in children at risk of dyslexia are predictive of later reading development. On a cautionary note, Ramus *et al.* (2018) conducted an overview of the literature relating to brain function and dyslexia which demonstrated that there is an over-reliance on small studies whose results tend to be inflated and not always replicable. They showed that the only robust finding is that that there is a demonstrable smaller brain volume in individuals with dyslexia, with language-related temporo-parietal regions mostly implicated. They concluded by highlighting the need for higher methodological standards and larger scale or meta-analytic studies to confidently demonstrate the causal link between specific brain functions and dyslexia.

The cognitive basis of dyslexia

In the previous chapter, we saw that phonological skills have a causal relationship with learning to read and spell. We might therefore reasonably hypothesize that a deficit in phonological processing would compromise reading development. This then raises the question as to whether a phonological weakness is the core cognitive deficit in children with dyslexia which then accounts for their slow progress in learning to read.

The *phonological deficit theory of dyslexia* is a simple causal theory that states that problems with phonology that pre-date reading are a cause of later reading problems. For such a theory to hold up, two claims that are both testable must be made. First, that the severity of the phonological deficit will predict variations in the severity of the reading deficit, and second, that children who develop dyslexia will show a phonological deficit before they begin to learn to read. We will look at the evidence for each of these claims in turn.

Phonological deficits in dyslexia have been extensively studied over the last 30 years and there are hundreds of published studies that have supported the theory that children with dyslexia have poorly developed phonological skills. The early research studies typically compared the language and phonological skills of children with dyslexia with children of the same age who did not have dyslexia; this is referred to as the 'chronological age matched research design'. However, this approach presents a major method-ological problem that can make it difficult to interpret the results of such comparisons. In the chronological age matched design, the experimental and control groups are of necessity reading at very different levels. Bearing in mind the reciprocal relationship between phonological skills and reading ability, it becomes very difficult to determine whether the phonological difficulties experienced by children with dyslexia arise from a core deficit or whether they are merely a consequence of their poor reading levels. One of the ways out of this conundrum is to employ a 'reading age matched design' in which the two groups are matched not on chronological age but on reading age. For instance, an experimenter might compare a group of nine-year-olds reading at the seven-year level with a group of seven-year-olds reading at their age appropriate standard. The aim of the experimenter is then to demonstrate that the control group of normally reading seven-year-olds is able to perform better than the nine-year-old poor readers on phonological or other reading-related tasks. If this proves to be the case, the experimenter has provided very stringent evidence of a core phonological deficit in the poor readers that cannot be accounted for by their reading level or their learning experiences. One particular problem of the reading age-matched design is that the poor readers are invariably three to four years older than the younger typically developing readers; it can be difficult to control for general maturational factors and the effects of teaching which might act to obscure differences between the two groups that can be difficult to interpret. Consequently, many studies employ two control groups – a chronological age-matched control group and a reading age-matched group. In general, these have shown that children with dyslexia perform poorly relative to controls on tasks that require them to blend, analyze or manipulate speech segments in words, whether at the level of the syllable, rime or phoneme.

Is there a particular component of phonological awareness that is especially compromised in dyslexia? Swan and Goswami (1997) compared the ability of children with dyslexia on tasks of syllable, rime and phoneme segmentation with that of chronological age-matched and reading age-matched control children. Although the poor readers were disadvantaged relative to the chronological age-matched controls on all three levels of segmentation task, they were impaired relative to the reading age-matched control participants only on the phoneme segmentation task. This suggests that in children with dyslexia (as with typically developing children) it is the ability to analyze speech at the level of the phoneme that is the most critical phonological determiner of their ease of learning to read.

There are also many studies that have demonstrated that children with dyslexia perform more poorly than chronological age-matched or reading age-matched controls on phonological processing measures such as naming speed, short-term verbal working memory and nonword repetition (see Hulme and Snowling 2009 for a fuller review of these studies). In general, it has been found that the greater the severity of phonological impairment in children with dyslexia the more severe the reading difficulty.

It is possible for a child with dyslexia to demonstrate relatively intact phonological awareness while struggling with tasks that measure phonological processing speed, and indeed vice versa. Wolf and Bowers (1999) view children who have both phonological awareness and phonological processing difficulties as having a 'dual deficit' which makes their literacy problems more severe than if only one of these phonological skills were impaired. From my own clinical experience, it is not unusual to see children who show a single deficit in which their phonological awareness is satisfactorily developed but whose naming speed is slow; these children typically read fairly accurately, albeit usually slowly, and they invariably have difficulties with spelling. Patterns of phonological skill may also change over time and with access to intervention. Phonological awareness is, as we shall see in a later chapter, a highly trainable skill, while phonological processing abilities (like naming speed and verbal working memory) are less likely to respond to direct intervention. Thus, a child who has a dual phonological deficit who then goes on to receive explicit phonological awareness training may well eventually overcome their phonological awareness difficulties but still be left with a single (naming speed) deficit; this changing phonological profile would be expected to be accompanied by improvements in reading accuracy but very likely persisting reading fluency and spelling problems.

Many children presenting with learning difficulties, including dyslexia, are not uncommonly diagnosed as having auditory processing difficulties. This diagnosis is a controversial one and indeed many researchers and practitioners are not convinced that such a disorder actually exists. However, it is not implausible to suggest that if a child has difficulty in processing auditory information this might result in phonological problems which would then in turn slow the development of reading skills. An important point to realize is that an auditory processing deficit implies that children have difficulty processing not just speech sounds but also non-speech sounds such as tones and musical notes. Perhaps the most influential of the auditory processing deficit theories is that proposed by Tallal and Piercey (1974) which was based on the findings of experimental studies that assessed children's ability to process tones at differing speeds of delivery. In their studies, typically developing children and those with developmental language disorders were readily able to make comparisons between pairs of tones when these were slowly presented. However, while the control children had no difficulty in making comparisons when the tones were presented at an increasingly faster rate, the performance of the children with developmental language disorder deteriorated markedly when the time interval between the two tones was decreased. It was suggested that children with developmental language disorders (and possibly also children with dyslexia) have what is termed an auditory temporal processing deficit, that is they find it hard to process auditory information when it is presented at rapid rates, which is of course the case when listening to speech. Unfortunately, it has proved difficult for other independent researchers to replicate these findings. Heath, Hogben and Clark (1999) found that when they asked children with developmental language disorders and children with dyslexia to carry out a similar tone comparison task, it was only the language-disordered children that demonstrated difficulties while the children with dyslexia performed similarly to the control group. Mody, Studert-Kennedy and Brady (1997) were able to demonstrate that children with dyslexia had no difficulty when required to process non-speech sound-based stimuli (in this case sine waves) but had difficulties processing phonological stimuli. The general consensus is that it is speech sound-related skills (not generalized auditory processing) that predict reading ability and that it is an impairment in these skills that causes reading problems experienced by children with dyslexia.

The second testable claim of the phonological deficit theory is that children with dyslexia will show a phonological deficit before they learn to read. There are number of family at-risk longitudinal studies that address this question. A good example of such a study is that of Hindson *et al.* (2005). These authors compared the language and phonological skills of pre-school children who came from families with a strong history of dyslexia with those in a matched control group whose families had no history of dyslexia. The at-risk pre-schoolers had significantly lower scores than the controls on measures of phoneme and rhyme awareness, emerging letter knowledge and verbal memory. This is clear evidence that the phonological deficit predates the reading problem, therefore suggesting a causal connection between delayed phonological development and the later onset of a dyslexia based literacy disorder. A further family at-risk study, which will be described in more detail in the next chapter, drew a similar conclusion. Snowling, Gallagher and Frith (2003) followed 56 children at high risk of reading difficulties from just before their fourth birthday until they were eight years of age. The children who went on to develop dyslexia (evident as poor reading at age eight) had shown delayed language development at three years nine months. Weaknesses were also evident in naming objects at speed, emergent letter knowledge and nonword repetition. Even at age six, they had persisting oral language impairments and their phonological awareness was poorly developed. We can thus conclude that the phonological deficit in dyslexia is evident before these children have begun to learn to read.

The phonological deficit theory of dyslexia meets its two testable claims, first, that the severity of the phonological deficit predicts variations in the severity of the reading deficit and, second, that the phonological deficit precedes the onset of the reading difficulty. We might be tempted to feel confident that the cause of dyslexia has been established once and for all. However, we will find in the next two chapters that this theory turns out to be rather simplistic and does eventually fail to explain the considerable individual variations we see in children with dyslexia.

Behavioural outcomes in dyslexia

The third level of study in Frith's causal model of dyslexia is the behavioural level which is the level at which the dyslexia is expressed educationally; in effect, how does a deficit in phonological processing affect children's reading and spelling? To answer this question, it is useful to revisit the connectionist model of reading that we looked at in relation to typical literacy development in the previous chapter. Connectionist models conceptualize dyslexia by providing a bridge between cognitive (phonological) and behavioural (reading) levels of explanation in the form of the mappings that develop between sounds and letters as children learn to read a given word. The differences in connectionist terms between the typical reader and the reader with dyslexia are diagrammatically represented in Figure 2.2.

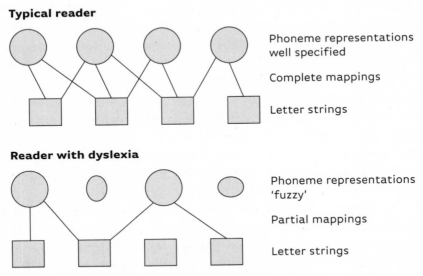

Figure 2.2 Dyslexia: a connectionist view

Phonological measures, whether derived from awareness or processing tasks, tap into the integrity of children's phoneme representations. In the typical reader, phoneme representations are well specified so that when the child is presented with a new word to read, it is easy for them to create complete mappings between the phoneme level and its printed letter string — so that the word is read correctly even after few presentations. In contrast, the child with dyslexia has phoneme representations that are fuzzy and non-segmented (or poorly organized). These poorly specified phoneme representations prevent the development of complete and secure mappings between phonemes and their corresponding letter strings. Thus, when the child with dyslexia comes to read a novel word they are able to achieve only partial or incomplete mappings, even with repeated presentations, which means that the word is unlikely to be read correctly. Indeed, many parents of children with dyslexia complain that their child finds it hard to read a given word even after they have seen it many times. Most children with dyslexia find spelling even more difficult than reading. While accurate reading, especially when reading in prose context, can sometimes be achieved on the basis of partial letter-sound representations, spelling requires full and complete letter-sound mappings.

At the behavioural level, one of the first signs of dyslexia is difficulty in acquiring alphabet knowledge, that is in learning the names and sounds of the individual letters of the alphabet. This is essentially a paired associate learning task in that the child has to associate printed letters with their sound representations; the connectionist approach, with its emphasis on creating mappings between letters and sounds, very much captures this associative learning. Children with dyslexia cannot easily achieve full knowledge of the alphabet because the mappings or associations between sounds and letters are incomplete.

The dyslexic child's inability to map alphabetic symbols to speech sounds means that they fail to develop phonic reading strategies. (In Brian Byrne's terminology, they fail to acquire the alphabetic principle: the realization that sounds and letters are systematically associated with one another, such that whenever a particular phoneme occurs in a word, and in whatever position, it can be represented by the same letter.) One direct way of measuring a child's level of phonic skill is to ask them to attempt to read nonsense words that cannot be recognized through previous exposure nor accessed through semantic clues. These words can be read only if the child is able to apply sound-to-letter correspondence rules in a systematic way. Indeed, there is a great deal of evidence that children with dyslexia have considerable difficulty in reading nonwords like 'fup', 'stip' and 'bolrik'. Two review papers of what is termed the nonword reading deficit pooled data from a number of studies of nonword reading in children with dyslexia (Rack, Snowling and Olsen 1992; Van Ijzendoorn and Bus 1994). These authors demonstrated that poor readers not only had problems in decoding nonwords when compared to chronological age-matched controls, but in a number of studies their nonword reading was poorer than that of younger children reading at the same level (i.e. reading age matched control group). Children with the most severe phonological difficulties tend to show the most severe nonword reading difficulties (Griffiths and Snowling 2002). As we shall see in later chapters, the use of nonword reading tests as an assessment tool is of enormous value in 'diagnosing' dyslexia and in quantifying the severity of the child's phonic decoding difficulty.

Dyslexia is a disorder that for many individuals is lifelong. Having said that, its presentation may change over the course of development, becoming altered with maturation, through experiential factors and as a result of developing compensatory strategies. Cognitive and educational expressions of dyslexia that are evident at one point in development may not be present at another. Indeed, a child identified with dyslexia at age seven may look very different by the time they are 16. Children with mild dyslexia can, after a late start, learn to read adequately by middle childhood and even develop basic spelling skills. And indeed, those children with dyslexia who receive appropriate targeted literacy intervention, preferably as early as possible and for as long as needed, may well overcome the worst of their reading difficulties by the time they are adolescents. Moreover, some children develop compensatory strategies, such as the verbally able child who learns to draw on their good language skills and the context clues available in continuous text to support accurate word identification. For other children who have severe dyslexia (especially those who do not receive appropriate intervention), the educational gap between them and their peers often widens as they get older; attention and behaviour problems may develop and their oral language (especially their vocabulary knowledge) can deteriorate due to their failure to read. Reading fluency and spelling problems usually persist into adulthood, even for those with mild dyslexia. This is well illustrated in a long-term follow-up study by Maughan *et al.* (2009). These authors had the opportunity to reassess three decades later individuals who had participated in a large-scale epidemiological study of reading problems when they were nine to ten years old. Eighty per cent of those who had been identified at age nine to ten with significant 'reading retardation' had spelling scores as adults that were well below the population average. Moreover, they had passed fewer school exams, obtained lesser qualifications and were in lower paid jobs than those in a matched control group who had not had reading problems as children.

The phonology-decoding-reading connection: an example

We will now look at a case study that demonstrates the salience and robustness of the phonology-decoding-reading connection in a child with dyslexia. Nicholas was a participant (along with 37 other children) in our first longitudinal study of early literacy development (Muter *et al.* 1998). There was no indication at the outset of this study that he would go on to develop severe dyslexia. He was first seen at age four during his last term at nursery school when he, along with his classmates, was determined to be a non-reader. He was a bright and articulate boy, enthusiastic, sociable and eager to please. He had not as yet established phonological or letter knowledge skills but then nor had his peers. Nicholas was seen again a year later at age five (towards the end of his Reception class year), and then at age six as he approached the end of Year 1. During those two years, his classmates made good progress in their phonological awareness, as demonstrated by their performance on an initial sound phoneme deletion task; by the end of Year 1, the average score for the group as a whole was five (out of ten items) while Nicholas was unable to score at all. By the end of Year 1, he was able to identify only five letters of the alphabet while the average for the group was 19. It was clear that he was not developing the skills required to underpin progress in learning to read, and more specifically to acquire the alphabetic principle. Not surprisingly, he performed poorly on a single word reading test at the end of Year 1 (he was able to read five words accurately from the reading list, while the group average was 17). His struggle to acquire alphabetic reading skills was clearly demonstrated by his inability to read simple nonwords, in contrast to many of his peers who were now beginning to develop this skill. Interestingly, he performed well in line with his peers on an arithmetic test. It was evident by age six that Nicholas was demonstrating the profile we might expect to see in a child with emerging dyslexia. His teachers were informed of the experimenter's concerns, and he went on to receive some literacy intervention.

We had the opportunity to follow up this sample of children when they were aged ten and in their penultimate year at primary school. Nicholas, along with 33 other children, returned to the study. Nicholas continued to display significant difficulties with phonological awareness, phonic decoding and literacy, with the performance gap between him and his peers appearing ever larger. On a phonological awareness test of 24 items which required the children to delete a specified sound from a spoken nonword in order to arrive at a real word (e.g. 'stip' without the /t/ says 'sip'), Nicholas obtained a raw score of only four, while the group average was 17. He was still very poor at decoding, as demonstrated by his score of only 2/20 on a one- and two-syllable nonword reading test, in contrast to the group average of 14–15/20. Not surprisingly, his reading and spelling were very poor indeed; he scored in the bottom 5 per cent for his age group on standardized measures of reading and spelling. However, his score on a maths test was within the normal range. Not only was Nicholas struggling in literacy, but he scored within the 'clinical range' on behaviour checklists completed by his parents and teachers. He had gone from being a happy, well-behaved four-year-old at the outset of the study to a disengaged, unhappy, anxious and defensive ten-year-old by the time the study was completed. The case of Nicholas clearly demonstrates the robust and persistent association between phonological skills and learning to read. On a practical note, it suggests that children at risk of dyslexia can be identified at an early age, as young as five (through the administration of simple phonological awareness and letter knowledge tests). It follows that delivering early targeted and robust intervention should at the very least help prevent the worsening of children's literacy problems and, equally as worrying, the potential deterioration in their motivation and behaviour.

Reading comprehension difficulties

In Chapter 1, we saw that reading comprehension can be viewed as the product of word recognition and listening comprehension. In this Simple View of Reading model, it would be reasonable to expect that if a child is struggling to comprehend what they read, they must have a difficulty either with reading the text accurately or with processing the language information contained in that text – or perhaps even both.

Children with reading comprehension disorders are defined as those whose reading comprehension skills are far worse than expected from their level of reading accuracy. This can be demonstrated by for instance administering a test such as the York Assessment of Reading Comprehension (YARC; Snowling, Stothard *et al.* 2011). The primary version of this standardized test requires the child to read out loud a page of text. The time the child takes to read the passage and their reading errors are recorded; scores are then provided for reading speed and accuracy. After the child has read the passage, they are asked eight questions which assess their understanding of what they have read. Some of the questions address stated facts within the text whereas others require inference. A reading comprehension score is obtained which can then be compared to the child's reading accuracy and fluency scores. Many children with dyslexia will score well on the reading comprehension measure but obtain low scores for reading accuracy and fluency. In contrast, the child with a reading comprehension difficulty will read the text accurately and even fluently, but fail to comprehend what they have read. It has been estimated that as many as 10 per cent of our child population has a reading comprehension difficulty that often goes unrecognized during their primary schooling, and is likely to persist well into their secondary school years.

How do we characterize the deficits seen in children with reading comprehension problems? First, it has been demonstrated that children with reading comprehension difficulties do not exhibit the phonological or decoding problems that one typically sees in children with dyslexia. Stothard and Hulme (1995) compared the phonological, decoding and spelling skills of a group of children with a reading comprehension impairment with those of a group of age-matched controls and also with a group of younger children matched for reading comprehension with the impaired group: a comprehension age-matched group. The comprehension-impaired group scored at a similar level to the age-matched controls on a phonological awareness measure, a nonword decoding test and a spelling test (and both groups were better than the comprehension-matched controls). This clearly demonstrates that reading comprehension-impaired children do not have difficulties with reading and spelling words or with the phonological and decoding skills that underpin these literacy skills.

Still bearing in mind the Simple View of Reading model, it seems reasonable to hypothesize that children with reading comprehension impairments will have difficulties with the listening comprehension component of the equation. This is indeed the case, with many studies showing that poor comprehenders show a wide range of oral language difficulties, measured in experimental studies and also demonstrable on standardized tests. In the Stothard and Hulme study, they found that the poor reading comprehenders obtained lower scores on a verbal intelligence test than those in the control group. Poor comprehenders have also been demonstrated to have more limited oral vocabularies as measured by standardized tests of vocabulary (Nation and Snowling 1998).

Experimental studies have explored in more depth the range and nature of the language difficulties experienced by poor reading comprehenders. Nation *et al.* (2004) compared a group of poor comprehenders with a group of equivalent age children who were matched for text reading accuracy and nonword reading skills. The children were assessed on a wide range of language measures, including tests of vocabulary, syntax (word order knowledge), morphology (knowledge of the units of meaning within words), and broader receptive and expressive language skills. The poor reading comprehenders experienced difficulty across all of these language measures compared to the typically developing children of the same age and level of reading accuracy. The authors found that a large proportion of the poor comprehenders, 35 per cent in fact (but none of the control children), met criteria that would qualify them for a clinical diagnosis of developmental language disorder. Yet, interestingly none of the children had previously been recognized as having language problems, a finding that clearly demonstrates that reading comprehension and associated language difficulties are not always obvious in children who appear (at least superficially) to read well. Indeed, reading comprehension disorders are often thought of as 'hidden' within the classroom because it is assumed that the child who reads out loud accurately must be making good progress in all aspects of literacy.

One of the largest studies of poor reading comprehenders is that conducted by Catts, Adlof and Weismer (2006) who compared 57 poor comprehenders with 27 poor decoders and 98 typically developing children of the same age. They were subjected to a large battery of language and literacy tests while in early high school. Not unsurprisingly, the poor comprehenders, but not the poor decoders, showed deficits in vocabulary and grammatical skills, though their phonological skills were normal. The poor comprehenders also showed deficits in listening comprehension and what is termed discourse processing. The latter might be measured by for instance asking children to tell stories and then scoring them for coherence and ordered structure (e.g. having a beginning, middle and end) and for using connective words like 'and', 'but' and 'therefore' which link components of the story together. Some studies have also shown that poor reading comprehenders find it hard to remember the meanings of words that they have been taught directly (new word learning), and that they have difficulties in inferring the meanings of new words from surrounding text (Cain, Oakhill and Elbro 2003; Nation, Snowling and Clarke 2007). Difficulties such as these will contribute to the vocabulary impoverishment that we typically see in poor reading comprehenders and that in turn affects their ability to understand what they are reading because they do not know the meanings of the words in the text.

As children get older, they encounter more complex texts which require that they not only understand and remember the factual information contained within them, but they also need to go beyond what is written, to read between and beyond the lines and therefore to make inferences. In the Catts et al. (2006) study, poor comprehenders had great difficulty making inferences. For instance, a text might state 'The bonfire began to burn uncontrollably. Jan rushed to pick up the garden hose.' An inferential question might ask 'Why did Jan pick up the garden hose?' The child needs to infer that Jan is planning to put out the fire by spraying water from the hose. The child with a reading comprehension impairment might be expected to have difficulty in linking the two sentences in order to make a causal inference.

Auditory/verbal working memory deficits are not infrequently found in children with reading comprehension difficulties. In a series of experiments, Nation *et al.* (1999) demonstrated that poor reading comprehenders performed more poorly on measures of verbal (but not visual/spatial) memory span and recall of abstract words than good comprehenders matched for decoding ability. The authors hypothesized that the memory difficulties experienced by poor reading comprehenders are specific to the verbal domain and as such are a concomitant aspect of broader language impairment rather than a specific cause of reading comprehension failure.

There is one particular language skill which is considered to be specific to reading comprehension (as opposed to being part of the broader language impairment). This is *comprehension monitoring*, which refers to the ability to detect when comprehension of a given piece of text has broken down, in other words the child loses the sense of what they are reading. In order to have effective comprehension monitoring the child needs to be able to appreciate that they are not understanding what they are reading and then to make the necessary correction; for good comprehenders, this would mean going back and re-reading the text so that it eventually makes sense. Poor comprehenders often fail to realize that they have 'lost the plot', nor do they appear to be prepared to re-read what they have not understood.

The causes of reading comprehension difficulties are presented diagrammatically in Figure 2.3.

Longitudinal studies have demonstrated a causal connection between early language deficits and later reading comprehension problems. A longitudinal study by Nation *et al.* (2010) demonstrated the stability and long-term persistence of both language and reading comprehension difficulties experienced by poor comprehenders. They studied 242 children at ages five, six, seven and eight years. At age eight, 15 children met criteria for being poor reading comprehenders and were compared to 15 age-matched control children, both concurrently and even more importantly retrospectively. The poor reading comprehenders' phonological skills were within normal limits throughout the study, but mild impairments in expressive and receptive language skills, listening comprehension and grammatical understanding were seen from an early age and persisted through to age eight.

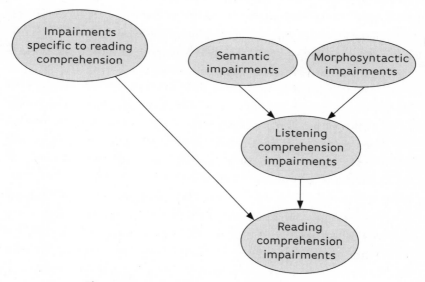

Figure 2.3 Causes of poor reading comprehension

Finally, Ricketts, Sperring and Nation (2014) tracked the educational progress of 15 poor reading comprehenders from age 11 through to 16 years. Educational attainments (based on national UK tests of English, maths and science) were lower in poor comprehenders at ages 11 and 16 years when compared to 15 controls matched for chronological age, nonverbal reasoning and decoding skill. When the attainments of the poor comprehenders were compared to national performance levels, they showed significantly lower levels at both age points. Clearly there is a link between difficulties in reading comprehension in middle childhood and poor educational outcome at secondary school.

Summary

- Disorders of literacy are grouped with mathematics disorders and disorders of written expression under a single over-riding diagnosis of specific learning disorders within the broader category of neurodevelopmental disorders; it is important to differentiate between disorders of word level reading (dyslexia) and of reading comprehension which together make up the category of literacy disorder.
- One influential model of dyslexia describes three different levels in a causal chain: the biological (genetic/neurological), the cognitive and the behavioural, each of which can in turn be influenced by environmental factors.
- Genetic variations seen in individuals with dyslexia act to influence the development of brain regions that underlie children's ability to learn to read; there is evidence of structural and functional differences in the left hemisphere brain regions that are specific to the development of language and literacy skills.
- At the cognitive level, problems with phonological analysis and processing that pre-date the development of reading skills are seen as the strongest causal basis of dyslexia.
- The poorly specified phoneme representations of the child with dyslexia prevent the development of complete and secure mappings between phonemes and their corresponding letter strings, with the result that the child fails to develop phonic reading strategies which can be tapped at the behavioural level by nonword reading tasks.
- Children with poor reading comprehension show a wide range of oral language difficulties, evident from a very early age, which have long-term implications for their educational progress and attainments.

Chapter 3

Beyond the Single Deficit Model
Explaining Individual Differences

Uta Frith's multi-level model of dyslexia has as its core the phonological deficit as the cognitive causal explanation of word level literacy disorders; this is usually termed the single deficit model of dyslexia. This model is based on a *modular* view of both brain and cognitive functioning, that is the theory that a specific brain region is responsible for a specific cognitive function. This approach has provided a very powerful and indeed influential perspective that has informed both research and clinical/educational practice over several decades. However, in this chapter and the next we will explore why the single deficit model ultimately fails to fully and comprehensively describe either the nature of dyslexia or how this disorder can present very differently from one child to the next.

Why the single deficit model fails at the biological level
Let us consider the biological level of explanation first. Because the multi-level model of dyslexia is modular based, it assumes that different sets of genes and separate brain regions underlie different learning difficulties. So, for instance, it is proposed that there is one set of genes that determines whether a child will have dyslexia and a different set of genes that determine whether they

will have a developmental language disorder. Similarly, the modular view states that a given brain region determines literacy function while a separate and different region controls language. We are beginning to see however that neither genes nor the human brain work in this simple modular fashion.

It is important to understand at the outset that genes do not cause dyslexia; rather they create 'risks' for developing the disorder. The concept of risk is probabilistic in the sense that being at risk for a given disorder means that the individual has an increased probability of developing that disorder, but that it is by no means inevitable that they will do so. In dyslexia, there are minor variants (or variations) in structure across multiple genes which create the risk for developing this disorder. However, there are also gene variants that play a protective role, and therefore help to reduce the probability of the disorder being expressed. It is the combination of these risk and protective variants in the individual child which, in interaction with their environment, determines whether they will show literacy difficulties sufficient to attract a diagnosis of dyslexia. Environmental influences that can modify the expression of dyslexic gene variants and influence outcome might include age of identification of the child's literacy difficulty, access to intervention, levels of print exposure, and so on. The exact combination of risk and protective variants will differ from person to person, which of course goes a long way to explaining the individual differences we see from one child with dyslexia to the next. (It is important to note that a single gene variant has only a small effect which can in itself be modified by environmental experiences. This is in sharp contrast to the effects of chromosome or gene deletions, duplications or mutations that we see in children with genetic disorders such as Down's Syndrome or Prader Willi Syndrome; in Down's Syndrome, the child has an extra chromosome, while in Prader Willi there is a deletion on chromosome 15. Deletions, duplications and mutations are rare but have very large effects which result in devastating compromises to the child's physical development and cognitive functioning.)

Research has shown us that there is not one set of genes that determines dyslexia, another separate set of genes that determines language disorder, and yet another that determines ADHD – and so on. This brings us to the important concept of *shared* versus *non-shared* genes. Bruce Pennington describes most genes as 'generalists' which means they are shared across disorders. So, the same gene variants could predispose a child to both dyslexia and language disorder. There are also non-shared genes that are specific to particular disorders; so for instance, there could be some gene variants that predispose a child only to dyslexia but not language disorder, while different genes might result in a child developing a language disorder but not dyslexia. It is of course difficult to accommodate the concept of genes being shared across disorders in a modular-based single deficit model.

We are now some way towards identifying shared versus nonshared genes in dyslexia. In the ALSPAC (Avon Longitudinal Study of Parents and Children) cohort of 15,000 children born in the Avon area of the UK in 1992 (Golding *et al.* 2002), longitudinal measures were taken of speech and language skills, IQ, reading and spelling, along with gene analyses. The findings of this study have resulted in the identification of genes that are susceptible in dyslexia and which confer risk; specific gene loci on chromosomes 2, 3, 6, 15 and 18 have been identified that appear to be 'markers' for dyslexia, and there are likely to be others that will be identified in due course. However, it is the number of specific risk genes a child has and their relationship to protector genes and their environment that ultimately determine whether they will go to develop dyslexia. These studies also aim to determine specific genes that are *shared* across disorders, and which can explain why many children with dyslexia have co-occurring (or additional) learning problems like language disorders or attention deficits (see Chapter 4). We are in the early stages of identifying shared genes, but two possible candidate-specific genes, labelled KIAA0319 and CMIP, appear to be susceptible genes in both dyslexia and developmental language disorder (Newbury *et al.* 2011; Scerri *et al.* 2011).

The single deficit model not only fails to work at the genetic level but also at the brain level. There is no convincing neurological evidence that a given cognitive module is located in a specific isolated brain region. Indeed, imaging studies have demonstrated that it is not only the integrity of a given brain region, but also the connections or interactions a brain region has with other regions, that determine cognitive functioning. This is nicely demonstrated in, first, a study by Silani *et al.* (2005) which adopted a particular form of MRI known as voxel-based morphometry that allows the study of patterns of grey and white matter density; the grey matter of the brain is made up of nerve cell bodies while the white matter is made up of bundles of nerve fibres that connect the grey matter regions of the brain. These authors found that there was less dense white matter between the left temporo-parietal and frontal regions of the brain in individuals with dyslexia than in controls. Given that these are speech sound processing regions of the brain, it follows therefore that what we are looking at here is *reduced connectivity* between these reading related areas (see Figure 3.1). In a further study by Saygin *et al.* (2013), the phonological awareness scores of 40 reading at-risk pre-schoolers correlated positively and significantly with the volume of the left arcuate fasciculus which is a tract of nerve fibres known to connect the frontal and temporo-parietal language regions of the brain. Both the pre-school phonological awareness scores and the brain volumes predicted the children's reading scores after they had started school. Thus, MRI studies have shown us that not only is there reduced activation in specific language-related brain regions in children with dyslexia but there is also reduced connectivity between the regions that are in involved in the processes of learning to read. This finding is difficult to accommodate within a modular perspective which proposes that separate and independent brain regions subserve separate cognitive functions.

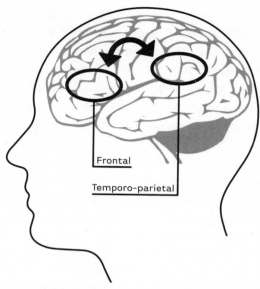

Figure 3.1 The connectivity between the reading-related regions of the brain

Why the single deficit model fails at the cognitive level

Not only does the single deficit model fail at the biological level, it also does so at the cognitive level. In this model, it is assumed that a single cognitive deficit is sufficient to explain the 'symptoms' of a given disorder and that different disorders have different single deficits. To demonstrate the failure of the model at the cognitive level, it is helpful to look in depth at the long-term longitudinal family at-risk study led by Margaret Snowling which I introduced in the previous chapter. This study commenced in the 1990s when the single deficit model was at its peak. Indeed, the hypotheses generated by the authors at the outset very much reflected the single deficit perspective. Seventy-three children were drawn from volunteer families in whom a first degree relative (most usually a parent, though occasionally a sibling) was reported to have dyslexia. At the same time, a control group was recruited in which no parent or sibling was known to have reading problems. Data from 56 of the at-risk children and 29 controls were analysed from the first three phases of the study which took place at ages three years nine months, six years, and eight years (Snowling *et al.* 2003). At all three phases, the children were administered a wide range of language-, literacy- and phonological-based tests. The authors hypothesized that significantly more children in the at-risk group would meet criteria for a diagnosis of dyslexia by the age of age eight when compared to the controls. Not surprisingly, this proved to be the case, with 37 of the at-risk children (66%) experiencing significant literacy difficulties at age eight compared with only four of the controls (14%).

The authors also hypothesized, in keeping with the single deficit model, that children in the at-risk group who had a significant phonological deficit would have dyslexia, while those in the at-risk group who did not meet criteria for dyslexia would not demonstrate a phonological deficit. In other words, they were expecting an all-or-none outcome: if you had poor phonology you had dyslexia; if you didn't have poor phonology you didn't have dyslexia. However, the results of the study did not confirm this hypothesis. While those children in the at-risk group who had reading problems demonstrated significant difficulties on the phonological tasks given, many of the at-risk children who were competent readers (and indeed performing at a similar level to the controls) also had phonological difficulties. Thus, these at-risk reading-unimpaired children were demonstrating a phonological deficit at the cognitive level but without the expected reading problems at the behavioural level. This flies in the face of the single deficit model which claims that a single phonological deficit is sufficient to account for the reading difficulties experienced by children with dyslexia. Having said that, many of the at-risk reading-unimpaired children, while reading sufficiently well, nonetheless had spelling problems and their speed of reading was slow. The authors were forced to conclude that dyslexia is not all-or-none, but rather a *dimensional* disorder which occurs along a continuum ranging from high risk to low risk.

An important finding within the at-risk group was that the reading-unimpaired children had far higher verbal IQs than the reading-impaired children. It was suggested that at-risk children with good oral language skills may be able to 'get round' their reading difficulties by using compensatory strategies that essentially protect them from failure. Such children might be able to take advantage of context and content clues contained in continuous prose text, while also drawing on their good semantic and vocabulary skills, to enable them to better 'guess at' words that they could not easily decode or recognize out of context. In contrast, the at-risk reading-impaired children had essentially two risk factors (a phonological deficit and low verbal IQ) which acted together to increase the likelihood of their having reading problems. This study clearly shows that the single deficit model, with its modular view, cannot easily explain the varied behavioural expression of the disorder, which is far better explained by the cumulative effect of (often multiple) risk and protective factors. The child with severe dyslexia will have wide-ranging literacy problems (which include difficulties with reading accuracy, fluency and spelling), with these occurring most usually within the context of broader oral language difficulties. In contrast, the child with mild dyslexia might well escape reading accuracy problems but is likely to be a slow reader and a weak speller; these children often have stronger language skills which provide a substantial compensatory resource that increases their reading accuracy.

Which children develop dyslexia?

We have seen that the development of dyslexia is determined by the accumulation of multiple risks interacting with strengths and protective factors. If a child has relatively few risk factors (perhaps even just one) and they have strengths that enable them to compensate for that risk, then they may not meet criteria for having the disorder. However, if a child is carrying multiple risks, there is an increased probability that these risks will accumulate to a critical threshold point that tips them over into the dyslexic category. We will now look at research that has determined what the primary risk factors for dyslexia are and that additionally provides evidence for this accumulating multiple risk model.

We have already seen that being born into a family where there are other members who have literacy problems confers a significant risk of developing dyslexia. What is the nature of that risk and are there associated and additional risks that make it likely that such a child will meet diagnostic criteria for having dyslexia? Maggie Snowling, Charles Hulme and their colleagues have conducted a number of research studies that have explored the nature of the risk for children born into 'dyslexic families'. In particular, they have looked at the important connection between oral language difficulties evident in young children from an early age and later emerging literacy problems. Before we look at some of these studies in depth, it is important to consider (albeit briefly) the characteristics of children who have a developmental language disorder as there is much overlap of this disorder with dyslexia.

In DSM-5, developmental language disorders (DLD) are subsumed under the broader diagnostic category of communication disorders. DSM-5 describes four main features of DLD (American Psychiatric Association 2013: 42). First, language disorders are evident as persistent difficulties in the acquisition of comprehension or production skills, which also include reduced vocabulary, limited sentence structures and impairments in discourse (i.e. using language to explain or describe events or topics). Second, the child's language skills are well below those expected for their age, resulting in limitations in effective communication, reduced social participation, poor academic attainment and restricted occupational opportunities. Third, the language difficulties are evident from the earliest stages of development, and finally, they cannot be attributed to hearing impairment, medical or neurological conditions or intellectual disability. More information about the nature of language disorders is provided in Box 3.1.

Box 3.1: Developmental language disorder (DLD)

The term developmental language disorder is most usually reserved for children whose oral language skills are much poorer than their nonverbal abilities, which are typically within normal limits. These children form quite a heterogeneous group. Some children have difficulty with understanding and producing language (receptive and expressive language disorders), others are able to understand spoken language but are unable to express themselves appropriately (expressive language disorder), some children have accompanying speech problems which makes their speech difficult to understand (speech sound disorder) and some have difficulty with the social aspects of language (pragmatic language disorder). Prevalence rates for language disorder are of the order 3–6 per cent, with boys more likely to be affected than girls.

The communication difficulties of children with a language disorder are likely to be recognized during their pre-school years. There are many studies that have demonstrated that around 50 per cent of pre-schoolers with delayed language development go on to resolve their difficulties by the time they reach school age. However, this also implies that around half the children presenting with language problems as pre-schoolers will have persisting language problems in middle childhood and beyond, which will in turn impact their educational progress and their social communication. A classic study by Bishop and Adams (1990) found that of 83 children identified with speech and language problems at age four, 37 per cent had resolved their difficulties by the time they were five and a half. These language resolvers who were followed up at age eight years showed generally good outcomes in terms of their oral language and their reading skills. However, those who had failed to resolve their language problems by five and a half showed significant impairment in a wide range of language skills, and also in reading, at age eight. A longer-term study of the language-resolved children into adolescence showed that they maintained their normal oral language skills, but there was an increased risk of these children developing later reading problems which in turn impaired their academic performance.

Understanding the cognitive basis of language disorders is more complex than understanding literacy disorders, and is indeed beyond the scope of this book. There are many theories about what causes language disorders. Some theories attribute the disorder to deficits in the development of grammatical structure, others claim that it is a consequence of slow and inefficient auditory processing, while still others emphasize problems within the short-term phonological loop. Suffice to say that we so far lack a clear and well-supported cognitive level of explanation for language disorders. It is the view of Dorothy Bishop (2006) that, given the complexity of language and the heterogeneity of the difficulties seen in language-disordered children, it seems likely that we are looking at multiple cognitive deficits that may have differing effects on the development of separate language components.

Nash *et al.* (2013) compared the pre-school language skills of 112 children at family-risk of dyslexia with children who had a language disorder and a control group of typically developing children. One third of the at-risk group resembled the language-disordered children, having broad-based language difficulties that also included phonological problems. At the individual level, some family-risk children had both broader language and phonological difficulties, some had phonological difficulties only, and there were some who appeared to be developing normally. This study clearly demonstrates that there is a considerable overlap (or co-occurrence) of dyslexia and language disorders, and indeed coming from a family of dyslexics means that a child carries an increased risk of having a language disorder. Fifty per cent of the family-risk children had phonological difficulties which placed them at risk for decoding (and of course reading and spelling) problems. At a practical level, the authors suggest that screening pre-schoolers from at-risk families on an early phonological measure (such as a nonword repetition test) and a broader language measure (such as a sentence comprehension or sentence repetition test) would enable practitioners to identify children at risk for different forms of language and literacy impairment.

Thompson *et al.* (2015) studied four groups of pre-schoolers: family-risk of dyslexia only, language disorder only, family-risk plus language disorder and typically developing controls. The children were recruited for the study at age three and assessed annually on a wide range of cognitive, language and literacy measures up to the age of eight years. After the last assessment phase, the children were classified as having dyslexia if their scores were significantly and substantially below the average score for the control group on a composite (reading and spelling) measure. The authors conducted a complex statistical analysis called logistic regression modelling which enabled them to first, predict individual risk of dyslexia and second, to investigate how risk factors accumulate to predict poor literacy outcome. They were able to demonstrate that dyslexia is the outcome of multiple risk factors which were essentially the measures taken earlier in this study that predicted whether the children were classified as having dyslexia at age eight. Pre-school language difficulties and being born into a dyslexic family were strong determiners of whether a child would develop dyslexia. Additional predictors in the pre-school years included the children's emerging letter knowledge, phonological awareness and rapid naming scores (and to a lesser extent their scores on a motor test). On further analysis, the authors found that speech and language delay is not a good predictor until close to school entry point; this is consistent with the view that many children with delayed language who resolve their difficulties by ages four to five years learn to read normally. In terms of the educational implications of these findings, the authors point out that screening does not reach an acceptable level of predictive reliability until close to school entry when letter knowledge, phonological awareness and rapid naming together provide sufficient sensitivity and specificity to function as a screening battery. Clearly, the early identification of dyslexia is difficult, and the closer the assessments are to school entry the more accurate predictions become.

A further study by Snowling *et al.* (2016) explored in more depth the relationship between early language and later reading in at-risk children. Three groups of children (language disorder, family-risk of dyslexia and controls) were followed at regular intervals from pre-school to middle childhood. The authors were especially interested in whether children had persisting or resolving language difficulty profiles as they proceeded from pre-school into middle childhood. The children were defined at all ages as having a language disorder if they scored significantly below the control group average on language measures. Not surprisingly, the language and literacy outcomes were relatively poor for those with persisting language difficulties but relatively good for those with resolving language problems. An interesting, and somewhat unexpected, finding was that some children who had average language abilities as pre-schoolers went on to exhibit language difficulties that emerged in middle childhood. Late-emerging language difficulties are relatively rare, they are associated with family-risk of dyslexia, they are difficult to detect and they usually result in significant reading problems. Snowling and her colleagues concluded that there are three trajectories of language impairment. First, there are those children who have persisting language impairment identified in pre-school which is severe and pervasive and invariably associated with poor literacy outcomes. Second are those children whose pre-school language impairment resolves by school entry and who have a generally good outcome in language and literacy. Possible protective factors that would improve outcome in this latter group include strengths in nonverbal ability and having less extensive vocabulary difficulties at pre-school. Third are the late-emerging language-impaired children identified in middle childhood who have poor language and literacy outcomes.

Hayiou-Thomas *et al.* (2017) looked at whether the presence of an early speech sound disorder confers a risk of developing dyslexia; here we are looking at children who have what are commonly referred to as articulation problems, such that their speech is difficult for others to understand. The authors found that children with pre-school speech difficulties were at risk for developing phonemic and spelling problems at age five to six years. This was especially the case for children whose speech was disordered (i.e. not following the usual sequence or pattern of speech development, with often odd sound substitutions being evident). Beyond the domain of speech, the presence of a co-occurring language difficulty was strongly predictive of early reading problems, and being at family-risk of dyslexia constituted a further risk. Early speech sound disorder considered as a single factor has only a modest effect on literacy development; however, when additional risk factors are present (family history, delayed language development), there are serious negative consequences for the child's later literacy development. This is consistent with the view that multiple factors accumulate to predict reading disorders.

Finally, there is a widely held belief that otitis media (glue ear), a common cause of hearing problems in pre-school children, can delay speech and language development and therefore indirectly impair progress in reading. However, a prospective study of over 6,000 children who suffered otitis media in the first one to three years of life showed that this condition resulted in only very minor, small and circumscribed impairments of receptive language and verbal cognition at age three years (Paradise *et al.* 2000). Moreover, the authors found that when otitis media is associated with language impairment, it is likely to be mediated by socio-demographic factors (e.g. low socioeconomic status of parents) which can result in late diagnosis or a failure to treat. They concluded that the impact of otitis media on children's language and cognition has been overstated.

Introducing Case Study 1: a longitudinal perspective of a child with developmental language disorder and dyslexia

Our first case study is Alex whose history and broad presentation is described in Box 3.2. His assessments and interventions will be discussed in depth in the later chapters that specifically address these topics.

Box 3.2: Case Study 1 – Alex

Alex was referred for assessment at age six. He had by then a complex history of language and learning difficulties. His parents reported that he was a very late talker and was in fact producing only single words at age two and a half years. He underwent hearing tests which proved normal. At age three, Alex was referred for a speech and language evaluation. This showed that his receptive and expressive language were both severely delayed. He went on to receive regular speech and language therapy up until the time that he started school as a rising five-year-old. Alex found it difficult to settle into school life because of his poor understanding of spoken language and his struggles to express himself. He continued to receive speech and language therapy during his Reception class and

Year 1. When he was referred to me for assessment, he was in Year 2 and making minimal if any educational progress. His parents and teachers observed that he seemed to be a little stronger in maths than literacy. He was able to read and spell only a few simple high frequency words. There was a strong family history of reading and writing difficulties on father's side of the family, including father himself who even as an adult was a very poor speller.

Alex's assessment at age six will be described more comprehensively in the later chapter on assessment. However, by way of summary, he demonstrated good, indeed well above average, nonverbal abilities. When given a verbal ability test (administered orally), he obtained below average scores on measures of verbal reasoning and expressive vocabulary. He was able to score only very minimally (at barely the five-year-old level) on standardized measures of reading and spelling accuracy. His maths was noticeably stronger, and indeed on a pencil-and-paper arithmetic test he scored within normal limits for his age. Diagnostically oriented testing revealed short-term auditory/verbal working memory difficulties and poorly developed phonological awareness. It was concluded that Alex was a nonverbally able boy with a language disorder who was clearly markedly at risk for developing dyslexia.

Shortly after the assessment took place, Alex's parents and his school applied for a statutory assessment and at the age of seven he received a statement of special educational needs (now called an education, health and care (EHC) plan). Even with continued speech and language therapy and targeted literacy intervention, he continued to struggle enormously within a mainstream primary school setting. At an annual review of statement that took place when he was eight, it was determined that his educational needs would be better met in a specialist setting. He was then placed at a school for language-disordered children where he had access to high levels of speech and language therapy input and individualized and small-group language and educational interventions delivered by specialist teachers. By the age of 11, Alex was deemed to have made sufficient progress for him to return to a mainstream school setting.

During his secondary school years, Alex has been observed by his teachers to cope fairly well with the oral language demands of the classroom. However, his progress in terms of basic literacy is very much slower, even though he is continuing to receive additional literacy support. Now aged 13 years, it is clear that he is unable to access his written curriculum, hence this new referral for a further evaluation. This assessment is described comprehensively in the later assessment chapter when we will pick up Alex's story again.

The foregoing discussion provides evidence that the single deficit model of dyslexia fails to accommodate the research evidence within both the biological and cognitive domains; nor does the single deficit model adequately explain the individual differences and varying degrees of severity seen in children with dyslexia. That is not to say that children with a single phonological risk factor will not necessarily have literacy problems, but it does mean that their difficulties are likely to be comparatively mild and largely restricted to problems of spelling and perhaps fluency; many such children will not even meet the threshold for a diagnosis of dyslexia. It appears that those children who do meet diagnostic criteria for this developmental disorder are those who are carrying multiple risks or deficits (with phonology and broader aspects of language being especially strongly implicated). In the next chapter, we will look at additional cognitive risk factors outside the language domain which result in other complex educational presentations of which dyslexia is but one component.

Summary

- The single deficit or phonological deficit model of dyslexia is based on a modular view of gene and brain function. However, here is no convincing neuroscientific evidence that a given cognitive module is determined by a specific set of genes or is located in a specific isolated brain region; it is not just the integrity of a given brain region, but also the connections or interactions a brain region has with other regions that determine cognitive functioning.

- The single deficit module at the cognitive level assumes that dyslexia is an all-or-none phenomenon; however, we have clear evidence from at-risk longitudinal studies of dyslexia that reading disorders occur along a continuum of severity, with their behavioural expression varying from child to child.

- Whether a given child develops dyslexia is determined by the accumulation of multiple risks that interact with strengths or protective factors; the more risks a child has, the more likely they are to achieve a critical threshold which will attract a formal diagnosis of dyslexia.

- Risks for developing dyslexia include being born into a family where other members have reading problems, having pre-school speech and language difficulties which persist beyond the point of school entry, having poor phonological skills, being slow to acquire alphabetic letter knowledge and having persistent speech sound difficulties.

- The impact of risk factors can be reduced by protective factors which may be inherent in the child (e.g. having good language skills or nonverbal abilities which provide important compensatory resources), or environmental (e.g. early identification through screening of at-risk pre-schoolers).

Chapter 4

Beyond the Single Deficit Model
Explaining Co-Occurrence

In the previous chapter, we saw that the single deficit model fails to adequately explain dyslexia at either the biological or cognitive levels of explanation. There is arguably an even more compelling reason why single deficit models don't work. This is because they cannot readily explain the high rate of co-morbidity (now more usually referred to as co-occurrence) of dyslexia with other learning disorders. Co-occurrence is evident when two different disorders or diseases are present in the same individual. How often should we expect dyslexia to co-occur with another disorder in the same child? As an example, let us assume that the incidence of dyslexia in the child population is 10 per cent and the incidence of maths disorders is also 10 per cent. If the disorders are separate and independent, as they are hypothesized to be in a modular-based single deficit model, the number of children expected to have both disorders is given by the product of the proportion of children with each disorder ($0.1 \times 0.1 = 0.01$ or 1%). However, as we shall see throughout this chapter, the rates of co-occurrence in developmental disorders are very much higher than this. Indeed, there is good evidence that about 40 per cent of children with one neurodevelopmental disorder will also meet diagnostic criteria for having another neurodevelopmental disorder. There are two forms of co-occurrence. The first is when one disorder is the forerunner of the other and pre-dates it; the overlap of dyslexia and language disorder described in Chapter 3 is an example of this. The second form of co-occurrence is when two distinct disorders co-exist at the same time; a good example of this would be dyslexia and co-occurring arithmetic disorder (dyscalculia).

To demonstrate the high levels of co-occurrence of dyslexia with other developmental disorders, we can return to the long-term longitudinal at-risk study conducted by Maggie Snowling and her colleagues, including myself. These children were followed up into their senior schools, undergoing final extensive assessment at age 13 years (Snowling, Muter and Carroll 2007). The children's literacy and language skills were assessed, and they were also administered standardized tests of mathematics, attention and nonverbal skills. Of the 21 children identified as at-risk poor readers, 16 (i.e. more than 70%) showed additional difficulties in respect of oral language, nonverbal skills, attention control or mathematics (and sometimes a combination of these). Indeed, in this sample of children, their numeracy problems were in most cases as serious as their difficulties in literacy. We shall shortly see that children with dyslexia show a significantly elevated risk of having co-occurring learning difficulties which are sometimes sufficiently severe as to attract a formal diagnosis of language disorder, attention deficit hyperactivity disorder (ADHD), developmental co-ordination disorder/dyspraxia (DCD) or specific arithmetic disorder/dyscalculia.

How do we account for the high level of co-occurrence of dyslexia with other learning disorders? At the genetic level, co-occurrence is explained by the concept of shared versus non-shared gene variants which was introduced in the previous chapter. To briefly recapitulate, when genes are shared across disorders it means that the same gene variants could predispose a child to both dyslexia and for instance dyscalculia. However, there are also non-shared genes that are specific to particular disorders; so for instance, there could be some gene variants that predispose a child only to dyslexia but not dyscalculia while different genes variants might result in a child developing dyscalculia but not dyslexia. Not only are genes shared across disorders but so also are cognitive risks – the same cause giving rise to different disorders. The same cognitive risk might predispose a child to dyslexia and dyscalculia. It is this shared cognitive risk that explains why different disorders commonly overlap. However, there are also non-shared cognitive risks that are specific to different disorders: for example, a cognitive risk that gives rise to dyslexia but not dyscalculia and a different cognitive risk that predisposes the child to dyscalculia but not dyslexia. It is the non-shared risks that explain why there is not total overlap of two disorders.

A disorder that frequently co-occurs with dyslexia, and indeed is usually viewed as a forerunner of it, is developmental language disorder, which was discussed in some depth in Chapter 3. Indeed, 50 per cent of children with pre-school language disorder go on to develop dyslexia. We could hypothesize that both genes and cognitive risks are shared across these disorders. At the cognitive level, it has been reported that short-term verbal working memory difficulties and phonological processing problems are frequently observed not only in children who have dyslexia but also children who have language disorders – which makes them good candidates for being shared cognitive risks in these two disorders. There may well be non-shared cognitive risks also, in that for instance we might expect to see grammar and vocabulary deficits in children with language disorders but not necessarily in children with dyslexia. And as we saw in Chapter 2, temporal auditory processing difficulties are not unusually seen in children with language disorders but they are not typically present in children with dyslexia. A recent family risk study by Gooch *et al.* (2014) highlighted executive skills and fine motor abilities as potential non-shared risks (executive skills are complex higher order skills needed to regulate behaviour – see the more comprehensive description of these skills in Box 4.3). The executive skills measured in this study were sustained attention, response inhibition (the ability to stop a prescribed motor response when specific conditions are present) and visual spatial memory. The children with pre-school language disorders demonstrated difficulty with the executive and motor tasks while the children who were at family risk for dyslexia but did not have language problems had fewer (though still some) difficulties with these tasks. A useful figurative means of representing co-occurrence of learning difficulties is in the form of a Venn diagram, which displays visually the partial overlap (i.e. co-occurrence) of two disorders and then relates this to shared and non-shared features evident at the cognitive through to the behavioural level. A hypothesized Venn diagram for dyslexia and language disorder is given in Figure 4.1.

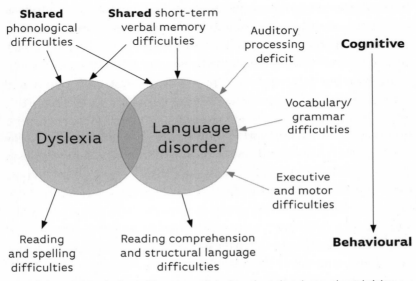

Figure 4.1 Dyslexia and language disorder: shared and non-shared risks

The partial overlap of the Venn circles indicates the shared status of dyslexia and language disorder, in other words the co-occurrence. At the cognitive level, short-term verbal memory and phonological awareness difficulties are seen to contribute to both disorders (shared risks), whereas vocabulary/grammar difficulties, auditory processing deficits, executive problems and motor weaknesses contribute only to language disorder (and are, therefore, potential non-shared risks). The two disorders are expressed differently at the behavioural level, with dyslexia resulting in word level reading and spelling difficulties while language disorder is expressed as structural language and (very likely also) reading comprehension difficulties.

Dyslexia and co-occurring maths problems/dyscalculia

The earlier discussed at-risk longitudinal study demonstrated clearly that dyslexia commonly co-occurs with arithmetic disorders, and that indeed the maths problems that many poor readers have may be as severe as their difficulties with literacy. DSM-5 categorizes arithmetic disorders, and the alternative descriptive label dyscalculia, as a specific learning disorder within the broader category of neurodevelopmental disorders. It is characterized by difficulties in acquiring number sense, number facts or calculation procedures; children may fail to appreciate number magnitude; they often count even single digits on their fingers; and they tend to become confused when carrying out computations. There may also be difficulties with mathematical reasoning (e.g. grasping and applying mathematical concepts, facts or procedures to solve quantitative problems).

For the diagnosis to be made, the difficulties should be evident as mathematical/numerical skills that are substantially below those expected for the individual's age and are expected to cause significant interference to academic or occupational performance. Moreover, they should be evident during the school years (but may not become manifest until the demands for those affected academic skills exceed the individual's limited capacities, e.g. in timed tests), and are not better accounted for by intellectual disability, sensory impairment or inadequate educational instruction. A brief summary of maths disorder/dyscalculia and its causal basis is given in Box 4.1; for a fuller discussion, see Hulme and Snowling (2009).

Box 4.1: Specific maths disorder/dyscalculia

Specific arithmetic disorder or dyscalculia are diagnostic labels used to describe children who find it inordinately difficult to acquire maths concepts and to calculate with numbers accurately. There have been some population studies of the incidence of maths problems which appear to have reached a consensus of a rough prevalence figure of around 6 per cent;

most of these studies have shown that arithmetic problems commonly co-occur with reading difficulties. Arithmetic disorders tend to run in families, and there is increasing evidence of them being moderately heritable. Recent neuroimaging studies have found that the intra-parietal sulcus (bilaterally) is the most critical brain region for arithmetic functioning.

The cognitive basis of arithmetic disorders is much less well understood than that of literacy disorders. There is, however, good agreement that many children who find arithmetic and maths difficult have a fundamental deficit in *numerosity* (which might be viewed as cognitively analogous to the phonological deficit seen in literacy disorders). Numerosity (sometimes referred to as number sense) describes a deficit in understanding the magnitude of number. Tasks that measure numerosity include counting dots accurately, deciding which of two numbers is the bigger (digit comparison), and deciding which of two boxes contains the most dots (dot comparison). Children with specific arithmetic disorders perform these tasks less accurately and more slowly than children who have no arithmetic problems. Tests of numerosity have also been demonstrated to be good longitudinal predictors of later arithmetic ability, even after controlling for the effects of IQ, memory and reading skills; this is suggestive of a causal connection between earlier-identified numerosity difficulties and later-emerging arithmetic problems. There are however other cognitive deficits that might be expected to contribute to the development of arithmetic problems. One possible candidate is working memory; of course, carrying out arithmetic computations would be expected to place a heavy load on auditory working memory skills. Working memory difficulties in children with arithmetic problems are usually evident on complex working memory tasks that require both the processing and storage of numerical information (e.g. mental arithmetic tasks), as opposed to simple working memory tasks (e.g. repeating a sequence of digits). Another possible cognitive candidate is a visual spatial difficulty which can impact selected visually based mathematical concepts like understanding geometry and symmetry, interpreting graphs and visual schema, calculating measurement and understanding the conceptual basis of fractions. Tests of visual spatial ability and nonverbal IQ typically correlate moderately with measures of arithmetic skill; it would thus be unsurprising to find that a substantial number of children with arithmetic problems have difficulty with nonverbal cognitive domains like visual spatial ability, nonverbal reasoning, visual memory and so on.

Arithmetic abilities are arguably more complex and diverse than reading abilities. It is likely therefore that arithmetic problems in a given child might stem from a number of underlying cognitive deficits that include verbal processes like counting and nonverbal abilities such as visual spatial awareness. Indeed, several single case studies have demonstrated very different patterns of underlying difficulty in children with arithmetic disorders.

What is the prevalence and nature of the common co-occurrence of dyslexia and specific arithmetic problems? This question was nicely answered in a series of studies conducted by Landerl, Moll and their colleagues. Landerl and Moll (2010) carried out the screening of 2568 children from Grades 2 to 4 in urban and neighbouring areas of Saltzburg, Austria. Of the total sample, 6.1 per cent had an arithmetic disorder, 7.0 per cent had a reading disorder and 8.8 per cent had a spelling disorder. This indicates that arithmetic problems are nearly as common as literacy disorders. Co-occurring reading and arithmetic disorders were evident in 23 per cent of the sample, this finding being indicative of a high degree of overlap between reading and arithmetic disorders. In a separate study, Landerl et al. (2009) determined the non-shared risks in a sample of 109 eight- to ten-year-olds, some of whom had only reading difficulties, some only arithmetic problems, and some difficulties with both reading and arithmetic (there was also a control group of unaffected children). Children who had only reading difficulties and those who had both poor reading and arithmetic demonstrated problems on measures of phonological awareness, while children who had only arithmetic difficulties performed at the same level as the control group on these measures. In contrast, when the children were administered tests that tapped numerosity (specifically dot comparison and digit comparison tasks), the children with reading problems only had no difficulties with these, while the children with arithmetic problems and those with both arithmetic and reading problems found these numerosity tasks very challenging. This study clearly demonstrated that phonological difficulties are associated with dyslexia while a deficit in basic number processing accounts for the difficulties seen in children who are termed dyscalculic. Phonological and numerosity deficits may be construed as non-shared cognitive features in these two disorders, which means of course that we would not expect a total overlap of dyslexia and dyscalculia. In some children, weaknesses in visual spatial abilities that impact the grasp of visual concepts in maths would be expected to function as a non-shared risk specific to dyscalculia.

The next question we should raise is: what is the shared cognitive risk factor which explains the overlap of dyslexia and dyscalculia? One explanation for this comes from a study of 93 children at family risk of dyslexia who were followed longitudinally from pre-school through to the first two years at school (Moll *et al.* 2015). These authors found that arithmetic skill in primary school was predicted by pre-school verbal number skills (specifically, number knowledge and counting), and these skills in turn were influenced by earlier oral language skills. Thus, early language problems, which could well include difficulties with verbal working memory, may explain the co-occurrence of literacy and arithmetic disorders. This conclusion was further reinforced by a recent study by Moll, Landerl, Snowling and Schulte-Korne (2019) which showed that there is higher co-occurrence of dyslexia and dyscalculia when the latter disorder is measured by subskills that build on language and verbal memory (e.g. arithmetic fluency) than when defined by deficits in basic number processing (e.g. dot and digit comparison tests). Thus, children with dyslexia who also have poor language skills will be especially vulnerable to having co-occurring dyscalculia. In the Moll *et al.* 2015 study, executive skills (specifically selective attention – the ability to focus on a specific stimulus while screening out distractors – and response inhibition) also predicted counting and number knowledge; this was not an unexpected finding, given that focusing attention while counting and inhibiting inappropriate responses would be important in accurate computation. In keeping with the findings of the Landerl and Moll study, the authors found that phonological awareness did not influence arithmetic development.

Thus, a likely candidate for the shared risk factor in dyslexia and dyscalculia is a language deficit, of which verbal memory is a probable component. The non-shared risks are hypothesized to be phonological difficulties specific to dyslexia, while numerosity deficits, visual spatial difficulties and executive problems are specific to dyscalculia. A proposed Venn diagram for dyslexia and dyscalculia is shown in Figure 4.2.

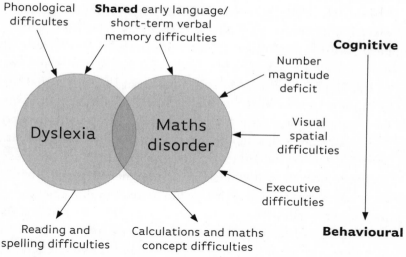

Figure 4.2 Dyslexia and maths disorder shared and non-shared risks: a proposed model

Introducing Case Study 2: a child with dyslexia and dyscalculia

Our second case study is Jyoti whose history and broad presentation are described in Box 4.2.

Box 4.2: Case Study 2 – Jyoti

Jyoti, aged nine years, was referred for assessment by her parents, with the support of her teachers at an independent day school where she is currently in Year 4. Her parents are concerned about her difficulties in understanding concepts in maths, her slow speed of working, her difficulties in transferring her thoughts to paper, her struggles with visualization (including spatial tasks) and her weaknesses in spelling. A helpful report from her class teachers described her as being currently average in her class in reading, after having made initially slow progress in Reception and Year 1. She is, however, performing below class standards in spelling, written work and maths. There are no teacher concerns about her overall concentration, though Jyoti has been observed to have difficulty in following instructions, processing information and planning strategies (especially in maths). Jyoti is described as a well-motivated, enthusiastic, co-operative and hard-working girl who gets on well with her teachers and her peers. She attends weekly spelling support groups, together with some lessons in perceptual skill and she has access to in-class support for maths. The school's SENCo has been working on her listening skills, her spelling, spatial abilities and maths. Jyoti has had six Individual Educational Plans (IEPs). The most recent indicated that she is working on mental maths recall, developing maths strategies, using a spelling dictionary and improving vocabulary usage in story writing. Previous IEPs have targeted specific aspects of maths and spelling. In addition to the learning support Jyoti has received at school, she had an outside school tutor in Years 1 to 3. In Year 4, she started at an external tutoring centre, which provided a helpful report, indicating that Jyoti has been working largely on maths, including her speed of working through numerical calculations.

Jyoti's early development was characterized by normal speech and language development in spite of her having early ENT problems. She had recurrent tonsillitis which caused hearing problems and she was not discharged from the hearing clinic until age five. Recent hearing tests have reported normal findings. Jyoti underwent an evaluation by a speech and language therapist when she was aged five years. It was reported that she had good listening, attention and social interaction skills and there were no concerns about her receptive language though her expressive language skills were a little underdeveloped. Some specific speech sound difficulties were observed, and it was noted that her phonological awareness was delayed. Jyoti went on to receive some speech and language therapy sessions over the course of the next year, with targets aimed at improving her pronunciation and developing better phonological awareness. There is a family history of reading and spelling difficulties (father).

Dyslexia and co-occurring attention problems/AD(H)D

Problems of attention control are frequently cited by parents and teachers as being evident in children who have literacy problems. One particular difficulty with this apparent co-occurring difficulty is that it can be hard for psychologists (myself included) to disentangle whether they are looking at a core deficit that would be sufficient to attract a formal clinical diagnosis of attention deficit hyperactivity disorder (ADHD) or whether one might be merely seeing a secondary behavioural consequence of the literacy disorder. Many children with reading problems become increasingly frustrated by their failure to learn to read and this can set the scene for deteriorating motivation and increasing disengagement, especially as they get older; in the classroom the child might well present as distracted, daydreamy and generally 'switched off'. It is these latter behaviours that parents and teachers might be tempted to describe as an attention problem, but they may be more appropriately described as an understandable secondary behavioural consequence of the learning difficulty. This can present a challenge when assessing a child with a literacy disorder who appears to also have difficulties in engaging and sustaining their concentration. An interesting study by Cooper *et al.* (2018) identified a small number of individuals they described as having 'late onset ADHD' – children who showed no features of ADHD in early childhood but who were doing so by mid-adolescence.

These children had shown low scores on reading and spelling measures at age nine. The authors speculated that:

> children with reading/spelling difficulties at age 9 years do not show mental health problems at this age but as they move through the educational system, they encounter higher academic demands and start to develop multiple mental health problems (including ADHD-like symptoms). (p.1110)

The essential feature of ADHD is persistent inattention and/or hyperactivity which, along with impulsivity, interfere with functioning and development. Being inattentive means that the child finds it difficult to maintain focus, lacks persistence, is distractible and is often disorganized. Hyperactivity refers to excessive motor activity when it is not appropriate and is often evident as fidgetiness, fiddling with objects and not sitting still when required. Impulsivity refers to hasty actions that occur spontaneously without forethought and which may be harmful to the child and to others. Being impulsive means that the child seeks immediate rewards and is unable to delay gratification when this would result in a better outcome.

According to DSM-5, the prevalence of ADHD is around 5 per cent of the child population, it is persisting and is more common in boys than girls (there is the increasing view that ADHD manifests itself differently in girls than boys). It frequently co-occurs with behavioural problems, in particular oppositional defiant disorder (ODD); in colloquial terms, these are children who 'don't do what they're told'. In later life, ADHD places the individual at risk of anxiety/depression, substance abuse and even mental illness. A brief summary of the features of ADHD, including its cognitive basis, is given in Box 4.3. For a fuller description, see Hulme and Snowling (2009).

● Box 4.3: ADHD

ADHD is a severe and persisting disorder that has considerable implications for children's learning and behaviour in a wide range of contexts, not just the classroom but the broader (including social) environment. It is highly heritable; meta-analyses have reported mean heritability rates as high as 0.75. Bearing in mind that many children with ADHD respond well to prescription medication (e.g. Ritalin), it is proposed that ADHD is a consequence of neurotransmitter (specifically dopamine) dysfunction within the brain.

What is the cognitive explanation for ADHD? One theory is that it is caused by executive dysfunction. Executive skills are frontal lobe brain-based skills required to execute tasks, get organized, control impulses and be adaptable and resilient; these are important to negotiating many everyday life and school demands. There are thought to be as many as 11 subskills that define executive function, which include response inhibition, emotional control, task initiation, planning and prioritizing, organization, time management, goal-directed persistence, flexibility and even cognitive skills like working memory and sustaining attention. A common criticism of the executive function deficit explanation of ADHD is that it is too vague and general an explanation, and that not surprisingly therefore some, though not necessarily all, executive subskills are deficient in children with ADHD. An alternative cognitive perspective might be described as motivational; most usually children with ADHD are seen as having problems in what is termed 'delay aversion'. This theory explains why children with ADHD are invariably impulsive and reward seeking. Experimental paradigms that have demonstrated this show that such children prefer the immediate gratification of an instant reward to a larger reward delivered after a delay. In a model proposed by Hulme and Snowling (2009), there are two risk factors that cause the behavioural symptoms of ADHD: executive deficits and motivation deficits (specifically delay aversion). Executive deficits contribute to *both* hyperactivity/impulsivity and the inattention aspects of ADHD, while the delay aversion contributes primarily to hyperactivity/impulsivity.

While ADHD is seen as a persisting neurodevelopmental disorder, its behavioural manifestation can change over time and in response to environmental factors and experiences.

Why do dyslexia and ADHD commonly co-occur? Certainly, literacy disorders and ADHD co-occur far more frequently than expected by chance, with co-occurrence rates of between 25 and 40 per cent. One study that has addressed this question compared the cognitive performance of children with dyslexia only, children with ADHD symptoms, children with both dyslexia and ADHD symptoms and a control group (Gooch, Snowling and Hulme 2011). The authors were interested in how the children performed in three separate sets of tasks: measures of phonological skills (phoneme deletion, nonword repetition, phonemic decoding and digit recall); tests tapping selected executive function (e.g. sustained attention, working memory); and tests of time perception which reflected the children's ability to judge the duration of time intervals (a time discrimination task using tones and a task requiring the reproduction of the duration of a visually presented stimulus). The children with dyslexia performed poorly on the phonological tasks, the children with ADHD symptoms performed poorly on the executive and time perception tasks, while the children with both dyslexia and ADHD symptoms performed poorly on the phonological, executive and time perception tasks. This study provides evidence for the non-shared characteristics in these co-occurring disorders, with a phonological processing deficit being specific to dyslexia while executive dysfunction and time perception difficulties are specific to ADHD.

A study by McGrath *et al.* (2011) provides even more direct evidence of shared versus non-shared risks in co-occurring literacy disorder and ADHD. A total of 614 children from the Colorado twin study were selected to generate a multiple deficit model of literacy disorder and ADHD. The potential predictors in this study were phonological awareness, response inhibition, verbal working memory, rapid naming and processing speed (mental efficiency of processing and matching symbols such as letters or numbers under speeded conditions). The authors then looked at which of these predictors contributed to reading ability, inattention symptoms and hyperactivity/impulsivity. They found that phonological awareness was a significant predictor of reading ability, but not inattention or hyperactivity/impulsivity. Response inhibition was a significant predictor of inattention and hyperactivity/impulsivity but not of reading ability. These are the non-shared deficits in the two disorders – phonological awareness being unique to reading ability and response inhibition to ADHD. Processing speed, rapid naming and verbal working memory contributed to both reading ability and the behavioural characteristics of ADHD, and were therefore potential shared cognitive deficits. These shared deficit candidates were investigated in more detail, with the final result being that the best shared predictor across the two disorders was processing speed. The Venn diagram describing the shared and non-shared deficits in dyslexia and ADHD is given in Figure 4.3.

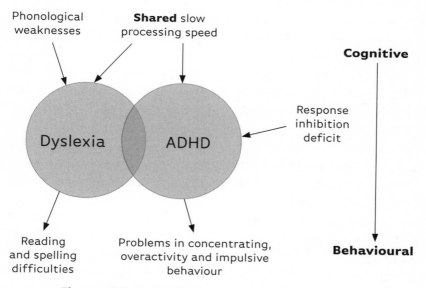

Figure 4.3 Dyslexia and ADHD: shared and non-shared risks

Introducing Case Study 3: a child with dyslexia and ADHD

Our third case study is Billy whose history and broad presentation is described in Box 4.4.

Box 4.4: Case Study 3 – Billy

Billy, aged seven years, was referred for assessment by his parents and teachers who requested an independent appraisal of his abilities, his educational attainments and the status of any learning difficulties he might be experiencing. Billy attends a state school where he appeared to do very well in the Nursery and Reception classes. However, by the end of Year 1, he was finding written work increasingly challenging and he was becoming somewhat distracted and tired. In Year 2, he demonstrated difficulties with writing and his progress in spelling was poor. These struggles continued through his Year 2 and now on into Year 3. Billy was not a late reader and in fact he loves books and he reads accurately with good comprehension. His mother has however noted that he will sometimes guess at unfamiliar words and he is not a confident decoder. A helpful report from his school described him as achieving averagely in his class in reading and maths, but below class expectation in spelling and written work. He is slow to produce written work and finds it hard to retain and apply spelling patterns. He is not as yet receiving any additional intervention. Billy's teachers commented on his demonstrating rather poor focus and stamina, and being easily distracted within the classroom context. He also finds it hard to follow multistep instructions. Nonetheless, his teachers recognize that he is a very bright and articulate little boy. His mother commented on Billy's confidence having declined over the course of the last year or so, with his at times being reluctant to do his homework. Although a generally generous and thoughtful child, he can exhibit occasional stubborn and oppositional behaviour.

Billy's early developmental history was characterized by good speech and language development. He is a generally healthy little boy. Billy has had some disruptive experiences in his life, with his grandfather being diagnosed with cancer a week after his birth. There is a family history of dyslexia on both sides (father's mother and three of father's cousins, together with a cousin on mother's side who has both dyslexia and dyspraxia).

Dyslexia and co-occurring motor disorders

Many children with dyslexia present with handwriting difficulties and problems of written presentation and organization. This raises the issue of such children having not only dyslexia but also a separate co-occurring disorder that specifically impacts their handwriting, perhaps as a result of difficulties with visual motor skills and motor organization. Difficulties in this domain are most usually referred to as developmental co-ordination disorders (DCD) and sometimes within the UK as dyspraxia.

DSM-5 lists four main features of DCD. First, the child's motor skills are substantially below those expected for a child of their age. Second, their motor difficulties significantly and persistently interfere with self-care activities and academic learning (especially handwriting); they may also restrict play, leisure and occupational opportunities. Third, the motor difficulties are evident from an early age and finally, they are not attributable to a neurological condition or to visual impairment or intellectual disability. According to DSM-5, the prevalence of DCD in children aged five to eleven years is 5–6 per cent, with boys being more likely to be affected than girls. Delayed motor milestones are usually the first sign of DCD in pre-schoolers. In the middle years, there are difficulties with handwriting, ball games, organization and motor sequencing. DCD is more common in pre-term and low-birth-weight children; indeed, being born extremely premature is a powerful risk factor. Most children with DCD have motor problems that persist well into late adolescence. DCD very commonly co-occurs with ADHD and perhaps a little less often (though not infrequently) with literacy disorders.

A brief summary of the features of DCD and its hypothesized cognitive basis is given in Box 4.5. Again, a fuller description can be found in Hulme and Snowling (2009).

Box 4.5: Developmental co-ordination disorder (DCD)

DCD is most obviously expressed as difficulties with motor function, including handwriting, handling tools and implements and so on. However, it needs to be borne in mind that virtually all movements are heavily dependent on perceptual input, particularly information from vision, the vestibular (balance) system and proprioception (sense of body movement). For this reason, it may be better to think of movement skills as perceptual motor skills rather than simply motor skills. There are no clearly defined subtypes within DCD, but some children show particular difficulties with fine motor skills (hand movement related) while others show mostly difficulties with gross motor skills (involving whole body movements). Because of the high co-occurrence of DCD with other disorders, it has been suggested that DCD should not be thought of as a discrete disorder, but as a manifestation of 'atypical brain development' that often leads to other disorders as well. One interpretation of this is that a variety of genetic and environmental factors adversely affect brain development that in turn has diverse effects. A recent Australian twin study showed that the heritability of DCD is a relatively high 0.65–0.7 (Martin, Piek and Hay 2006).

Hulme and Snowling (2009) have suggested that the reason that children with DCD show a range of perceptual, balance and body movement problems is they have what they term a 'noisy sensorimotor map'. They define the sensorimotor map as a system that 'relates positions of objects in visual space to positions in motor space i.e. a system that relates "seen" positions to "felt" positions' (p.235). The clearest cognitive deficit in children with DCD appears to be that of processing spatial information in the visual modality; so these children have difficulty with size, length and shape information when they are presented with a visual task. This means that in cognitive terms visual information about spatial location is degraded or blurred so that positions are only represented in a very approximate way. This leads to a difficulty in producing movements that are guided accurately in space. Deficits in the sensorimotor map very likely cause problems for both fine and gross motor skills as both involve moving the body through space, whether fingers and hands in fine motor control or larger body parts like legs and arms in gross motor control.

Hulme and Snowling acknowledge that some children with DCD may have additional problems with balance not readily explained in terms of a deficit in the sensorimotor map; these children are likely to have particular problems learning and executing gross motor skills.

Dyslexia and DCD frequently co-occur. In a study by Ramus, Pidgeon and Frith (2003), nearly 60 per cent of eight- to twelve-year-olds with dyslexia also had motor difficulties, as demonstrated on tests of postural stability, bead threading and finger to thumb movements. In the longitudinal study by Gooch *et al.* (2014), pre-schoolers at family risk of dyslexia performed slightly worse than controls on measures of motor skill, though the effects were more pronounced for at-risk children who also had language problems.

Why do dyslexia and DCD co-occur? Unfortunately, it is not as easy to explain the co-occurrence of these two disorders in terms of the interaction or overlap of shared and non-shared characteristics as it is for dyslexia and maths disorders or dyslexia and ADHD. It seems obvious that the non-shared deficits in these co-occurring disorders would be a phonological deficit explaining the dyslexia and a visual/spatial/perceptual deficit explaining the DCD. Finding a shared deficit that explains the overlap of the two disorders is more challenging. We saw that with dyslexia and maths disorders the shared risk factor might be early language (including verbal working memory) difficulties, while in dyslexia and ADHD the shared risk factor is almost certainly a processing speed deficit. What might be the shared risk in dyslexia and DCD? It seems that processing speed deficits are evident across a wide range of developmental disorders, and indeed these (along with memory and attention problems) are often regarded as 'domain general deficits'. It could be, therefore, that slow processing speed is the shared feature in dyslexia and DCD, though as yet we have no direct evidence for this. This hypothesized view of the co-occurrence of dyslexia and DCD is conveyed in the Venn diagram shown in Figure 4.4.

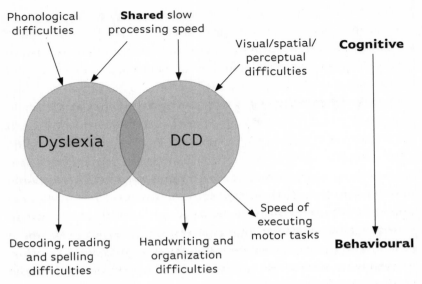

Figure 4.4 Dyslexia and DCD: shared and non-shared risks

It could be however that the shared/non-shared risk model of co-occurring difficulties does not work as well in explaining the co-occurrence of dyslexia and DCD as it does for dyslexia and maths disorders and for dyslexia and ADHD. The association between dyslexia and DCD may stem from multiple genetic and environmental factors that place a child at risk for a range of disorders that include motor as well as more cognitively based difficulties. Certainly, in the Gooch *et al.* (2014) study and also in the Thompson *et al.* (2015) study (described in Chapter 3), early motor difficulties were (an admittedly minor) risk factor for some children who developed later reading problems. However, it has been suggested that the link between dyslexia and DCD may have more to do with generalized neurodevelopmental immaturities than with identifiable shared and non-shared cognitive risks. It seems that more research is needed to clarify the nature of the overlap between these two disorders.

Introducing Case Study 4: a child with dyslexia and DCD
Our fourth case study is Freddie whose history and broad presentation is described in Box 4.6.

Box 4.6: Case Study 4 - Freddie

Freddie, aged 12 years, was referred for assessment by his parents, on the advice and recommendation of Ms B, his special needs and English teacher, at Smith state comprehensive school where he is now in Year 8. His parents and teachers first became aware of his difficulties with reading and writing by the end of Reception. He continued to struggle in Years 1 and 2 but did manage to pass his Key Stage 1 SATs. The family moved Freddie from Jones School, where he commenced his primary schooling, to Australia where they spent the next three years and he attended a local primary school. He very much 'bumped along' the bottom of the class and his parents arranged for him to have outside school phonics tuition. The family returned to the UK and he commenced Year 6 at Brown School where his literacy difficulties were quickly identified. He was fortunate to be provided with one-to-one targeted literacy tuition on a regular weekly basis during Year 6 and he also had extra time allotted during his Key Stage 2 SATs. He passed his English and maths but just failed the SPAG (spelling and grammar) component of the assessment.

Freddie commenced Smith School in 2017 and by halfway through the year his English teacher had identified him as a student needing extra support. He attended the Reading Wise intervention programme after it was found that he scored at a very low level on a standardized reading test. Considerable improvements took place and his teachers view him as now reading at a much higher level. Freddie seems to be finding maths easier than literacy and he is in the middle sets in this subject at Smith. He is not currently receiving any additional targeted support though an informative report from his teachers acknowledged his continuing difficulties with spelling, handwriting and written work. This has caused increasing frustration over the years, which can result in disengagement at school and even occasionally spill over into anger outbursts at home. His teachers suspect that his difficulties are consistent with a dyslexic profile. Freddie's mother and Ms B felt it important to have a more comprehensive understanding of the nature and extent of Freddie's written output difficulties, hence the current referral.

Freddie's early developmental history seemed advanced with respect to his milestones for walking, talking and so on. There are no health problems. There is a possible family history of spelling difficulties (mother).

Summary

- Evidence shows that about 40 per cent of children with one neurodevelopmental disorder will also meet diagnostic criteria for having another neurodevelopmental disorder, indicating a high rate of co-occurrence.
- It is hypothesized that 'shared' causes at both the genetic and cognitive levels explain the partial overlap of disorders while 'non-shared' factors specific to individual disorders account for the lack of a total overlap.
- In dyslexia co-occurring with language disorder, short-term verbal memory and phonological awareness difficulties contribute to both disorders (shared risks), whereas vocabulary/grammar difficulties, auditory processing deficits, executive problems and motor weaknesses appear to be more specific to language disorder (and are, therefore, potential non-shared risks).
- In dyslexia co-occurring with arithmetic disorders/ dyscalculia, it is hypothesized that the shared cognitive risk accounting for their overlap is an early language (including verbal working memory) difficulty, while the non-shared risks are in the domains of phonological awareness (for dyslexia) and numerosity, visual spatial and executive skills (for dyscalculia).
- In dyslexia co-occurring with ADHD, it has been shown that the best shared predictor across these two disorders is slow processing speed, while the non-shared deficits are phonological awareness, which is unique to reading ability, and response inhibition, which is unique to ADHD.
- In dyslexia co-occurring with DCD, it seems obvious that

the non-shared deficit in these co-occurring disorders is a phonological deficit explaining the dyslexia and a visual/spatial/perceptual deficit explaining the DCD; finding a shared characteristic that explains the overlap of the disorders has proved more challenging, with more research being necessary to establish why these disorders are frequently seen in the same child.

Chapter 5

Assessment and Formulation of Literacy Difficulties

In this chapter, I will describe general principles of assessment and report writing for children presenting with literacy disorders, with a specific focus on the assessment process for children with dyslexia, including those with co-occurring language and reading comprehension difficulties. Chapter 6 will look in depth at the additional assessments that are needed for children suspected of having co-occurring difficulties in the domains of maths, attention and visual motor skill.

However, before embarking on a description of what amounts to a test-based model for assessing literacy disorders, we should digress briefly to look at whether testing is needed at all to determine if a child has a literacy difficulty. There is a strong movement in educational psychology which questions whether testing is either necessary or indeed pedagogically useful. This is based on a dissatisfaction with psychometrics, especially IQ testing, which it is claimed confers labels on children which can restrict their educational opportunities. The preferred method is said to be one of *consultation* and *systems work*. In this approach, the child is seen as embedded within a family, school and community; the educational psychologist's role is to identify barriers to progress and to remove these by changing the context of the child's learning environment. This usually involves classroom observation and curriculum-based assessment (essentially looking at what the child should know and what indeed they do know). The psychologist then *consults* with teachers (and parents) to consider what factors need to be altered within the school and home to facilitate the child's improved progress. Essentially, the psychologist *works with the existing school system* to develop strategies and classroom modifications that can support the child's learning. My own view of this approach is that in omitting test-based assessments and avoiding diagnostic labels, the child's personal barriers to learning can go unrecognized; it then becomes difficult, if not impossible, to develop a prescriptive teaching programme that addresses directly the underlying cause and the educational expression of their failure to learn to read.

Before launching into a description of how to assess the child with a literacy disorder, let us consider how definitions of dyslexia and models of literacy disorder that were discussed in Chapters 2 to 4 might inform the assessment process. To begin with, we will revisit Margaret Snowling's definition of dyslexia from 2000:

> Dyslexia is a specific form of language impairment that affects the way in which the brain encodes the phonological features of spoken words. The core deficit is in phonological processing and stems from poorly specified phonological processing. Dyslexia specifically affects the development of reading and spelling skills but its effects can be modified through development leading to a variety of behavioural manifestations. (pp.213–214, my emphasis)

This definition is largely based on the (now rather discredited) single deficit perspective of dyslexia, but it is nonetheless useful in that it draws attention to the fact that we need to address three critical components when we assess a child presenting with what might be a dyslexic problem, specifically aspects of language, phonology and literacy. Another similar perspective of assessment can be drawn from the model of dyslexia proposed by Uta Frith which focuses on three levels of study: biological, cognitive and behavioural; it follows that we might expect to assess at the *cognitive* (phonological) and *behavioural* (literacy) levels (the *biological* level is one which is not of direct relevance to psychologists and teachers, and at any rate much further research and development is needed before neuroscanning tools would be seen as clinically and economically viable).

It is important, however, not to lose sight of the multiple deficit model of dyslexia for which we have argued a strong case in Chapters 3 and 4. Single deficit models would predict that assessing whether a child has dyslexia or not requires no more than the testing of literacy and phonological skills. However, the multiple deficit model implies that first, it is important to take account of the dimensional/continuity factor which means that dyslexia presents in differing degrees of severity and with various behavioural expressions from one child to another. Second, there is the strong likelihood that a given child will have additional risk factors and even co-occurring learning difficulties, important aspects that should not be overlooked in assessment in order to provide a full and complete picture of the child's difficulties. Third, we need to assess for protective factors which can help to ameliorate the child's difficulties and which can positively impact outcome. Finally, bearing in mind the criticisms of dyslexia testing raised by Elliott and Grigorenko (2014), we need to develop an assessment methodology that describes comprehensively the child's individual profile of strength and weaknesses which should then in turn inform management (including intervention methodologies and accommodation practices).

When to assess

Of course, a child can present for assessment at any age. Anxious parents may make contact about a five- to six-year-old who seems to be making slow progress in beginning to learn to read. At the other age extreme, some children's literacy difficulties do not appear to attract parent and teacher attention and concerns until they are in their secondary school years. Obviously, the earlier a child's literacy difficulties are assessed and identified, the earlier intervention programmes can be set in place. Also, very importantly, children whose learning problems are detected when they are young are less likely to experience frustration-based behaviour problems or declining motivation, which can inhibit their receptivity to teaching and intervention and perhaps even set the scene for later mental health problems.

In 2009, a Government-commissioned report conducted by

Sir Jim Rose, *Identifying and Teaching Children and Young People with Dyslexia and Literacy Difficulties*, was published (accessible online as well as in hard-back version). This report provided a systematic three-tier methodology for identifying children with literacy difficulties as early as possible and ensuring they have access to structured and evidence-based interventions from a young age. The report called for children who made a slow response to high-quality literacy instruction (that included systematic phonics in the context of a language-rich curriculum) to be systematically monitored during their first two years of schooling (Tier 1). This process would be expected to include classroom observation and the maintenance of progress records. The child's performance on the Phonics Screening Checklist (which was introduced by the UK government for all Year 1 children by 2012) would provide more specific information about their sound-letter knowledge after two years of formal schooling. If the child's difficulties persisted, a skills assessment would be conducted by the school's special educational needs co-ordinator (SENCo) which would determine whether the child should have access to group-based intervention programmes that targeted their specific gaps (Tier 2). Children who failed to respond to these literacy programmes would then be more comprehensively assessed and intensified learning support made available (Tier 3). Rose and his colleagues advised against blanket screening because in their view screening tests are not optimally reliable and may not be economically viable. Rather, they suggested that it is better that teachers identify children at risk of reading difficulties and then closely observe and assess their response to pre-and early-reading activities. We have seen in Chapter 3 that family risk is a strong pre-school predictor of children with dyslexia and that children with language difficulties at school entry are also at high risk of developing dyslexia (Thompson *et al.* 2015). Teachers who identify at-risk children according to these criteria can then monitor closely their development of reading skills during their early school years.

Assuming that a child has failed to progress in response to high-quality literacy instruction during the first two years at school and is also making slow progress when provided with additional intervention programmes, a more comprehensive evaluation could be called for. Whether this is conducted by a SENCo, specialist teacher or psychologist will depend on assessment resources that are available and on parent preference. The protocols suggested in this chapter will describe test materials that can be used to assess literacy and related (including language) difficulties, some of which have restricted access (and are therefore available for use only by psychologists) and others that are more widely available to teachers.

Starting the assessment process: obtaining background information

An assessment will most usually begin by exploring the reason for the referral while also obtaining background information about the child; this process can identify at-risk features, highlight the nature of parental and teacher concerns, and determine whether there are any additional factors that might influence the child's presentation (these might include potential co-occurring learning difficulties, medical problems, family or schooling factors). Such information would typically be obtained at the outset from parent and teacher questionnaires and perhaps standardized checklists.

A completed *family questionnaire* should address:

- developmental history, including milestones, in particular asking whether the child has a speech and language delay or disorder
- parental perspective of the child's literacy difficulties
- family history of literacy (and/or language) problems
- health problems, including birth history, any evidence of head injuries, presence of sensory (hearing or sight) problems
- potential co-occurring difficulties, through asking questions about whether the child has weaknesses in motor skill, attention or maths
- interventions the child has already accessed, e.g. school-based educational interventions, speech and language therapy, occupational therapy.

A completed *school questionnaire* should seek information from teachers about:

- the child's educational performance relative to their peers
- attention and behaviour in the classroom
- current learning support and classroom accommodations
- response to interventions to date.

Behaviour ratings made by parents and/or teachers through checklists or screening questionnaires may be relevant, especially when considering and providing evidence for co-occurring difficulties, for example Strengths and Difficulties Questionnaire, SDQ (Goodman 2007), Conners' questionnaire which screens for ADHD (Conners 2008) and the Children's Communications Checklist (Bishop 2003) which screens for language difficulties, especially in the social and pragmatic language domains.

On meeting the child and family, it is useful to spend 15 to 20 minutes with them to discuss in more depth the content of the completed questionnaires; to ask targeted questions in order to obtain more specific information; to clarify the concerns that parents want addressed by the assessment; and to describe the format of the assessment session. Whether the child is included in this preliminary meeting is dependent on their age and level of maturity; for younger children, it is usual to speak only to the parents, while for adolescents, it would be appropriate to include the child in some (if not all) the discussions.

Developing an assessment protocol

What protocol is used to assess a child with a presenting literacy disorder will very much reflect the theoretical perspective of the examiner and indeed also their own personal preferences for specific tests and procedures. However, some general considerations need to be borne in mind. For instance, the age of the child will impact the content of the protocol; with younger children, there is likely to be a stronger emphasis on foundation literacy skills such as letter knowledge, word level reading and spelling and handwriting, while for older children timed tasks that assess reading and writing speed and fluency and quality of written narrative assume increasing importance. Reading comprehension is an important assessment domain at all ages. Furthermore, the information contained in the questionnaires and the outcome of the preliminary discussion will help the examiner develop hypotheses about additional testing that might be needed to address in more depth co-occurring difficulties, such as attention problems or visual motor weaknesses. In this sense, while much of the protocol content may be standard for each and every child, there may be a proportion of tests which are selected according to the examiner's hypotheses about what specific difficulties that individual child might have.

Most psychologists and specialist teachers who assess a child presenting with concerns about their literacy development will conduct tests that cover ability/intelligence (IQ), educational attainments, underlying cognitive functioning, and perhaps some aspects of behaviour. Now, bearing in mind the definitions and models of literacy disorder we discussed in the earlier chapters, there is potentially one 'outlier' in this list, and that is ability or intelligence. DSM-5 excludes IQ/educational attainment discrepancies from its definition of dyslexia and indeed other specific learning difficulties and disorders too; this means for instance that it is no longer considered acceptable to diagnose dyslexia as being present if a child's word reading level is below that predicted from a knowledge of their chronological age and IQ. Also, many psychologists (including Elliott and Grigorenko 2014; Stanovich and Siegel 1994) argue against the need for, and indeed use of, IQ tests as part of the assessment procedure. In addition to the arguments against discrepancy definitions raised in Chapter 2, there is the view that because dyslexia (and other specific learning difficulties and disorders) are evident across the full ability range, and are best understood as arising from deficits within specified cognitive domains (phonology in the case of dyslexia), there is no need to assess IQ at all. However, in the real world of assessment, there is no doubt that IQ assessments can provide a wealth of information about the pattern of a child's learning difficulties.

First, IQ tests enable us to determine whether a child's

presenting literacy difficulty is a selective and specific problem or whether it is a component of a global learning difficulty. Thus, an assessor might ask for instance: is the child's reading ability at a far lower level than their other cognitive and educational skills, or do they have difficulty with all learning and educational domains (of which reading and phonology are just two)? Using IQ tests in this way indirectly implies a 'discrepancy perspective' but does not explicitly define dyslexia/literacy disorder in these terms. Second, IQ scores are informative in enabling parents and teachers to have appropriate expectations of the child. Some children with poor literacy skills may be labelled incorrectly as 'slow learning' or 'not very bright', but obtaining a high score on an IQ test can help parents and teachers view the child in a very different and indeed more positive light. Conversely, if a child is of low ability and feels under pressure from too high academic demands, providing parents and teachers with information regarding their IQ can 'take the pressure off' and encourage the setting in place of educational expectations that are lower and more appropriate to the child's needs. Moreover, IQ tests can provide information that directs parents and teachers towards the right type of schooling and level and range of interventions that are appropriate. Third, intelligence tests can help localize co-occurring difficulties. Most IQ tests have verbal and nonverbal scales of ability; a low verbal IQ could suggest the presence of oral language difficulties which would warrant further testing and intervention, while a low nonverbal IQ could be indicative of visual spatial and possibly motor problems. Finally, IQ tests can help to localize strengths and compensatory resources. Knowing that a child has a high verbal IQ can direct teachers to encourage them to draw on their good vocabulary knowledge so that they are able to make informed guesses about word pronunciations when word recognition and decoding fail; such a verbal-based word attack strategy can significantly improve word identification when the child reads in prose context. Similarly, recognizing that a child has highly developed visual spatial skills can help teachers direct students to select option subjects at secondary school that capitalize on their strengths within that domain, subjects like art, design and technology, and physical geography.

Arguably, the ability test most usually employed by psychologists is the Wechsler Intelligence Scale for Children, WISC, now in its fifth version (Wechsler 2016). The WISC is viewed as a 'gold standard' assessment instrument that is adopted worldwide; it is based on a large core US standardization sample but also draws on country-specific (including UK) standardization samples. The WISC V is a 'closed' or restricted access test which is available only to chartered clinical, educational or occupational psychologists. In its most recent version – the WISC V – there are five subscales of ability, each comprising two subtests: a Verbal Comprehension Scale which is composed of oral question and answer tests and which addresses verbal language skills; a Visual Spatial Scale which consists of puzzle and pattern materials and which assesses spatial constructional and visual spatial organization abilities; a Processing Speed Scale in which the child has to complete pencil-and-paper visually based processing activities under timed conditions; a Working Memory Scale which evaluates short-term verbal and visual working memory; and a Fluid Reasoning Scale which assesses the child's ability to think abstractly, reason, identify patterns and problem solve. The individual subtest scores are given as scaled scores (with a mean of 10) and the index scores as standard scores (with a mean of 100); see Box 5.1. As well as providing index scores for each ability scale separately, the WISC V allows for the calculation of a Full Scale (or overall) IQ which is based on seven subtest scaled scores, covering verbal and nonverbal abilities, processing speed and working memory. It is also possible to calculate a General Ability Index that is based on five subtest scaled scores from the Verbal Comprehension Scale and the two nonverbal scales of ability: Visual Spatial and Fluid Reasoning (but excluding processing speed and working memory scores). The WISC V is a very comprehensive ability test in that it provides information that goes way beyond merely calculating an IQ figure. Indeed, it provides valuable information about a child's verbal (language-based) skills, their nonverbal abilities and also crucially their processing speed and working memory; either or both of the latter are often compromised in children with specific learning difficulties/developmental disorders, including dyslexia. Some educational psychologists in the UK prefer to use the British Abilities Scales, now in its third version (Elliot and Smith 2011), which is standardized in the age range 3 years to 17 years 11 months. The BAS consists of 20 short tests, covering knowledge-based attainments (including literacy and numeracy tasks), thinking skills and processing abilities.

For specialist teacher assessors who do not have access to the WISC V, a very useful and well validated, though not as comprehensive, ability measure is the Wide Range Intelligence Test, WRIT (Glutting, Adams and Sheslow 2000) which has a US standardization sample but is adopted worldwide. This provides two subscales of ability, Verbal and Visual (nonverbal), which contain four subtests that are not dissimilar in content to those of the WISC V. Verbal and nonverbal ability indices may be calculated, along with a Full Scale IQ.

The current perspective on assessment draws on the multiple deficit model of dyslexia in that it emphasizes first, that testing should take the form of cognitive/behaviour profiling, rather than IQ/literacy discrepancy scores. This means that it is necessary to assess the child's literacy skills at both the *cognitive* (phonological/language) as well as the *behavioural* (reading and spelling) levels. Second, it is important to determine a pattern or profile of the individual child's *strengths* and *weaknesses* which can inform teaching decisions and intervention provision. Finally, it is important to recognize and indeed to test for *co-occurring learning difficulties* in order to arrive at a complete and fully comprehensive picture of the child's learning.

Assessing at the behavioural level

Behavioural level skills refer to educational attainments which are important to understanding how the child achieves within the classroom context. Psychologists and teachers will most usually choose attainment tests that have been developed within their own country because these are standardized on local populations and are based on that country's specific school curricula. Most obviously in relation to dyslexia, this means assessing reading and spelling/writing skills, though maths should also be included. For some children with dyslexia, maths is a relative strength which parents and teachers would want to highlight and promote so that the child is able to achieve academic success in an important curriculum-based subject; importantly, children who perceive themselves to be good at maths are likely to develop improved confidence and self-esteem. Maths tests are also important for the identification of co-occurring specific arithmetic problems/dyscalculia. Assessing at the behavioural level (expressed diagrammatically in Figure 5.1) is conducted using standardized educational attainment tests based on large representative samples of children; the presenting child's score is compared to that of their matched age group and may be expressed in a number of different ways, most usually as standard scores or centiles (see the glossary in Box 5.1 for an explanation of test scores).

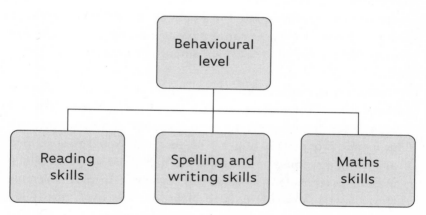

Figure 5.1 Assessment: the behavioural level

Box 5.1: Glossary of test scores

A **percentile** (or centile) indicates the percentage of the distribution that is equal to or below that particular score. For example, if a child obtains a percentile of 60, this means that 60 per cent of children in the same age range of the normative (or standardization) sample scored at or below that child's score.

Scaled or **standard scores** give the clearest indication of a child's reading level because they are based on a distribution that has a prescribed mean (or average) and standard deviation. The standard deviation reflects the variation or spread of scores around the mean. Because the standard deviation becomes the unit of measurement, it is, therefore, possible to make comparisons across different tests and at different ages. Scaled scores usually have a mean of ten and a standard deviation of three, while standard scores have a mean of 100 and a standard deviation of 15.

Index scores are composite or compound statistics based on two or more test scores and which provide an aggregate or summarization measure. IQ scores are examples of index scores. It is usual to quote the 95 per cent confidence limits of index scores, that is the range of values that you can be 95 per cent certain contain the true mean of the population.

A **reading age equivalent** is calculated by finding the average reading level for a group of children of a given age. Thus, an eight-year-old poor reader who obtained the same reading score as a group of six-and-a-half-year-olds would be described as having a reading age of six and a half years. In general, the use of age equivalent scores is discouraged by experts because they can be very difficult to interpret and even positively misleading. An age equivalent tends to convey the impression that any child who scores below age level has a problem when in fact a large proportion of children must score below average by definition. To illustrate, after excluding those children whose reading age is precisely at age level, 50 per cent or the remainder will read below age level and 50 per cent above. Also, reading ages may be difficult to interpret because the clinical significance of a discrepancy between chronological age and reading age depends on the variation in scores for a given test at a given age. This variation or spread of scores around the mean (i.e. the standard deviation) may vary according to age and also the particular test being used. This makes it very hard to compare children's reading performance at different ages and across different measures.

A single word reading test is not enough!

Reading is a multicomponent skill. Consequently, administering a single word reading test is not sufficient on its own to capture the complexity of the reading process. Nor does it recognize that in many children with literacy disorders, some components of the reading process will be impaired while others will remain relatively intact. To capture an individual child's profile of reading skills and indeed to determine their pattern of relative strength and weakness, a number of different types of reading tests are needed.

Arguably, the most widely used measures of reading are those contained in the Wechsler Individual Achievement Test (WIAT), now in its third version WIAT 3 (WIAT 3; Wechsler 2017). Like the WISC, the WIAT is a gold standard measure, with a large US standardization sample but with additional specific country-based samples that ensure that it can be confidently adopted worldwide. The WIAT is a (mostly) closed test for use only by psychologists, though having said that, there is a teacher version of the WIAT 3 that has five literacy subtests (the maths and cognitive tests remain closed and are for use by psychologists only). The Wide Range Achievement Test (WRAT), now in its fifth version, WRAT 5 (Wilkinson and Robertson 2017) is an open test with a US standardization sample that is available for use by teachers as well as psychologists. There has of late been an increasing interest amongst practitioners in attainment instruments that additionally assess underlying cognitive abilities as these can help to inform decisions about appropriate intervention. An example is the Feifer Assessment of Reading (Feifer 2016a) which is a US-based test in the age range 5–21 years. In addition to measures that cover aspects of literacy (including decoding and fluency), there are language-, phonological- and processing-based measures that enable the assessor to comment on the type of literacy difficulty the student has and then to relate this to proposed specific interventions.

A good starting point in the assessment of a child's reading skills is the administration of a single word reading test, such as those featured on the WIAT or the WRAT. These provide a measure of whether the child is able to accurately read a word in isolation without the benefit of content or context to guide their pronunciation; individual children might read some words through whole word recognition while other words may be attempted through a whole or partial decoding strategy. However, in the real world, children rarely read words in isolation. They do so mostly in the context of reading continuous text. Consequently, it is important to administer a test that allows you to arrive at a reading accuracy score that is based on *reading prose*, for instance the UK-based York Assessment of Reading for Comprehension (YARC) primary test (Snowling *et al.* 2011), for use by teachers as well as psychologists. Many verbally able children with dyslexia obtain a higher score on a prose reading accuracy test than they do on a single word reading test; this is because they draw on their good language skills and the context and content clues available in the text to make informed 'guesses' at word pronunciations. For instance, a child might encounter the orthographically complex word 'yacht' while reading a story about boating. Even a child with a severe decoding deficit is likely to be able to identify the initial and final letters of the word 'yacht' i.e. 'y' and 't'; combining that information with the boating content and taking note of the surrounding text and position of the word in the sentence, the child is likely to arrive at the correct reading of the word that they would otherwise find very difficult to read out of context.

As children get older, being able to read not just accurately but also rapidly and fluently becomes an important goal, and *measures of reading speed* should therefore be included in the assessment protocol. The slow reader is not only unable to access the same amount of reading material as the fluent reader, but they are also likely to be disadvantaged in time constrained situations such as sitting tests and exams. Moreover, they may become increasingly 'turned off' reading because it is such an arduous and effortful process, so becoming reluctant and even avoidant readers. The YARC allows the examiner to calculate a prose reading speed by timing the child as they read a passage out loud (primary version) or silently to themselves (secondary version). The Oral Reading Speed and Fluency subtests of the WIAT 3 also provide measures of reading speed while reading prose passages out loud. The Sight Word Efficiency subtest of the Test of Word Reading Efficiency, TOWRE (Torgesen, Wagner and Rashotte 2012), now in its second version (TOWRE 2), permits a very quick assessment of reading speed by calculating the number of single words a child is able to read accurately during a 45-second time period (this test is available to teachers as well as psychologists).

Children with dyslexia should be assessed for decoding deficiencies because this is a core, and indeed defining, deficit in this developmental disorder. In Chapter 2, we saw that the most usual means of assessing a child's decoding ability is to ask them to read pronounceable nonsense words. Examples of *nonsense word reading tests* are those available on the WIAT (Pseudoword Decoding, which is untimed) and on the TOWRE 2 (Phonemic Decoding Efficiency, which is timed).

Of course, the main goal of reading text is to understand its content and in so doing to acquire knowledge. Consequently, measuring *reading comprehension* is an important component of the assessment process. In verbally able children with dyslexia, it is rare for reading comprehension to be severely impaired, except in special instances where the child is an unusually slow and effortful reader whose 'cognitive energy' is largely devoted to struggling through reading the passage. Indeed, many verbally able children achieve remarkably high scores on reading comprehension tests. But we would of course expect reading comprehension to be negatively impacted in the child who has either a specific reading comprehension disorder or who has both dyslexia and co-occurring language problems. The most usually adopted tests of reading comprehension are those that feature in the WIAT 3, WRAT 5 or the YARC. In the first, the child reads a short passage silently or out loud (according to preference) and then answers a series of questions about the content. The Sentence Comprehension subtest of the WRAT 5 involves a 'cloze' procedure in which the child supplies a missing word from a written sentence they read.

The primary version of the YARC requires the child to read out loud two pages of text while in the secondary version the student reads the texts silently to themselves; they are then asked questions, some factual and some inferential, about the content (while being able to refer back to the text). The Feifer Assessment of Reading also includes a silent reading comprehension test.

Assessing spelling skills

For most children with dyslexia, even those regarded as having mild difficulties, spelling is invariably significantly impaired and for many will be a lifelong handicap. Spelling skills are most usually assessed through single word spelling-to-confrontation tests such as those that feature on the WIAT and the WRAT. It is not unusual to find that children with dyslexia obtain a lower score on a word spelling test than on a single word reading or prose reading test. Of course, the ability to read accurately draws on *recognition* skills within the memory domain. Moreover, the child who adopts a partial decoding strategy, combined with semi-recognition and a little informed guesswork, may come to accurately read the word. Put in connectionist terms (see Chapter 2), the existence of partial sound-to-letter mappings may be sufficient to enable the child to identify the word when reading. However, spelling requires complete and accurate *recall* of the letter sequence of a given word; this not only places a greater demand on memory but also necessitates complete letter-to-sound mappings which are rarely available to children with dyslexia.

Is there anything to be gained diagnostically from studying children's spelling errors? There is the widely held view that children with dyslexia tend to make more non-phonetic spelling errors than typical readers, spelling a word in such a way that when it is read out loud it does not match the standard pronunciation of the word. For instance, we might expect to see a child with dyslexia write 'wack' for 'walk', 'brith' for 'bridge', 'firend' for 'friend'. However, there is not a lot of evidence that supports this understandable view. Cassar *et al.* (2005) compared the spelling errors of children with dyslexia with those of younger children who were spelling at the same level (a 'spelling age matched' research design). They found that the children with dyslexia made essentially the same types of spelling errors as the younger non-dyslexic children. It was concluded that children with dyslexia learn to spell in the same way as younger typically developing children, only more slowly. However, there are two important caveats to this broad conclusion. First, there is evidence that children with persistent speech disorders show a higher incidence of non-phonetic spelling errors (Stackhouse 1982). This is not entirely surprising as we might expect such children's speech sound substitution or omission errors to be reflected in similar errors when they come to write the word they have spoken incorrectly. Second, clinical experience (including my own) tells us that children with very severe and persistent phonological difficulties are likely to produce a higher incidence of non-phonetic spelling errors than those will milder phonological problems.

Assessing writing skills
Some though not all children with literacy disorders will struggle with the mechanics of handwriting. Those that do will most usually have co-occurring visual spatial and motor difficulties that impair pencil control. A sample of handwriting is of course available from the child's spelling test. In the absence of normative information regarding handwriting skill, the examiner most often makes a qualitative judgement as to handwriting ability, based on consistency of letter formation, letter spacing and, of course, legibility. There are however standardized tests that assess speed of writing, the most usually adopted in the UK being the Detailed Assessment of Speed of Handwriting, DASH (Barnett *et al.* 2007). For the Free Writing subtest of this measure, the child writes a short essay on the topic 'My Life', conducted over a timed ten-minute period, and their speed of writing is recorded in words per minute. Children who have a literacy disorder, together with co-occurring handwriting problems, will typically obtain a low score on the Free Writing subtest. However, it is not unusual to see children with literacy disorders who have no handwriting

problems to also obtain a low writing speed score, this being due to their difficulties in finding words they know how to spell, their struggles with organizing their thoughts and ideas, and their general disengagement with the writing process. Many examiners will want to make qualitative evaluations of the child's written narrative skills, which might include comments on their paragraph organization, sentence constructions, vocabulary usage, grammar and syntax, spelling accuracy, and punctuation usage.

What does the literacy profile of a child with a literacy disorder look like?

Having carried out a range of reading, writing and spelling tests, we need to interpret the literacy pattern or profile of the child. Children with severe dyslexia, especially those with accompanying language difficulties, are likely to perform poorly on all of the literacy tests administered; in other words, they will obtain low scores on measures of single word reading, prose reading accuracy, reading speed, decoding ability, spelling, writing speed, and very likely reading comprehension also. Children with milder dyslexia may achieve scores within normal limits on measures of reading accuracy and sometimes even a high score on a measure of reading comprehension, but perform poorly on the tests of spelling, reading fluency, decoding and writing speed. Within the literacy profile, we often find that children with dyslexia (whether mild or severe) show a characteristic pattern of scoring. Typically, their lowest scores are on the decoding and spelling measures (which are often strikingly similar); this is hardly surprising since spelling and nonword reading have a very high correlation of around 0.9. Single word reading is often the next lowest score (along with reading and writing speeds). Verbally able children with dyslexia will usually obtain a relatively high score on the reading comprehension measure because this skill draws heavily on their good language abilities. They also very often record a higher prose reading accuracy than single word reading score because they are able to use their good language skills to better identify words that are read in a contextual framework. This pattern of scoring for reading and spelling accuracy is expressed diagrammatically below:

prose reading accuracy > single word reading > decoding nonwords = spelling

Assessing maths skills

For children about whom few concerns are expressed regarding their mathematical ability, it may suffice to merely 'screen' their numeracy skills, using one of the two maths subtests from the WIAT or the arithmetic subtest of the WRAT 5. However, for children who appear to have co-occurring difficulties in numeracy, more comprehensive testing is needed. Psychologists would then usually administer both the Numeracy and Maths Problem Solving subtests of the WIAT 3. Numeracy is a pencil-and-paper test that evaluates the child's grasp and application of the standard numerical operations of addition, subtraction, multiplication and division (and also includes calculating with decimals, negatives, fractions and percentages, as well as simple algebra). Maths Problem Solving covers a broader range of mathematical concepts and principles and also addresses the child's written problem-solving abilities. The British Abilities Scales and the Feifer Assessments also provide maths attainment tests.

Assessing at the cognitive level

Assessing the child presenting with a literacy difficulty at the cognitive level most obviously necessitates evaluating their phonological abilities. However, many psychologists and teachers will also want to explore potential co-occurring learning difficulties by assessing the child's underlying abilities in other non-phonological cognitive domains. Assessing at the cognitive level is expressed diagrammatically in Figure 5.2.

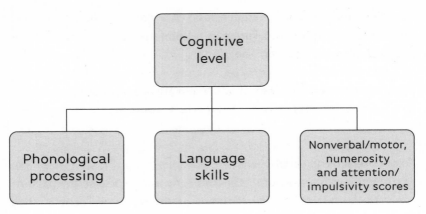

Figure 5.2 Assessment at the cognitive level

In this chapter, we will concentrate on cognitive testing of phonological skills relevant to dyslexia, together with language skills that will be compromised in children with reading comprehension disorders and co-occurring developmental language disorders. Cognitive testing relevant to identifying the co-occurring disorders of dyscalculia (numerosity), DCD/dyspraxia (visual motor skills) and ADHD (attention/impulsivity) will be addressed in the following chapter.

Assessing phonological skills

The model of phonological processing that has most relevance for psychologists and teachers is that developed by Wagner and his colleagues from their large-scale correlational and longitudinal studies of typical literacy development (see Chapter 1). Indeed, these authors went on to develop a test available to psychologists and teachers that enables them to assess comprehensively the phonological abilities of the individual child. The Comprehensive Test of Phonological Process, now in its second version, CTOPP 2, (Wagner *et al.* 2013) assesses three components of phonological ability – phonological awareness, phonological working memory and phonological access in long-term memory. There are two age-related versions of the test: one developed for children in the five- to six-year age range and the other developed for use with older individuals aged from seven to 24 years. The CTOPP 2 was normed on 1900 individuals across the USA, according to a stratified sampling procedure that ensures that it represents the nation as a whole.

In the five- to six-year age range, there are three core *phonological awareness* subtests: Elision (deletion of a specified phoneme in a spoken single syllable word); Blending Words (joining sounds together to form single and multisyllabic words); and Sound Matching (asking the child to choose from an array which word begins with the same sound as the target word). For the seven years plus age group, the core phonological awareness subtests are Blending Words, Elision and Phoneme Isolation (identifying a named sound, usually the first or last, in spoken words). There are also two supplementary subtests, Segmenting Nonwords and Blending Nonwords. The phonological awareness measures correlation with standardized reading tests is 0.48.

Phonological working memory is most usually assessed using a symbol memory span test; the CTOPP 2 has a Memory for Digits task that requires the child to repeat accurately a sequence of random digits spoken by the examiner. Nonword Repetition is also designated as a phonological working memory measure on the CTOPP 2 and it does indeed have a strong working memory component (though it also assesses other components of speech and language, including segmenting of speech sounds and the ability to articulate sequences of speech sounds). The phonological working memory subtests of the CTOPP 2 have a correlation with standardized reading tests of 0.34.

Phonological access in long-term memory is assessed using naming speed tasks. Children in the five- to six-year age range name colours and/or shapes as rapidly as they can in a 30-second time limit, while children from seven years upwards name letters and/or numbers. The correlation of the naming tests with standardized reading tests is 0.45.

Children with severe and persisting reading problems are likely to experience difficulties with all three types of phonological tasks. However, there are some children who may have difficulty with one or two of the phonological tasks, but not all three. Phonological awareness tests are particularly strongly diagnostic of dyslexic difficulties, but it is not uncommon to assess children who are able to blend and segment phonemes within words, but who exhibit phonological working memory limitations or naming speed problems or both. Of course, phonological abilities such as blending or deleting phonemes are 'trainable' skills, and are a key feature of many literacy intervention schemes; indeed, they are the primary skills that are targeted in programmes like Sound Linkage (Hatcher, Duff and Hulme 2014). If a child has had access to phonological training before they are assessed, they may score higher on the phonological awareness measures than they would have done had they not had such an intervention. Working memory and naming skills are less responsive to training, and thus for children with dyslexia who have benefited from intervention they may prove more reliable indicators of an underlying phonological deficit.

In assessing the child who is suspected of dyslexia, there are four types of tests that essentially function as *markers* (or diagnostic indicators) for this developmental disorder. Three of these are cognitive level tests – phonological awareness (often a phoneme deletion or elision test), phonological working memory (most usually a digit span measure) and phonological processing or phonological access in long-term memory (a naming speed task). The other marker test is most appropriately described as being at the behavioural level: a nonword reading test that assesses phonic decoding ability. Employed together, these measures can determine the presence, and also to some extent the severity, of the phonological deficit. The child who obtains very low scores on all four measures may be viewed as having a severe phonological/decoding deficit and is likely to be struggling with all aspects of literacy, in other words reading and spelling accuracy and fluency (though not necessarily reading comprehension). The child with only slightly depressed scores on these four measures, or who performs poorly on some though not all of them, may have less marked and pervasive literacy difficulties. For instance, the child who obtains acceptable scores on the phonological awareness and nonword reading measures but who scores poorly on the working memory and naming speed measures may read fairly accurately, but could well struggle with spelling and fluency of reading and writing.

Assessing language skills in children with severe dyslexia and those with reading comprehension difficulties

We saw in earlier chapters that some children who meet criteria for having severe dyslexia are likely to be carrying a further risk factor beyond their weak phonological skills; this is the additional risk of having poor oral language skills. These children's language difficulties may need to be explored in more depth in order to better understand the nature of these. Knowing the child's verbal comprehension index (or verbal IQ) provides information about their breadth of vocabulary and their verbal reasoning but does not tap into more structural aspects of language like grammar and syntax. For a more comprehensive evaluation of the child's language difficulties, especially if it is suspected that they have a yet to be recognized language disorder, a referral to a speech and language therapist would be advised. Tests such as the Comprehensive Evaluation of Language Fundamentals, CELF (Wiig, Secord and Semel 2006), which are most usually employed by speech and language therapists, assess structural aspects within both the receptive and expressive language domains; such tests provide a broader evaluation of the child's communication difficulties which would inform an opinion as to whether or not the child meets criteria for a formal diagnosis of developmental language disorder.

Children who obtain low scores on the WIAT 3 or YARC reading comprehension measure also need to undergo assessments that target their language skills. The great majority of children who fail to comprehend what they read will have underlying difficulties across a broad range of language domains (receptive and expressive), and also including vocabulary knowledge and grammar.

As part of their overall evaluation of children with severe dyslexia and/or poor reading comprehension, psychologists and teachers may want to administer supplementary cognitive or diagnostic *marker* tests which could indicate that a language disorder is present, and which would then warrant a referral for more extensive investigation by a speech and language therapist. Conti-Ramsden, Botting and Faragher (2001) have suggested that a low score on a sentence repetition test, of which versions appear on the CELF and the WIAT 3, may function as a marker for language disorder; this is because it assesses awareness of morphological and syntactic structures as well as verbal working memory, these being frequently compromised skills in children with language disorders. Bishop, North and Donlan (1996) have further suggested that a nonword repetition test, such as that found on the CTOPP, might also achieve marker status in that it captures the phonological memory, articulatory programming and word segmentation difficulties evident in many children with language disorders. Bearing in mind the Simple View of Reading model, useful information relating to the language basis of a child's reading comprehension difficulty might be obtained by administering a test of listening comprehension, of which the WIAT 3 has an example. In this test, the child listens to a short piece of oral discourse and then answers either one or two questions about its content. If testing time is limited, questionnaires or checklists such as the Child's Communication Checklist (Bishop 2003), which can be completed by parents or teachers and scored by the examiner later, provide information about pragmatic aspects of language as well as the child's social communication skills.

A summary of the tests described in this chapter and their core attributes is given in Box 5.2.

Box 5.2: Tests and their core attributes

IQ tests provide measures of broad cognitive skills which can help to distinguish generalized learning difficulties from specific learning difficulties; most will cover verbal and nonverbal abilities, and some also address processing speed and working memory (WISC and WRIT).

Reading tests should capture the complexity of the reading process by addressing the following subskills:

- single word reading accuracy (WIAT and WRAT)
- prose reading accuracy (YARC)

- reading speed and fluency (YARC, WIAT, TOWRE, Feifer)
- reading comprehension (YARC, WIAT, WRAT, Feifer)
- phonic decoding ability (WIAT, TOWRE, Feifer).

Spelling and writing tests should address written output skills by assessing:

- individual word spelling (WIAT and (WRAT)
- handwriting legibility and speed (DASH)
- written narrative skills.

Maths tests are needed to determine if the child has co-occurring maths problems or conversely, has a strength in this educational domain. Some tests assess pencil-and-paper arithmetic skills, while others address concepts and maths problem solving (WIAT, WRAT, Feifer).

Phonological tests function as 'markers' of the underlying deficit in children with dyslexia, to include tests such as the CTOPP, featuring:

- phonological awareness (e.g. Elision, and Blending Words)
- phonological working memory (e.g. Memory for Digits and Nonword Repetition)
- phonological access in long-term memory (e.g. Rapid Letter Naming).

Language tests determine if the child might have a co-occurring DLD and are also relevant for children who have reading comprehension disorders; tests could include:

- language scales such as the CELF
- vocabulary tests (WISC and WRIT)
- sentence repetition (CELF and WIAT)
- nonword repetition (CTOPP).

Assessing for cognitive strengths and protective factors

We saw in earlier chapters that verbally able dyslexic children may be able to draw on their good language skills to support correct word identification, particularly when they are reading in context. It follows that language-based testing (whether a verbal IQ test or a vocabulary measure) might well indicate whether a particular child will be in a strong position to take advantage of this compensatory mechanism. Children with strong language capabilities may be prescribed a teaching programme that includes drawing their attention to the information contained in surrounding context as an aide to precise word identification. Some children with dyslexia may have other strengths they can draw on as effective compensators for their deficient phonological and decoding skills. For instance, the single case JM described by Hulme and Snowling (1992) had very good visual memory skills which enabled him to learn to read by building up a visual memory store of words. Consequently, there may be a place for visual memory tests in an assessment protocol in order to decide whether 'visualization' learning techniques have a role in the prescribed teaching programme of a given child. Snowling and Melby-Lervåg (2016) have suggested that other cognitive skills might be identified as protective factors, including having rapid processing speeds or acquiring letter knowledge at an early age. In practice, it is not usual to carry out specific tests aimed at determining strengths but rather to *eyeball* the child's overall test profile to detect patterns of scoring that could indicate a domain that constitutes a relative strength they might draw on by way of compensation. Sometimes strengths from within the child come from outside the cognitive domain and yet still play an important compensatory role that positively influences outcome – these might include high levels of resilience, persistence, motivation and frustration tolerance. Strengths within non-academic domains, such as sports or art, are also important to recognize as they can allow the child to experience success beyond classroom-based learning – which in turn may boost their self-esteem and self-confidence and so enhance their motivation and levels of engagement. Finally, there are family/schooling factors that can function as protective factors, in particular early identification which means the child receives targeted intervention from a young age, and high levels of parental support, including the provision of a rich home literacy environment (Dilnot *et al.* 2017).

Developing a diagnostic formulation

Once information is gathered from family and teacher question-naires, interviews, and the test protocol, the next step is to develop a diagnostic formulation which describes the child's learning difficulties in the context of their broader environment. A formulation is not merely a restatement of test results. It requires first, the *interpretation* of what the test results mean in terms of the child's presenting difficulty and second, the *contextualization* of the findings in relation to their schooling and sociocultural environment. Without clear interpretation and contextualization, it is difficult to make meaningful and relevant recommendations for intervention and management that truly reflect and meet the individual child's special needs. While some would see arriving at an accurate and comprehensive formulation as 'something of an art', it is my view that successful interpreting and contextualizing stems from having a sound knowledge of the evidence base for learning disorders, combined with the experience of working with children with a wide range of learning difficulties.

The first part of the formulation might consist of a re-iteration of parental and teacher concerns and a brief summary of the test findings and most importantly their interpretation. The second part of the formulation should specify the primary disorder, for our purpose dyslexia because this is the primary focus of this book. The underlying cognitive deficit and its behavioural expression then need to be stated, in other words a deficit in phonological processing which results in poor decoding and consequent reading and spelling impairment. Any co-occurring difficulties, and the evidence for these, should be made explicit; in this chapter, we focus on dyslexia occurring in the context of early developmental speech and language difficulties: essentially dyslexia with co-occurring language disorder/delay. Our case study, Alex, is an example of this, and his assessment is described in depth at the end of this chapter. It is important to comment on the availability of compensatory resources or strengths, such as being highly verbally articulate or having strong visual abilities or being good at maths. The child's temperament and their levels of self-esteem and confidence need to be considered because these can significantly influence their motivation and engagement with learning; if these are adverse factors, and are not addressed, they can impact the child's well-being and even ultimately their mental health.

One of the biggest challenges in formulating a child's learning presentation is to arrive at a comment or statement about severity that might also include prognosis. The severity of the presentation will depend on a number of factors, including extent of the underlying phonological deficit, how far behind the child is in their educational attainments, the number of additional 'risk' factors present, and the presence of co-occurring learning difficulties. The more severe the underlying phonological deficit (as indicated by the child's level of scoring on measures of phonological awareness and processing), the more severe the literacy difficulty is likely to be. Children who have significantly delayed speech and language development are carrying an additional risk factor, especially if the language difficulties persist into the years of formal schooling. Children who have co-occurring learning difficulties are usually viewed as having more severe educational problems overall; indeed, the more co-occurring difficulties the child has (some may have two or three of these over and above their dyslexia), the more severe and complex their presentation. An important caution to bear in mind is that it can be difficult to determine the severity of a child's learning problem if they are very young. Children presenting with a literacy disorder at age six or seven are likely to show smaller gaps in their educational attainments when compared with age- or peer-expectations, which may tempt the assessor to conclude that their difficulties are comparatively mild. It is however important to bear in mind that for many children, this performance gap may widen with increasing age, such that on re-assessment some years later their literacy difficulties may present as more severe. The case of Nicholas, presented in Chapter 2, is an example of the educational gap widening over time. Consequently, we need to be appropriately cautious about expressing views on severity of learning disorders in young children.

Determining prognosis (predicting outcome) is an even greater challenge. Obviously, this will be heavily influenced by the severity of the child's disorder together with the number of additional risks or co-occurring difficulties that are present. The able and articulate child with mild dyslexia and no co-occurring difficulties could potentially do well at school and indeed go on to achieve high academic results, even in tertiary level studies. The child with severe dyslexia and co-occurring learning difficulties is far more likely to find academic study a considerable challenge and may well leave school with few qualifications. However, there are several non-cognitive factors that can also substantially influence whether the child achieves well in school and indeed on into adult life – or not! These include early versus late identification, having a stimulating versus impoverished learning environment, high quality intervention versus little or no intervention, having a low frustration tolerance and lack of resilience versus being motivated and resilient, and good versus poor parental support. Non-literacy cognitive skills, additional risk factors and environmental experiences that impact prognosis and outcome are sometimes referred to as *moderator variables*, which can be either positive or negative. The impact of moderator variables on outcome is expressed diagrammatically in Figure 5.3.

Report writing

The final stage of the assessment is to provide feedback to families, schools and other professionals, which may include face-to-face discussion and of course the writing of a report. The report should provide data from the evaluation, interpret these data, provide a diagnostic formulation (which should include strengths as well as weaknesses) and then conclude with a series of recommendations aimed at addressing the child's difficulties and supporting them within their learning environment. Most experienced report writers will have developed their own structure and style of report that they feel best conveys the information derived from the assessment and which parents and those working with the child find accessible.

Dyslexia
Same predisposition but different outcomes

Good outcome

Good parental support

Motivated and resilient

High quality intervention

Early identification

No co-occurring learning difficulties

Stimulating learning environment

High verbal IQ/good language

Poor outcome

Low parental support

Disengaged/low resilience

Lack of quality intervention

Late or no identification

Co-occurring learning difficulties

Impoverished learning environment

Low verbal IQ/language difficulties

Moderator variables
Positive   Negative

mild

severe

Phonological deficit

Genetic/neurodevelopmental predisposition

Figure 5.3 The impact of moderator variables on outcome

In response to concerns that learning evaluations do not always achieve the expected high standard they should, there are moves from professional organizations to standardize procedures in assessment and report writing so as to achieve 'best practice'. One such organization, SASC (SpLD Assessment Standards Committee) has as its aim 'to support and advance standards in SpLD (specific learning difficulties) assessments, training and practice in the assessment of specific learning difficulties'. SASC recommended reports have as their guiding principles that they should:

- be *accessible*, that is, easily understandable to persons and organizations
- be *consistent* with principles of best practice
- be *reliable*, thus ensuring that the conclusions are reliable and robust and are based on converging evidence from the developmental history, background information, observations and test results and are related to relevant definitions and diagnostic criteria
- achieve *clarity* in reporting test results by increasing the emphasis on interpretation of key test results and linking these to resultant cognitive/educational profiles
- be *efficient and useful* through achieving clarity, transparency and succinctness while presenting sufficient detail to support the conclusions reached.

SASC has now developed a recommended report-writing format for pre-16 and post-16 age groups. The basic structure of the pre-16 report is given in Box 5.3. The Department for Further Education (DfE) has indicated that reports prepared for a student at any age that meet SASC guidelines, and are presented in their recommended format, may be used as evidence for the application for a tertiary years Disability Student Allowance (DSA). For further information about SASC, refer to their website.[1]

---

1   sasc.org.uk

Box 5.3: SASC report format

Cover sheet: with assessor statements, signature and date.

Overview: potentially detachable and with five sections:

- *Referral* (referrer and reason for referral)
- *Diagnostic Outcome* – to include formulation (and descriptors as needed) and whether further testing, additional information or onward referral is needed
- *Profile* – summarizes key features of testing, developmental history and background to provide evidence for conclusions and diagnoses reached
- *Impact* – describes how the child's difficulties are affecting their educational and broader functioning and how they are coping with (including compensating for) these difficulties
- *Key Recommendations* – to include interventions, accommodations and other support.

Background information: which provides the context for the assessment, should cover health and developmental history, family history of SpLD or other developmental conditions, linguistic history, educational history and current situation.

Main body of the report: for which there are three sections:

- *Cognitive Profile* – to include tests of ability (verbal and nonverbal), working memory, phonological processing and processing speed
- *Additional Diagnostic Evidence* – attention-related difficulties, visual difficulties, motor difficulties and maths-related difficulties, for example deficits in numerosity
- *Attainment* – single word reading, prose reading, reading comprehension, spelling, writing, typing, numeracy.

Confirmation of Diagnostic Decision: diagnostic formulation.

Recommendations: must be tailored to the needs of the child.

Appendices: Five appendices are recommended – explanation of statistical terms, summary table of test results, definitions of SpLDs as applicable, explanation of tests and tasks, other references as applicable.

Case Study 1: Alex – assessment and formulation

Recall that Alex had presented for assessment at age six, with significant speech and language problems and delay in starting to read. He had received speech therapy as a pre-schooler. Following his receiving an EHC plan at age eight, he attended a special language school for three years. He was reassessed at age 13, having returned to mainstream school, but continuing to experience severe literacy problems. The test scores obtained at his assessments conducted at ages six and 13 years are presented in Boxes 5.4 and 5.5. Alex's test profiles from ages six through to 13 years demonstrate how the behavioural and educational expression of a specific learning difficulty can alter with development and in response to moderator variables discussed earlier in this chapter.

Box 5.4: Alex's test results at six years nine months
Wechsler Pre-school & Primary Scale of Intelligence IV (WPPSI IV) (Wechsler 2014)

Verbal Comprehension	*Visual Spatial*
Index = 81 (75–91)	*Index = 114 (104–121)*
Similarities = 7	Block Design = 12
Vocabulary = 6	Object Assembly = 13

Average scaled score = 10; 95 per cent confidence limits given in parentheses.

Wechsler Individual Achievement Test II (WIAT II)
1. Single Word Reading – Standard score = 75
2. Pseudoword Decoding – Standard score < 60
3. Spelling – Standard score = 70
4. Numerical Operations – Standard score = 110
5. Mathematics Reasoning – Standard score = 90

York Assessment of Reading for Comprehension (YARC)
1. Reading Accuracy standard score = 80
2. Reading Comprehension standard score = 80

Comprehensive Test of Phonological Processing 2 (CTOPP 2)
1. Blending Words – Scaled score = 8
2. Elision – Scaled score = 6
3. Memory for Digits – Scaled score = 6
4. Rapid Colour Naming – Scaled score = 6
5. Nonword Repetition – Scaled score = 7

CELF IV
Sentence Repetition – Standard score = 80

Visual Motor and Writing Skills
1. Beery Test of Visuomotor Integration – Standard score = 105
2. Handwriting – good letter formation, legible printing script

Alex's summary and formulation at age six
Alex is a six-year-old boy who scored at an above average level on measures of nonverbal ability (WPPSI IV Visual Spatial Index = 114). However, he scored at a significantly lower level on the oral language measures of the WPPSI Verbal Comprehension Scale which evaluate verbal concepts, verbal reasoning and vocabulary

knowledge (WPPSI Verbal Comprehension Index = 81). The size and direction of the verbal-nonverbal discrepancy is consistent with that typically seen in children with speech and language delay or disorder. Given that verbal abilities are important predictors of literacy development, it is unsurprising that Alex has made a very slow start in learning to read and spell; he obtained below average standard scores (ranging from below 60 through to 80) on measures of single word reading, prose reading accuracy, phonic decoding ability (Pseudoword Decoding), and spelling. He also has weak reading comprehension (standard score = 80). However, Alex is making better progress in maths; he scored well on a test that assessed pencil-and-paper computation skills (Numerical Operations standard score = 110), though rather less well on a test which tapped into maths concepts and the language of maths (Mathematics Reasoning standard score = 90). His handwriting and his visual motor skills are developing well (see Chapter 6 for a fuller description of the Beery Test). Alex's short-term verbal working memory and phonological processing and analysis abilities are significantly underdeveloped (scaled scores of between six and eight on CTOPP 2 Blending Words, Elision, Rapid Colour Naming and Memory for Digits subtests). He also obtained a low score on a test known to be a 'marker' for language delay or disorder (Sentence Repetition standard score = 80).

Alex is a little boy of above average ability (assessed non-verbally) who has a developmental language disorder (DLD) together with emerging dyslexia. He was delayed in his speech and language development, and at the present assessment scored at a below average level on measures of oral language skill and on 'markers' of language impairment (verbal working memory, nonword and sentence repetition). His poor language skills would be expected to have far-reaching effects on his ability to learn within the classroom and of course they contribute to his reading comprehension difficulties. Alex's slow progress in learning to read and spell, his poor decoding and his underlying phonological deficits point to him also having dyslexia. Indeed, 50 per cent of children with early speech and language impairment will go on to develop dyslexia because these two disorders share causal risk factors, specifically deficits in phonological processing and short-term verbal memory. Alex was not observed to have attention control or visual motor difficulties. Nor does he have maths problems though he does struggle a little with the language of maths, which is likely to be a consequence of his language impairment. There is a family history of literacy difficulties which is indicative of a genetic or familial predisposition.

Box 5.5: Alex's test results at 13 years 9 months
Wechsler Intelligence Scale for Children V (WISC V)

Verbal Comprehension
Index = 92 (85–101)
Similarities = 9
Vocabulary = 8

Visual Spatial
Index = 114 (104–121)
Block Design = 12
Visual Puzzles = 13

Fluid Reasoning
Index = 115 (107–121)
Matrix Reasoning = 13
Figure Weights = 12

Auditory Working
Memory Index = 84 (77–94)
Digit Span = 6
Letter Number Sequencing = 8

Processing Speed
Index = 100 (91–109)
Coding = 10
Symbol Search = 10

Wechsler Individual Attainment Test (WIAT III)
1. Single Word Reading Test – Standard score = 82
2. Pseudoword Decoding – Standard score = 70
3. Spelling – Standard score = 72
4. Numeracy – Standard score = 105
5. Maths Problem Solving – Standard score = 90
6. Sentence Repetition – Standard score = 84

York Assessment of Reading for Comprehension (YARC – secondary version)
1. Reading Comprehension Standard score = 90
2. Reading Speed (silent) Standard score = 75

Detailed Assessment of Speed of Handwriting (DASH)
Free Writing Standard score = 68; content poor, with grammatical errors evident and limited range of vocabulary used.

Comprehensive Test of Phonological Processing 2 (CTOPP 2)
1. Phoneme Elision – Standard score = 95
2. Rapid Letter Naming – Standard score = 65
3. Nonword Repetition – Standard score = 80

Alex's summary and formulation at age 13
Alex continues to present as a young man of above average nonverbal ability, as reflected in his high index scores on the Visual Spatial and Fluid Reasoning Scales from the WISC V. His verbal abilities have significantly improved over the course of the last six to seven years, having risen from a below average level at age six (Verbal Comprehension Index = 81) to a currently low-average level (Verbal Comprehension Index = 92). However, the verbal-nonverbal discrepancy remains significant and is again of the size and direction typically seen in children with developmental language disorder. Reading, writing and spelling remain a considerable challenge for Alex; he scored at a below average level on measures of word reading, speed of reading, phonic decoding ability, spelling and speed of writing. His reading comprehension skills have developed relatively well alongside his improvements in oral language. Alex's maths continues to be an educational domain of relative strength (especially his pencil-and-paper computational skills), though some difficulties with the language of maths are still evident (Maths Problem Solving). It is probable that Alex's phonological awareness has improved in response to speech and language therapy and literacy intervention, though difficulties in phonological processing and efficiency remain (CTOPP 2 Rapid Letter Naming). Alex continues to register low scores on 'markers' of language impairment (Sentence Repetition and Nonword Repetition) even though improvements in his oral language skills have taken place.

Alex is an intelligent young man with a history of early developmental language delay and a diagnosis of developmental language disorder. His oral language skills have substantially improved in response to intensive speech and language therapy and are now within normal limits for his age. Having said that, some mild residual language difficulties remain in respect of vocabulary knowledge, reading comprehension, quality of written narrative, and the language of maths. Now at secondary school, Alex's primary difficulty is his severe dyslexia which is having a pervasive effect on all components of literacy skill, with his progress being noticeably slow. Alex continues to present as a young man who concentrates well and is motivated and engaged. His teachers report that he displays strengths in science, art and technical drawing.

Summary

- Assessments of children with literacy disorders should target primarily the behavioural (educational) and cognitive (phonological/language) levels of difficulty, though arguably useful information regarding broader learning profiles can be obtained through also carrying out IQ tests.
- A single word reading test is not enough; literacy is a multi-component skill and this should be reflected in the administration of a wide range of tests that cover also prose reading accuracy, reading speed, reading comprehension, decoding ability, spelling and written narrative skills.
- Phonological tasks that function as cognitive 'markers' for dyslexia measure phonological awareness (e.g. phoneme deletion tests), short-term verbal working memory (e.g. memory span tests) and phonological processing (e.g. rapid naming tests).
- Cognitive level testing that targets language skills is needed for those children who have reading comprehension difficulties and for those whose dyslexia is occurring in the context of developmental speech and language delay or disorder.

- When formulating a child's learning presentation, it is important to consider protective as well as additional risk factors as these 'moderator variables' impact both severity and prognosis.

Chapter 6

Assessing Children with Co-Occurring Difficulties

In Chapter 5, we looked at a comprehensive assessment framework and methodology that could be used to evaluate the child presenting with literacy problems. Case Study 1, Alex, illustrated the assessment process for a child with severe literacy difficulties occurring in the context of early developmental speech and language impairment. In this chapter, the emphasis is on assessing the child who has multiple risk factors that are likely to result in a presentation that includes simultaneously co-occurring disorders, specifically from within the arithmetic, attention and visual motor domains. We have already looked at evidence that shows that as many as 70 per cent of children presenting with a literacy problem will have at least one co-occurring learning difficulty, a figure that clearly indicates the need for assessing beyond the literacy impairment. Assessing for co-occurring difficulties in a time-limited assessment session may indicate the need for what I call 'hypothesis driven testing'. This means that the assessor draws on existing test results, specified concerns of parents and teachers, and behavioural observations during the course of the test session to determine whether further testing is needed to identify the presence of additional learning problems. Low scores on maths tests and expressed concerns on the part of parents and teachers about the child falling behind in maths at school would warrant a consideration of whether the child could have dyscalculia or specific arithmetic disorder. Observations of fidgety, restless and impulsive behaviour during the test session, especially if this is backed by parent and teacher comments about poor concentration, would raise the issue of the child having an attention deficit disorder. Samples showing poor handwriting obtained at the assessment and parent observations of clumsiness and immature drawing skills would suggest that the child needs testing for developmental co-ordination disorder/ dyspraxia. We have already looked at cognitive-based 'marker' tests for dyslexia (i.e. phonological processing measures) and also for developmental language disorder (i.e. nonword repetition and sentence repetition measures). There are also 'marker' tests for arithmetic, attention and co-ordination disorders which tap into the underlying cognitive bases of these. Where testing time is limited, the use of parent and teacher questionnaires can be considered, these being particularly relevant to the assessment of attention disorders.

Assessing co-occurring arithmetic disorder/dyscalculia

In Chapter 4, we saw that that 23 per cent of children with a literacy disorder also present with a disorder of arithmetic or numeracy, indicating a relatively high level of co-occurrence (Landerl and Moll 2010). Adopting the Pennington model of shared versus non-shared risks in co-occurring disorders, there is evidence to suggest that a non-shared deficit in arithmetic disorder is a deficit of numerosity; to recapitulate, this refers to the child's appreciation of the magnitude of numbers. Standardized maths tests, such as those that appear on the WIAT III and WRAT 5, would be expected to demonstrate that the child with an arithmetic disorder performs below the level of their peers in terms of their understanding of maths concepts and numerical operational procedures. However, these attainment tests do not assess the cognitive deficit of numerosity which may be viewed as a 'marker' for dyscalculia. Tests that perform this function are The Butterworth Dyscalculia Screener (Butterworth 2003) and the more recently developed Test of Basic Arithmetic and Number Skills, TOBANS, (Hulme, Moll and Brigstocke 2016), both of which are available to teachers as well as psychologists. The Butterworth Dyscalculia Screener is a 30-minute digital test standardized in the age range six to 14 years. There are five subtests: a simple reaction time test, two *capacity* tests

(Dot Enumeration in which the child matches a collection of dots to its number and Number Comparison in which the child selects the larger of two numbers), and two achievement tests that assess simple addition and multiplication. Low performance on the capacity and achievement tests is considered to be indicative of dyscalculia. The TOBANS consists of a series of timed pencil-and-paper tests of arithmetic skill and numerosity and is standardized in the age range seven to 11 years. The arithmetic tests cover simple addition, subtraction, multiplication and division which assess arithmetic fluency, while the numerosity tests are Dot Comparison (which of two boxes has the most dots?), Digit Comparison (which of two numbers is the bigger?) and Count the Dots (how many dots are in each box?). Low scores on the TOBANS measures, especially those that assess numerosity, would be consistent with a formulation in terms of dyscalculia. The Feifer Assessment of Mathematics (Feifer 2016b) is designed to evaluate the underlying neurodevelopmental processes that support the acquisition of proficient maths skills. It comprises 19 subtests, measuring skills such as maths fact retrieval, numeric memory, perceptual estimation skills, linguistic maths concepts and core number sense development. Standardized on students aged four to 21 years, it purports to not only determine whether a child has a maths disorder but also identifies specific subtypes according to which component maths subskills are selectively impaired. Performance on arithmetic *fluency* tasks (such as those featured on the WIAT III, TOBANS, the Butterworth Dyscalculia Screener and the Feifer) may capture the underlying verbal difficulties that explain the co-occurrence of dyslexia and dyscalculia in children with a history of language problems (see Chapter 4).

It is important however not to lose sight of the fact that some children with maths problems may have other underlying difficulties (or risks) that are not conceptualized as a numerosity deficit. A child with an impairment of auditory working memory (captured for instance by a test of repeating digits backwards) would be expected to struggle with mental maths and to have difficulty in retaining verbal number facts. Alternatively, a weakness in visual perceptual and spatial abilities (captured by nonverbal tasks like Matrix Reasoning or Block Design from the WISC V or WRIT) would put the child at risk for difficulties with visual aspects of maths such as geometry and symmetry; time calculation; measurement; calculating volumes, areas and perimeters; understanding angles; and interpreting graphs, charts and calendars.

Case Study 2: Jyoti, a child with dyslexia and dyscalculia – assessment and formulation

Recall from Chapter 4 that Jyoti is a nine-year-old girl referred because of concerns about her spelling and written output skills, slow processing and weak maths. Her educational progress was slow in spite of her being a hard-working girl who has received both in-class and out-of-school intervention and tuition. Jyoti's test scores are given in Box 6.1.

Box 6.1: Jyoti's test results at nine years
Wechsler Intelligence Scale for Children V (WISC V)

Verbal Comprehension
Index = 111 (103–119)
Similarities = 11
Vocabulary = 13

Visual Spatial
Index = 86 (77–94)
Block Design = 6
Visual Puzzles = 9

Fluid Reasoning
Index = 88 (82–95)
Matrix Reasoning = 9
Figure Weights = 7

Auditory Working
Memory Index = 85 (74–96)
Digit Span = 7
Letter Number Sequencing = 7

Processing Speed
Index = 106 (96–116)
Coding = 9
Symbol Search = 13

Wechsler Individual Attainment Test (WIAT III)
1. Single Word Reading – Standard score = 103
2. Pseudoword Decoding – Standard score = 105
3. Spelling – Standard score = 88

4. Numeracy – Standard score = 90
5. Maths Problem Solving – Standard score = 80

York Assessment of Reading for Comprehension (YARC)
1. Reading Accuracy Standard score = 104
2. Reading Comprehension Standard score = 116
3. Reading Speed Standard score = 105

Detailed Assessment of Speed of Handwriting (DASH)
Free Writing Standard score = 100; fair expression of ideas, sentence construction and vocabulary usage.

Comprehensive Test of Phonological Processing 2 (CTOPP 2)
1. Elision – Standard score = 75
2. Rapid Letter Naming – Standard score = 80

TOBANS
1. Dot Comparison – Standard score = 79
2. Count the Dots – Standard score = 89
3. Digit Comparison – Standard score = 100

Beery Test of Visuomotor Integration
Standard score = 100

Jyoti's summary and formulation
Jyoti is a little girl of slightly above average verbal intelligence (WISC V Verbal Comprehension Index or Verbal IQ = 111, top 23 per cent of same age children) who does therefore have the language skills to support good academic development. In fact, standardized educational testing revealed that Jyoti is doing well in respect of her progress in reading; she achieved average to above average scores on measures of single word reading, prose

reading accuracy, reading comprehension, reading speed/fluency and phonic decoding ability (standard scores in the range 103–116). She is, however, a relatively weak speller (standard score = 88). Her mathematical skills are below both age- and verbal ability-expectation (standard scores = 80–90). Her handwriting is a nicely formed mix of printing and cursive scripts and is executed at an average speed. Her written expression skills are now beginning to develop quite well.

Jyoti is a verbally able girl who has a specific learning difficulty that comprises two separate disorders: dyslexia (specific literacy disorder) and dyscalculia (specific arithmetic disorder). As is typical of children with dyslexia, Jyoti exhibits underlying phonological processing and analysis difficulties, together with a weak short-term auditory/verbal working memory. However, her phonic decoding is far better than we would expect given her weak phonological skills. This suggests that she has responded very well indeed to targeted phonic decoding programmes delivered both in and out of school. Jyoti's improved decoding is likely to have fuelled her good progress in reading, but clearly spelling problems remain. Co-occurring alongside the dyslexia, which may well be of genetic/familial origin, is developmental dyscalculia. It is hypothesized that Jyoti's dyscalculia is partly a consequence of her poor visual spatial skills (note her low scores on the two nonverbal subscales of the WISC V, i.e. Visual Spatial and Fluid Reasoning); these appear to be impacting on visual subitizing (a component of numerosity that is captured by her poor performance on Dot Comparison and Count the Dots from the TOBANS). She also has short-term auditory/verbal working memory difficulties which would be expected to impair her mental maths and her ability to retain verbal number facts. Dyslexia and dyscalculia are two specific developmental disorders that commonly co-occur. The reason that Jyoti's dyslexia and dyscalculia are co-occurring is because they share a common cognitive cause or 'risk': a short-term auditory working memory limitation. The non-shared cognitive causes are phonological difficulties in the case of yslexia and visual subitizing/visual spatial problems in the case of dyscalculia. Jyoti has important strengths in respect of her verbal abilities, her reading and her high levels of motivation.

Assessing co-occurring attention disorders

The co-occurrence rate of dyslexia and ADHD is thought to be as high as 25–40 per cent. While many children demonstrating this co-occurrence will attract a clinical diagnosis of ADHD, we should not lose sight of the fact that a proportion of them could have (likely later diagnosed) attention problems which are a behavioural reaction to their long-standing literacy failure. In the Pennington multiple deficit perspective of co-occurrence, the shared causal risk in dyslexia and co-occurring attention problems is slow processing speed. Non-shared risks would be phonological deficits in dyslexia and difficulties with response inhibition in attention disorder.

The assessment of ADHD is a complex process and is best conducted in a multidisciplinary framework, especially if the child's presenting symptoms are sufficiently serious to warrant a consideration of prescription medication. A diagnosis of ADHD is arrived at following comprehensive interviews with parents and teachers, as well as behavioural observations of the child which may take place in a school visit context and/or within a one-to-one assessment. Rating scales and diagnostic tests are also frequently used.

The most widely adopted rating scale to inform the diagnosis of ADHD is that developed by Conners; now in its third version, the scale may be completed by parents and/or teachers. It consists of six subscales: inattention, hyperactivity/impulsivity, learning problems, executive function, aggression and peer relationships (Conners 2008). There are 110 items spread across the six subscales to which the parent or teacher responds by deciding how well each statement describes the child. Children with severe ADHD who also have behavioural problems are likely to obtain clinical range scores on all six subscales, while children with milder problems (perhaps without the hyperactivity and behavioural problems) will score in the clinical range on say just two to three subscales. Another frequently used rating measure in the assessment of attention difficulties is the Behaviour Rating Inventory of Executive Functioning-Second Edition (BRIEF-II) which assesses aspects of executive functions (Giola, Isquith and Guy 2015). As we saw in Chapter 4, executive functions are a collection of processes that are responsible for guiding, directing and managing cognitive, emotional and behavioural functions. The scales that this questionnaire covers are as follows: Inhibit (i.e. the ability to inhibit, resist or not to act on impulse); Self-Monitor (i.e. the ability to keep track of the effect of one behaviour on others); Shift (i.e. the ability to move freely from one situation or activity to another); Emotional Control (i.e. the ability to control emotional responses); Initiate (i.e. to begin a task or activity as well as independently generate ideas); Working Memory (i.e. the capacity to hold information in mind for the purpose of completing a task); Plan/Organize (i.e. the ability to manage current and future-orientated task demands); Task-Monitor (the ability to check work, assess performance during or after finishing a task to ensure attainment of goal); Organize Materials (i.e. the ability to engage in work-checking exercises); and Monitor (i.e. the ability to asses one's own behaviour or performance). These executive function processes form three broader indices of *Behaviour Regulation* (Inhibit, Self-Monitor); *Emotion Regulation* (Shift, Emotional Control) and *Cognitive Regulation* (Initiate, Working Memory, Plan/Organize, Task-Monitor and Organize Materials). The three index scores make up the overall score the *Global Executive Composite*.

Tests of attention that may be conducted within the context of a one-to-one assessment include the Test of Everyday Attention for Children, TEA-Ch (now in its second version) (Manly *et al.* 2016) and the Conners Continuous Auditory Test of Attention (CATA) (Conners 2014), both of which are digital and cover a wide age range (5–18 years in the case of the TEA-Ch, and eight years and above in the case of the CATA). The TEA-Ch 2, developed in Australia, consists of a series of computer 'games' which assess three domains of attention: *selective attention* which is the child's ability to focus on a specific activity while screening out distractor stimuli; *sustained attention* which describes the child's ability to maintain an 'attention set' while carrying out a lengthy activity that requires continued vigilance; and *switching attention* which refers to the child's capacity to switch from one task or mental set to another while inhibiting a previously acquired set. The American-devised CATA assesses auditory processing and attention-related problems in children and adults. The assessment lasts for 14 minutes, during which the child is presented with 200 high tones, which are either preceded by a low tone (warning sound) or presented alone. The child is required to respond when there is a warning tone presented with the high tone and not when the high tone is presented alone.

The results from rating scales and tests of attention need to be combined with information from other sources and then confirmed by a qualified clinician (usually a psychiatrist, paediatrician or clinical psychologist) before a firm diagnostic conclusion is reached.

Case Study 3: Billy, a child with dyslexia and attention disorder – assessment and formulation

In Chapter 4, I introduced Billy, a seven-year-old boy who is competent in reading and maths but making slow progress in spelling and written work. His parents and teachers also expressed concern about his lack of focus and his restless and distracted behaviour. Billy's test scores are given in Box 6.2.

Box 6.2: Billy's test results at seven years five months
Wechsler Intelligence Scale for Children V (WISC V)

General Ability Index = 132 (124–137)

Verbal Comprehension Index = 127 (117–123)
Similarities = 14
Vocabulary = 16

Visual Spatial Index = 135 (123–140)
Block Design = 13
Visual Puzzles = 19

Fluid Reasoning Index = 134 (125–139)
Matrix Reasoning = 15
Figure Weights = 17

Auditory Working Memory Index = 91 (83–101)
Digit Span = 8
Letter Number Sequencing = 9

Processing Speed Index = 89 (81–99)
Coding = 8
Symbol Search = 8

Wechsler Individual Attainment Test (WIAT III)

1. Single Word Reading – Standard score = 100
2. Pseudoword Decoding – Standard score = 90
3. Spelling – Standard score = 95
4. Numeracy – Standard score = 110
5. Maths Problem Solving – Standard score = 115
6. Written Expression – able to write simple sentence of his own.

York Assessment of Reading for Comprehension (YARC)

1. Reading Accuracy Standard score = 111
2. Reading Comprehension Standard score = 123
3. Reading Speed Standard score = 108

Comprehensive Test of Phonological Processing 2 (CTOPP 2)

1. Elision – Standard score = 105
2. Rapid Letter Naming – Standard score = 85

Beery Test of Visuomotor Integration

Standard score = 101

Test of Everyday Attention for Children 2 (TEA-Ch2)

1. Sustained Attention (Vigil) - Scaled score = 6
2. Switching Attention (Red and Blue Bags and Shoes) – Scaled score = 7

Billy is a young man of high intelligence; his WISC V General Ability Index (based on five subtest scores covering verbal and nonverbal abilities, but excluding processing speed and working memory) is 132, placing him in the top 2 per cent of same age children for overall intelligence. He has very well-developed verbal abilities (WISC V Verbal Comprehension Index/Verbal IQ = 127, top 4 per cent of same age children for language skills). On the basis of his high cognitive ability, we would expect his educational attainments to be developing well. In fact, standardized educational testing revealed that first, in general, Billy is a capable mathematician, achieving at an above average level on two standardized maths tests (standard scores of 110–115). Billy's single word reading is average (standard score of 100 on WIAT III single word reading), although below ability expectation. He does, however, read well in prose context (he obtained a standard score of 111 on YARC reading accuracy). His speed of reading is of a good standard (standard score = 108) and he has excellent reading comprehension (standard score = 123). He does, however, show some insecurities in terms of his phonic decoding skills (WIAT III Pseudoword Decoding standard score = 90). Billy's spelling is within the normal range for his age (standard score = 95), though again below his expected level. In handwriting, he is developing fair letter formation and is making an effective transition from printing to cursive writing, executed at a good speed. His written expression skills are however underdeveloped for such a verbally able child. Owing to concerns about Billy's concentration, his parents and teachers completed the Conners questionnaire; of the six subscales, he scored within the clinical range on three of these, specifically hyperactivity/impulsivity, inattention and executive function.

Billy is a very bright and articulate little boy with considerable academic potential, which he is now beginning to fulfil across a wide range of educational subjects. Having said that, there is evidence of mild dyslexia, though he is already beginning to show signs of developing compensatory strategies. As expected of a child with dyslexia, Billy exhibits mild relative short-term auditory/verbal working memory and phonological weaknesses. These in turn have impaired his ability to develop the sequential decoding skills necessary to underpin the normal expansion of his reading and spelling lexicons. It is of interest to note the family history of literacy difficulties which may be considered indicative of a genetic or familial predisposition. It must be emphasized though that Billy's dyslexia is mild and is mainly expressed as underachievement in spelling. Billy is compensating well for his dyslexia within the literacy domain of reading because he is drawing on his good language skills and the context cues available in prose reading material to aid and support both word identification and reading comprehension. Co-occurring alongside the mild dyslexia are attention problems, evident on formal testing as difficulty in sustaining his concentration over lengthy periods of time, and in switching attention and inhibiting his responses appropriately according to task demands (TEA-Ch 2). He was observed during the test session to find it hard to focus, and there were periods of restlessness and distractibility. Finally, he scored within the clinical range on three out of the six subscales of the Conners questionnaire. As is often found in children with attention difficulties, Billy is a slow processor (note his relatively low scores on WISC V Processing Speed Scale and on CTOPP 2 Rapid Letter Naming); slow processing speed is the shared risk factor in co-occurring dyslexia and attention problems/ADHD. Billy shows considerable strengths in respect of his verbal and nonverbal abilities, his reading comprehension and his maths; these constitute protective factors which could be considered predictive of a good overall academic outcome.

Assessing co-occurring visual motor disorders

In Chapter 4, we saw that dyslexia commonly co-occurs with motor difficulties, with one study showing a co-occurrence rate as high as 60 per cent. It seems obvious that the non-shared deficits in these co-occurring disorders would be a phonological deficit explaining the dyslexia and a visual/spatial/perceptual deficit explaining the DCD. However, finding a shared characteristic that explains the overlap of the disorders is less straightforward, and may not be obvious on formal assessment.

Most children with visual motor difficulties have problems with establishing well-formed, consistent and legible handwriting scripts, their written output is often messy and disorganized and their speed of writing slow. It is useful to explore the nature of a child's handwriting and written presentation difficulties in more depth through the administration of what might be termed 'marker' tests for DCD/dyspraxia. A universally used measure is the Beery Developmental Test of Visuomotor Integration (Beery, Beery and Buktenika 2010) which can be administered (by psychologists and teachers) to adults as well as children and which is composed of three subtests; a *Visuomotor Integration* test which requires the copy drawing of increasingly complex geometric shapes, a *Visual Perception* subtest which requires the child to visually match one of a series of presenting geometric shapes with a stimulus shape, and a *Motor Co-ordination* test which has the child drawing accurately a geometric shape within prescribed boundary lines. Low scores on these tests are indicative of visual perceptual, motor and visuomotor integration difficulties that characterize the child with handwriting problems and would be considered consistent with a presentation of DCD. Another useful test is the Rey Complex Figure Test (Meyers and Meyers 1996) which is most usually adopted as a measure of short- and long-term visual spatial memory, but whose copy version provides an admittedly rough (but nonetheless often useful) index of motor organization ability which is a core deficit in DCD. Children with severe motor and handwriting problems may need a referral to an occupational therapist or physiotherapist for a detailed appraisal of their difficulties which should provide a more definitive diagnosis and comprehensive treatment/management plan.

Case Study 4: Freddie, a child with dyslexia and visual motor difficulties – assessment and formulation

In Chapter 4, I introduced Freddie, a 12-year-old boy with a long-standing history of literacy difficulties who had shown recent improvements in his reading but who had considerable difficulty in expressing himself on paper in an accurate, coherent, legible and sufficiently rapid fashion. Freddie's parents are becoming increasingly concerned about both his disengagement in lessons and his moodiness and occasional anger outbursts. Freddie's test scores are summarized in Box 6.3.

Box 6.3: Freddie's test results at 12 years
Wechsler Intelligence Scale for Children V (WISC V)

Pro-rated General Ability Index = 112 (105–118)

Verbal Comprehension Index = 111 (102–118)
Similarities = 13
Vocabulary = 11

Visual Spatial Index = 86 (79–96)
Block Design = 6
Visual Puzzles = 9

Fluid Reasoning Index = 109 (102–115)
Matrix Reasoning = 11
Figure Weights = 12

Auditory Working Memory Index = 88 (81–98)
Digit Span = 7
Letter Number Sequencing = 9

Processing Speed Index = 83 (78–94)
Coding = 7
Symbol Search = 7

Wechsler Individual Attainment Test (WIAT III)
1. Single Word Reading – Standard score = 90
2. Oral Reading Speed – Standard score = 85
3. Spelling – Standard score = 79
4. Numeracy – Standard score = 105
5. Maths Problem Solving – Standard score = 110

York Assessment of Reading for Comprehension (YARC - secondary version)
1. Reading Comprehension - Standard score = 112
2. Reading Speed - Standard score = 95

Test of Word Reading Efficiency 2 (TOWRE 2)
1. Sight Word Efficiency – Standard score = 71
2. Phonemic Decoding Efficiency – Standard score = 73

Detailed Assessment of Speed of Handwriting (DASH)
Free Writing subtest – Scaled score = 6

Comprehensive Test of Phonological Processing 2 (CTOPP 2)
1. Elision – Standard score = 95
2. Rapid Letter Naming – Standard score < 79

Beery Test of Visuomotor Integration
Standard score = 81

Rey Complex Figure Test (copy version)
6–10th centile

Freddie is a young man of above average intelligence; his pro-rated General Ability Index of 112 (top 20% of same age children for overall intelligence) is based on four subtests from the WISC V, covering verbal and nonverbal abilities (though excluding the Block Design score as being an 'outlier' and therefore considered unrepresentative of his general ability). He has well-developed verbal language capabilities (WISC V Verbal Comprehension Index/Verbal IQ = 111, top 23% of same age students for language skills). On the basis of these ability indices, it was expected that he should be performing and progressing well educationally. In fact, standardized educational testing revealed that first, Freddie is a generally competent mathematician; he scored at a good-average level (WIAT III standard scores of 105–110) on two separate maths tests. He is however struggling with a number of aspects of reading. There are gaps in his word reading recognition (WIAT single word reading standard score = 90) and he is a slow reader, especially when reading out loud (note his low scores on WIAT III Oral Reading Speed and TOWRE 2 Sight Word Efficiency). He has markedly underdeveloped phonic decoding ability (TOWRE 2 Phonemic Decoding Efficiency standard score = 73). Reading comprehension is however very well preserved and is above average (YARC standard score = 112). Freddie is a very weak speller (standard score = 79). His handwriting shows rather uneven letter formation and can at times be difficult to read; he holds the pen incorrectly and he also writes very slowly. His written sentence constructions and vocabulary usage were noted to be immature and do not reflect his above average abilities nor his good verbal language skills. Freddie showed some signs of disengagement during the assessment, which included presenting as being 'off hand' in his manner, looking bored and giving up all too readily when he found an activity challenging. The Strengths and Difficulties Questionnaire was completed by his parents and teachers, with Freddie scoring within the clinical range on the Emotional Symptoms and Conduct Problems subscales but not on the Hyperactivity/Inattention or Peer Relationship Problems subscales.

Freddie is an able young man with a cognitive/educational profile that is indicative of developmental dyslexia. He exhibits short-term verbal working memory and phonological processing limitations that have impaired his ability to acquire phonic decoding strategies that are necessary for the development of word level reading and spelling skills. It may be that Freddie's reading has improved of late in response to intervention and it is likely that he has developed compensatory strategies. Certainly, his functional reading skills (his reading comprehension and his speed of reading silently to himself for content) are now within the normal range. He is however continuing to have great difficulty in reading accurately and fluently out loud, and he has marked spelling difficulties. Co-occurring alongside his dyslexia are visual spatial, motor organization difficulties and visual processing problems, evident from his low scores on the WISC V Visual Spatial and Processing Speed Scales, and also on the Beery Test of Visuomotor Integration and the Rey Complex Figure Copy tests. These difficulties, consistent with a diagnosis of developmental co-ordination disorder/dyspraxia, adversely affect his handwriting speed and quality, and also his general written presentation and organization. Freddie demonstrates strengths in his overall reasoning skills and his verbal abilities which are likely to provide a compensatory resource that is already contributing to his good reading comprehension and his well-developed maths problem-solving ability. Freddie's long-term educational struggles have caused him increasing frustration over the years which is currently resulting in moodiness and angry behaviour at home, and disengagement in lessons at school.

Summary

- Assessing for co-occurring difficulties can be achieved through 'hypothesis driven testing', with the assessor drawing on existing test results, specified concerns of parents and teachers, and behavioural observations during the course of the test session to determine whether further testing is needed to identify the presence of additional learning problems.
- The child who scores at a low level on standardized maths tests warrants further investigation of their *numerosity* skills (as well as their auditory working memory and visual spatial abilities) to determine if they have co-occurring dyscalculia or a specific arithmetic difficulty.
- Assessing aspects of attention (such as sustaining and switching attention, inhibiting responses as tasks demand) through standardized tests or rating scales, together with processing speed measures, can indicate whether the child should be referred for a clinical evaluation for co-occurring attention deficit with hyperactivity disorder.
- Measures of visual spatial, visuomotor and motor organization abilities can help to clarify whether the child's struggles with handwriting quality and speed and written presentation are attributable to co-occurring DCD/dyspraxia.

Chapter 7

Literacy Interventions

Chapter 6 began by revisiting definitions and models of literacy impairment in order to see how these can inform the process of evaluating a child presenting with a literacy difficulty. It is helpful to take the same approach when looking at intervention. Let us look one last time at Margaret Snowling's definition of dyslexia from 2000:

> Dyslexia is a specific form of *language* impairment that affects the way in which the brain encodes the *phonological* features of spoken words. The core deficit is in phonological processing and stems from poorly specified phonological processing. Dyslexia specifically affects the development of *reading and spelling skills* but its effects can be modified through development leading to a variety of behavioural manifestations. (pp.213–214, my emphasis)

Putting aside for the moment that this definition draws on a single deficit perspective of dyslexia, it is nonetheless useful in that it draws attention to the fact that we need to address three critical components when we plan intervention programmes for a child with a literacy difficulty, specifically aspects of language, phonology and literacy. In Uta Frith's model that emphasizes the levels of study in literacy disorders, we would expect to intervene at the cognitive (phonological/language) and behavioural (literacy) levels. Some alternative therapies claim to address literacy disorders at the biological level, and we will look, albeit critically, at these also.

Interventions need to be based on a strong causal model which recognizes the processes involved in typical literacy development and which in turn offers an explanation for how it might go wrong (as in the case of dyslexia), precisely what I aimed to do in Chapters 1 and 2. Indeed, it is crucial to have a very clear idea about the nature and origins of the child's difficulties in order to plan an intervention programme that is specifically tailored to their individual needs.

How do we know when an intervention works?

Demonstrating whether a proposed treatment or intervention actually does what it claims to do requires what scientists and researchers refer to as a *randomized control trial (RCT)*. Properly conducted, such a trial should determine unequivocally whether the proposed intervention is leading to the observed improvements and cannot be attributed to any other factor. Importantly, RCTs are, as Barbara Maughan has put it, 'the building blocks of evidence-based practice' (Maughan 2013, p.1). Indeed, when any new intervention appears on the market, it is important for professionals, teachers and parents to feel confident that first, their investment in terms of time and money is being well spent and, even more critically, that the child with a learning difficulty who receives the intervention will actually improve. It is only interventions shown to be effective through RCTs that can instil this confidence.

How do we carry out an RCT? The criteria that need to e satisfied in the well-conducted RCT are given in Box 7.1. Additionally, methodologically sound intervention studies are usually submitted to scientific journals that subject them to rigorous scrutiny through peer review before they are considered publishable. One final point to take away is that training or treatment studies require replication by other, preferably independent, researchers. There have been situations in which a treatment method has been apparently scientifically validated and then reported in a reputable journal, but thereafter other researchers have been unable to replicate the results. It is, therefore, important not to be overly enthusiastic about a one-off treatment study that describes dramatic results from a new treatment or training method. All new interventions await the reassurance that can only come through replication studies carried out by independent researchers.

Box 7.1: Criteria for conducting randomized controlled trials (RCTs) in the field of reading research

- Participants (Ps) must be selected by objective criteria, preferably by quoting test scores that indicate that the participants are achieving below expectation in, for our purposes, reading.
- Ps must be randomly allocated to groups in order to avoid allocation bias (an example of bias would be to assign the poorest readers to the intervention group).
- There must be an appropriate control group (which receives no treatment or an alternative intervention) against which the performance or progress of the primary intervention group can be compared.
- There must be pre-test data to ensure the groups are equally matched at the outset of the study, in other words are beginning the trial all at the same level of reading.
- The sample must be a good size; it should be fairly large in order to ensure that the statistics will be sufficiently powerful to detect differences between the groups.
- It is important to provide information on 'drop-outs' from the study – are they representative of the 'remainers' as a group or is there something special about why they failed to continue that warrants explanation?
- Assessors (i.e. those carrying out the pre- and post-intervention evaluations) must be 'blind' to treatment versus control group status, in other words they must not know to which group each child they assess is allocated (in order to avoid assessor 'bias').
- Teachers delivering the treatment or intervention must not be the assessors – again in order to prevent personal bias of those carrying out the intervention.

- The intervention must be fully and clearly described so that it can be replicated by other researchers.
- *All* data must be reported so that they are representative of the performance of the group as a whole ('outlier' scores that do not behave like the others in the group cannot be omitted from analyses without a good reason).
- Statistics must be appropriate to the type of data collected, with 'effect sizes' quoted as well as level of statistical significance.

Intervention at the cognitive level
Training phonological skills

In Chapter 1, we argued a strong case for phonological awareness being a powerful predictor and determiner of ease of learning to read. Chapter 2 looked at evidence that clearly demonstrates that most children who have word level literacy difficulties have an underlying deficit in phonological processing. It follows, therefore, that if we are to effectively treat a child with a disorder of this sort, we will need to provide training in phonological skills. The first phonological training studies took place in Scandinavia in the 1980s (for instance, the large-scale study of Olofsson and Lundberg 1985), with one very critical and highly influential study conducted in the UK (Bradley and Bryant 1983). The early studies of the 1980s hypothesized that if you trained phonological skills in children with reading disorders (who had demonstrably poor phonological abilities before training), it would result in an improvement in their reading skills by the end of training. While a number of Scandinavian studies showed this to be true, the gains in reading skill following training were disappointingly small.

A classic study by Lynette Bradley and Peter Bryant (1983) threw considerable light on why the results of these early studies were disappointing. They carried out a training study with 65 young poor readers having what they termed 'sound categorization difficulties' who were randomly allocated to one of three groups: a sound categorization training group, a control group that was trained in the meanings of words (semantic group), and a combined group that had sound categorization training in conjunction with linking (plastic) alphabetic letters with the trained sounds. Sound categorization training on its own produced no significant improvements in reading over the semantic control condition. It was only the children who had the sound categorization training *combined with* experience of letters who improved in their reading and also spelling. It seems that for phonological training to be effective in improving a child's reading, it needs to be linked with their experience of the printed word. This is very much in keeping with Brian Byrne's 'alphabetic principle' which was introduced in Chapter 1: that for children to learn to read, they need a minimum level of phonological awareness that enables them to break spoken words into sounds, they need to learn the letters of the alphabet and importantly they need to forge a 'link' between sounds and letters.

A study which further clarifies how phonological training impacts learning to read is that conducted by Hatcher *et al.* (1994); this is an excellent example of a well-constructed RCT that aimed to demonstrate empirically the efficacy of a phonological training programme conducted within the context of learning to read. It meets all the criteria listed in Box 7.1 and we can therefore be confident that improvements seen in the intervention groups are unequivocally a consequence of the teaching the children received. In this study, 128 poor readers aged seven years who had reading quotients of less than 86 on a standardized word recognition task (constituting the poorest 18% of readers) were randomly allocated to one of four groups. The authors ensured that the groups were carefully matched at the outset for age, IQ and reading age. The four groups were:

- Reading + Phonology group who received phonological awareness training, reading experience and activities that linked the two components
- Phonology alone group who experienced the same phonological training given the Reading + Phonology group, but had no explicit reading instruction or phonology linkage exercises
- Reading alone group who read books, had multisensory

training and learned letter names, but had no phonological training
- Control group who received conventional classroom instruction.

The children were pre-tested on a wide range of cognitive, phonological awareness and educational measures. Those in the three experimental groups received forty 30-minute sessions of individual instruction over a 20-week period. Twenty-three teachers trained specifically to implement the teaching programmes worked with children in all three experimental conditions; that is, each teacher taught the same number of children from each of the experimental conditions. At the conclusion of the teaching phase, the children were re-tested. To determine whether the effects of the intervention were long lasting, measures of reading were taken again nine months after the teaching programme was completed. It is important to note that the tests given at the pre-test, post-test and follow-up phases were administered by an assessor who had not taught any of the children and who was also 'blind' to the group to which each child belonged. At post-test, the Reading + Phonology group scored significantly higher than the other groups on measures of reading that included word recognition, text reading and nonword reading. The improvements in reading shown by the Reading + Phonology group were sustained at the nine-month follow-up.

Hatcher, Hulme and Ellis wanted to make two important points from the results of this study.

- First, they had demonstrated that a structured phono-logically based reading programme can significantly improve the reading standards of delayed seven-year-olds; indeed, the Reading + Phonology group made over a year's progress in text reading accuracy and reading comprehension over a seven-month period, although the teaching lasted for just 20 sessions. This amounts to gains of approximately 1.7 months for each month of elapsed time. In contrast, the Control group made gains in reading of just 0.9 months per month elapsed.

- Second, the authors wanted to reinforce the point that phonological training is most effective in enhancing progress in literacy when it is combined with the teaching of reading and writing. The Reading + Phonology group made far more dramatic progress in reading than either the Phonology alone or Reading alone groups. Also, the beneficial effects of the Reading + Phonology intervention were not purely mediated by changes in phonological skill. Larger improvements in phonological skills at post-test were obtained for the Phonology alone group without an equal improvement in literacy skill. Thus, phonological training is at its most effective when it encourages the formation of explicit connections or links between children's underlying phonological skills and their experiences in learning to read.

The materials used in this study eventually formed the basis for a commercially available phonological awareness training programme, *Sound Linkage*, now in its third edition. The programme begins with a series of short *phonological tests* that enable the teacher to determine what specific phonological skills the child has at their disposal and their overall level of phonological ability. The phonological activities that make up the training component in Sound Linkage are divided into nine sections and are graded in order of difficulty that then determines the sequence in which they are taught. Early introduced *phonological exercises* include identifying and manipulating syllables and identifying and discriminating phonemes, which eventually lead on to more advanced phonological skills such as deleting, substituting and transposing phonemes. *Linkage exercises* are presented after the phonological training activities which aim to make explicit the link between sounds and letters; these include learning letter-sound associations, relating spellings to sounds using plastic letters and writing words while paying attention to letter-sound relationships.

Including language skills

We saw in Chapter 3 that the multiple deficit model points to many children who have dyslexia having additional spoken language problems. If these are present when the child starts school they are considered to be at significant risk of developing literacy problems. We will now look at an RCT that targeted at-risk four-year-olds who were starting school with very weak speech and language skills (Bowyer-Crane *et al.* 2008). In this study, 152 such children were randomly allocated to one of two intervention groups: Oral Language (OL) training or Phonology with Reading (P + R) training (there was no control group as the aim of the study was to look at the differential effects of two different types of intervention). The P + R programme was similar in structure and content to Sound Linkage but also included work on sight words and reading in context. The OL programme targeted the following language domains:

- *listening activities* which included the child responding with an action when they heard a key word in a story read to them, getting the child to repeat sentences back and having the child follow instructions
- *vocabulary enrichment* that was based on a programme developed by Beck, McKeown and Kucan (2002) which involved introducing the child to a new word, asking them to repeat it, defining it for them and then giving them the opportunity to use the word in a wide range of different contexts and situations
- *oral narrative* in which the child told stories based around for instance sequences of pictures, with a strong emphasis placed on 'beginning-middle-end' structure and 'who-where-when-how' concepts
- *independent speaking* which required the child to talk with the experimenter about aspects of a book and engage in group-based 'show and tell' and 'guess what I'm describing' activities
- *generating inferences* which included asking questions of the children such as 'What will happen if I...?', 'If...then...?', 'What could happen next in this story?'

For a fuller description of the programmes and how they were implemented, see Carroll *et al.* (2011). The children engaged in daily teaching sessions which were delivered by teaching assistants over a 20-week period, with some group-based and some one-to-one lessons. The assessors who administered a range of language- and literacy-related tests before and at the end of the study were 'blind' to group membership. The children in the P + R group made significant improvements in their reading and related skills (including phonological awareness) but not in their language skills, while the children in the OL group made significant progress in their oral narrative, vocabulary knowledge and grammar but not in their reading or phonological awareness. This study clearly demonstrates that it is possible to substantially improve young children's language and literacy skills with a short-term targeted and specific intervention, even when this is delivered by lowly qualified (albeit trained and supervised) teaching assistants. The children in this study undoubtedly reaped considerable benefits from this very early intervention, which would be expected to significantly reduce their risk of later educational problems.

Is auditory working memory trainable?

Many children with literacy and language problems show deficits in their auditory/verbal working memory. It is therefore tempting to ask: would training working memory skills lead to improvements in literacy and language? Professor Susan Gathercole has suggested that working memory is strongly related to learning. Children with working memory difficulties may fail to follow and to remember instructions, they tend to have more limited spoken vocabularies, they struggle with activities that combine processing and storing information (such as mental arithmetic), they have difficulty in place keeping and are error prone, and they may often be mis-labelled as having attention problems because they fail to respond to (or more accurately remember) instructions. Gathercole and Packiam-Alloway (2008) have suggested that there are accommodations and strategies that can be set in place to support the child with a weak auditory/verbal working memory in both school and home contexts. These include the following:

- *Reducing working memory loads* – this can be done by limiting the amount of presented material (e.g. reducing the number of steps, shortening sentences, using accompanying actions to make verbal content more memorable); increasing the meaningfulness and familiarity of the material by reviewing a previous topic and then adding the new information to that; reducing mental processing demands by for instance simplifying the grammatical structure of the sentences used; and restructuring complex tasks by breaking them into small, simple steps or by guiding the child through the task using prompts.
- *Encouraging the child to request repetition* when they need it is an accommodation that can be individually tailored to their needs.
- *Supplying memory aids* can be helpful. These might including writing aids (such as spelling flashcards or charts, reminders of how a sentence is structured), mathematics aids (such as number lines, learning mathematical rules, multiplication grids, calculators and even finger counting for younger children), audio devices (such as tape recorders that can be replayed for reinforcement), and computer software (such as digital notepads). For these aids to be effective they need to be in close and easy proximity to the child and they will additionally need teacher-led instruction, practice and encouragement to use them.
- Developing the *child's own use of strategies* can allow them to prevent or overcome memory problems. Effective child-led strategies include: requesting help from a nominated person, rehearsing verbal information (initially out loud and eventually sub-vocally), developing a personalized and abbreviated note-taking style, using long-term memory aides like 'chunking' information, incorporating headings or prompt acronyms and using organizational devices such as flow charts, diagrams, bullet point lists and so on.

For a fuller description of the above, look at *Working Memory and Learning: A Practical Guide for Teachers* by Susan Gathercole and Tracy Packiam-Alloway (2008).

There has been enormous interest of late in computer-based programmes which claim to train working memory, in particular CogMed[1] and Jungle Memory™. These programmes consist of graded tasks of visual spatial and verbal working memory that are conducted over many repeated trials and which are aimed at or slightly above the child's current memory capacity. The authors of CogMed claim that working through these activities eventually results in benefits to the child's educational attainments, language skills, attention and even IQ. Melby-Lervåg and Hulme (2013) reviewed the results of a large number of CogMed and Jungle Memory™ intervention studies. They found that most of the programmes led to short-term improvements in working memory but these were not sustained long-term. Even more seriously, positive effects were found for only those measures that were close in content to the trained tasks, but there was no evidence of transfer to measures that were less directly related, including scholastic attainments and IQ. This means that the working memory training did not generalize to targeted skills such as reading and spelling. The authors contrast this to the good evidence from RCTs that clearly demonstrate the efficacy of phonological/language-based interventions for literacy difficulties.

Intervention at the behavioural level

Learning to read at the behavioural level involves giving children instruction in a wide range of reading-related skills including letter knowledge acquisition, phonic decoding strategies, orthographic conventions and rules of spelling, and reading comprehension – usually within the context of continuous text reading and written narrative. We will look first at teaching phoneme-grapheme correspondence, phonics and related teaching strategies, and then consider separately and in turn teaching reading fluency, spelling, reading comprehension, written narrative and study skills.

1   www.cogmed.com

Teaching grapheme to phoneme correspondence/phonics

There have been numerous studies that have demonstrated the efficacy of teaching reading using systematic phonic-based programmes. The most productive way of evaluating these is to look at meta-analytic studies which pool together the results of many individual studies into a single large-scale statistical analysis that increases the reliability and validity of the conclusions drawn. Recent meta-analytic studies have usually concentrated on studies that contain both cognitive (phonological) and behavioural (phonics and reading) interventions. For instance, Lonigan, Schatschsneider and Westberg (2008) pooled the findings from 83 RCT or experimental studies (with a control group and pre- and post-test design) that aimed to develop the phonological awareness, letter knowledge and phonic decoding skills of either unselected children or those with learning disorders in the early years of learning to read. The meta-analysis showed that these interventions produced large improvements in children's phonological awareness and their word reading when compared with a no treatment control group. A recent meta-analysis which focused on children and adults with reading difficulties showed that phonic reading instruction improved reading accuracy and reading fluency, whether the intervention included phonological awareness training or not (McArthur *et al.* 2012). Arguably, we might expect that incorporating a cognitive (i.e. phonological-based) element in training will increase the efficacy of the programme especially for children who have compromised phonological systems. Indeed, in the Lonigan *et al.* (2008) meta-analysis, the best intervention results were achieved when phonological awareness training was combined with the teaching of letter names and sounds or phonically based decoding instruction. Moreover, phonological awareness training appeared to be more effective when the instruction focused on small units in words (most usually phonemes) rather than larger units such as syllables or rimes.

Can we agree on what are the key elements of a phonological/phonic based intervention? Rose (2009) suggested that such an intervention should contain the core features described in Box 7.2.

Box 7.2: Core features of a systematic phonological/phonic literacy programme

The programme should be:

- *phonetic* – phonologically and phonically driven in terms of content
- *multisensory* – achieved through the child seeing the word in written form, hearing it in spoken form and writing the word
- *cumulative* – building up from a small base and expanding on pre-existing knowledge
- *sequential and progressive*, which implies the systematic and structured ordering of presented letters and words
- *conducted in small steps* so the child makes few errors and experiences success
- *logical*, with for instance phonological awareness instruction preceding phonic instruction, and
- with opportunities for *overlearning through repetition*; indeed, for all interventions, regular practice is crucial.

There are a plethora of commercially available structured phonological/phonic programmes. A comprehensive survey of such programmes is provided by Brooks (2016) and is a useful reference source. Of course, the personal preference of the individual teacher plays a part in selecting which programmes are to be used. Even more important is the matching of teaching materials to the individual child's difficulties and needs, but more of that later.

We saw in Chapter 1 that our English orthography is partly based on phoneme-grapheme correspondence and partly on more complex orthographic units like morphemes and rimes. A problem in teaching standard phonics to English-speaking children is that the 'sound out the word and blend' strategy (sometimes called 'synthetic phonics') does not always work as children are frequently confronted by what appear to be irregularly constructed words. Robert Savage recently introduced the concept of a 'set for variability' (SfV) which might function as a supplementary strategy in a standard phonic programme (Savage *et al.* 2018). He proposes that children need to develop such an adjustment strategy for when they mispronounce irregular words while they are attempting to decode them, for example, reading 'muscle' as 'muskle'. He suggests that children should be encouraged to adopt a two-process model of assembly: first, phonically assembling the word, for example, d-o-g, and second, matching a specific pronunciation to a known word (dog). Note that the child's ability to adopt the second (i.e. matching) process would be strongly predicted by their vocabulary knowledge. Savage and his colleagues asked: can you teach decoding as a two-process model? To answer this question, they carried out a randomized controlled intervention trial with Year 1 children (five- to six-year-olds). After screening, 201 at-risk poor readers were selected. They were randomly allocated to one of two groups: 1) phoneme mapping + SfV, or 2) best practice teaching (phonic decoding and sight word teaching but not SfV). In group 1, the children were taught synthetic phonics: sound out the word and then blend the sounds to arrive at a proposed reading + SfV. The latter involved using alternative phonic rules in context-based reading when synthetic phonics doesn't completely work; so for instance, trying an alternative vowel sound and supplementing with surrounding context of real text to identify what the word should be. The children were taught five steps:

1. Sound out the letters of an unfamiliar word and blend them, for example, 'salt', which the child might sound out as 's-a-l-t' (short 'a' sound) and then pronounce 'salt'.
2. Evaluate the produced word – they ask themselves 'is this a word I know?'
3. If the answer is 'no' (as in this example), replace the vowel sound with an alternative pronunciation: short 'o' sound.
4. Synthesize (blend) the revised string to arrive at the correct pronunciation, in this case 'solt'.
5. If it leads to a real word they know, it's likely to be correct.

The children in the phoneme mapping + SfV group achieved significantly higher scores at post-test on measures of real word reading and spelling than the best practice teaching group, with moderate effect sizes reported.

There is now convincing evidence from many RCTs that teaching that targets phonological awareness and decoding within a structured multisensory teaching framework is very effective in improving children's reading and spelling skills. Having said that, for children with dyslexia who are learning to read in English, the phonological/phonic-based approach does not provide all the answers. Supplementary strategies such as SfV in reading and, as we shall see in the next section, learning about larger orthographic units in spelling are needed to achieve higher levels of accuracy in reading and spelling.

The special challenge of spelling

Most children with dyslexia are at risk of having persisting spelling difficulties, even though they may have responded well to a systematic phonological/phonic teaching programme and attained an acceptable level of reading accuracy. Spelling in English provides an especial challenge because it is an orthography that is complex and based on units that go beyond the level of simple sound-to-letter correspondence.

Because spelling, like reading, is underpinned in phonology, it is important in a spelling programme to begin with phonological awareness training and the learning of letter names and sounds. From there, graphemes such as consonant clusters (bl, st, fr) and digraphs (sh, th, ch) can be introduced. Jamieson and Jamieson (2006) suggest that more complex spelling patterns should be presented in a systematic order that is based on the consistency, complexity and usefulness of the patterns. It should be adapted for the individual learner, and be based on their level of spelling and their current understanding of spelling-to-sound consistencies and rules. They advise that only one pattern should be introduced at a time, and patterns previously taught should be regularly reviewed and revised. (For a fuller description of spelling patterns, their order of teaching and methodology, see Jamieson and Jamieson 2006.)

An important aspect of teaching spelling to children with

dyslexia is that of introducing them to *key words*. These are very high frequency words such as *was, in, of, me, because*. It has been estimated that just 12 words make up 25 per cent of everything we read and write: *a, and, he, it, of, that, I, in, is, the, to, was*. And there are a further 88 words that make up half of the total words we write – words like *but, because, on, down*. Unfortunately, a sizeable proportion of key words are irregularly spelled (e.g. *could, when, some, said*), but because of their importance, they need to be taught early. A commonly used approach to teaching key words is the multisensory method of Simultaneous Oral Spelling developed from Bradley's (1981) adaptation of the Gillingham and Stillman method (1956). Put simply, the child looks at the printed word (visual input), hears and speaks the word as a whole word and through letter naming (auditory input) and then writes the word (kinaesthetic input). The word is covered and written again from memory, with the process repeated several times. Mnemonic strategies may be helpful for some important key words. These might involve making up a sentence using words that start with the letters of the word to be learned (e.g. BECAUSE: 'because eggs cause accidents, use special effort').

Many spelling programmes emphasize teaching at the smallest unit level – the phoneme. However, we have seen that many children with dyslexia have great difficulty in establishing and retaining grapheme-phoneme connections. A second problem is that grapheme-phoneme relations at this small unit level are often highly inconsistent and irregular. It is suggested, therefore, that it may be helpful to supplement standard phonic spelling programmes with interventions that encourage the child to focus on larger units in words. One of the advantages of this approach for children with dyslexia is that it reduces the load on the processing and memorizing of lengthy speech sound sequences. Additionally, there is emerging evidence that larger units in words (i.e. units such as rimes and morphemes) show greater orthographic consistency and regularity than do smaller unit graphemes (e.g. grapheme clusters, individual vowels) within the English language; consequently, it should be easier for children to learn and apply generalizations about these larger letter units without being confused and confounded by exceptions.

An example of a large unit teaching approach in spelling is that of *analogy* (teachers may be more familiar with the term 'word families'). An analogy involves using the spelling-sound relationships of a known word, for instance 'beak' to predict the pronunciation of an unknown word which shares a similar spelling pattern, such as 'peak'. Analogy is most usually applicable to words which share a common rime structure. Examples of rimes which have many onsets and which enable the predictive spelling of a large number of words include: *ang* (fang, bang, sang), *end* (bend, send, mend), *ight* (fight, sight, slight, might), *ay* (may, stay, lay) and *ump* (jump, bump, stump). To ensure that analogies are spontaneously and reliably used by children in their day-to-day spelling, it is necessary to have a training programme that is sufficiently lengthy (no shorter than a month and usually much longer) and in depth (i.e. using a number of analogous examples, together with explicit training in the pronunciation of individual onsets and rimes and in segmenting or blending the onset-rime pairs).

There is also increasing evidence that suggests that teaching children morphemes (units of meaning) can improve children's spelling. Terezina Nunes and Peter Bryant (2009) demonstrated this by carrying out a randomized controlled intervention trial of 200 nine- to nine-and-a-half-year-olds. This study focused on the children learning about the -ion/-ian distinction, using both real and nonwords. The 'schwa' sound in the affix 'un' is very common in multisyllabic English words – and there are few exceptions in regard to how it is spelled – which means that it is a very useful morpheme to teach children learning to spell. When 'un' occurs at the end of a multisyllabic word and the word refers to a person or an animal it is spelled 'ian' as in 'magician'. When the word does not refer to a person or animal it is spelled 'ion' as in 'situation'. The children in the study were randomly assigned to one of four spelling training groups: an *explicit morphology* group (these children were told whether their -ian or -ion spelling response was right or wrong *and* importantly also why), an *implicit morphology* group (the children were told whether they were right or wrong but not why), a *mixed morphology* group (with half the children given implicit and half explicit feedback) and a *control* group (who received text comprehension training). The children's spelling was tested at pre- and post-test and also at long-term follow-up. The experimental groups did better than the control group on the spelling tests at post-test and follow-up; the explicit training strategy (telling the children the -ion/-ian rule or principle) was the most effective. Nunes and Bryant went on to develop a teaching programme which involved teaching explicitly a morphemic principle or rule and giving the children plenty of practice in using it. In addition to the -ion/-ian principle, they were also taught:

- -ment and -ness suffixes for abstract nouns, for example, 'excitement, richness'
- prefixes that make negatives: in, un, dis, as in 'uninteresting, disabled'
- suffixes that indicate a person such as -er, -or, -ist, for example, 'doctor, psychologist'
- /y/ endings that can form adjectives as in 'thirsty, funny' or abstract nouns as in 'misery, poverty'
- -less and -ful endings as in 'careless, meaningful'
- adjectives with -al and -able endings as in 'comfortable'
- the prefix /re/ as in 'reapply, resume'.

The teaching programme was implemented in a study where the teachers could use the morpheme components in any way and as much as they wanted, so incorporating a high level of variation and flexibility. Even used in this way, the children who had morphemic training achieved higher spelling scores than those who had no morphemic instruction (and this effect was demonstrated for both high and low achievers). Nunes and Bryant make a strong case for spelling not being about learning to spell specific words but about acquiring spelling *principles*. Interestingly, learning about morphemes not only helps children's spelling but there is now emerging evidence that it helps them develop a broader vocabulary knowledge because large numbers of words are derived from other words by adding morphemic units like prefixes and suffixes.

Achieving reading fluency

We have seen that learning to spell accurately is a considerable challenge for children with dyslexia, as is also achieving good reading fluency, that is, being able to read quickly, fluently and with ease. Even when children with dyslexia come to read accurately, their fluency lags behind. Being a slow and effortful reader disadvantages children in time-constrained situations such as exams, it may adversely affect their reading comprehension because they 'lose track and fail to memorize' what they are reading, and it can be sufficiently discouraging to result in them avoiding reading activities. Interventions designed to specifically target fluency usually involve some form of guided repeated oral reading, sometimes referred to as *repeated reading intervention*. Typically, the child reads the same piece of text over and over again until they reach an acceptable (usually pre-determined) level of fluency; this is essentially a form of 'massed practice'. Two meta-analyses of repeated reading intervention studies (Samuels 2000; Therrien 2004) have shown that this training results in moderate to large effects on reading speed (and also to some extent reading comprehension). For repeated reading intervention to be effective, it needs to be conducted on a frequent basis, using a wide range of reading materials and over a sustained period of time. Short-length training sessions combined with incentive (reward) programmes may be necessary for many children in order to engage (and in particular, maintain) their motivation and commitment.

Improving reading comprehension

While verbally able children with dyslexia rarely have difficulty in comprehending and remembering what they read, this is not the case for either those children who have dyslexia occurring in the context of language difficulties or children who are poor reading comprehenders. These children will need an intervention programme that targets their ability to understand what they have read.

An important randomized controlled trial was conducted by Clarke *et al.* (2010) with 170 eight- to nine-year-old poor reading comprehenders who were randomly allocated to one of four groups: text comprehension, oral language, combined (i.e. oral and text comprehension) and control. After pre-testing on a range of standardized language and literacy measures, the children in all groups received 30 hours of training delivered by teaching assistants over 20 weeks. The children in the oral language condition worked exclusively in the oral language domain and received instruction in vocabulary knowledge, listening comprehension, figurative language and spoken narrative. The children in the text comprehension condition worked with books and were taught metacognitive strategies, inferencing, reading comprehension and written narrative. The children in the combined group received a mix of oral and text training. At post-test, the children in all three experimental groups performed at a significantly higher level than the control group on a standardized test of reading comprehension (but not on a control task, which was a maths test). Immediately after the intervention, the biggest improvement was in the combined group. However, at an 11-month follow-up, it was the oral language group who went on to make further gains in their reading comprehension and who had the best overall long-term outcome. The authors especially emphasize the important causal role of vocabulary knowledge in mediating the children's improvements in reading comprehension.

Clarke and her colleagues went on to develop a reading comprehension teaching programme which contains both oral and text level intervention techniques (Clarke *et al.* 2014). The oral level component contains many of the key features of the oral language programmed developed by Bowyer-Crane and colleagues (2008) which was described earlier in this chapter. The text level programme contained the following teaching strategies:

- *Metacognitive strategies*, the components of which are:
  - reading and then re-reading the text (mainly used for factual information)
  - re-reading to find the comprehension question's key word/s in the text and then using the surrounding

information to work out the meaning and to answer the question
- stopping from time to time to think about and discuss what has been read (teachers may 'scaffold' by asking prompt questions, modelling what to say, breaking the text into smaller, more manageable chunks and providing feedback)
- using mental imagery (a mind picture) about what is being read so as to provide cues to support memory
- thinking aloud as a strategy for monitoring comprehension (often conducted in peer groups to develop discussion and sharing of ideas around the content of the passage)
- explaining, reflecting on and summarizing the main point or theme of the passage.

- *Reciprocal teaching* which takes the form of a dialogue between teacher and student that follows the reading of a passage of text. There are four key strategies:
  1. asking questions about the passage and its content (typically, who, where, when, what, and why questions)
  2. clarifying: finding difficult words in the passage and looking for clues in the surrounding text to help explain them
  3. predicting: making guesses about what the passage is about and what might happen next
  4. summarizing: the student uses their own words to explain and summarize the key ideas of the passage.

(This is based on *Reciprocal Teaching at Work: Strategies for Improving Reading Comprehension*; Oczkus 2018.)

- *Inferencing from text* in which there are three key steps to making 'bridging inferences':
  1. picking out key ideas in the text and underlining them
  2. linking the key ideas to the questions being asked, and
  3. linking what is already known (background knowledge) to give clues.

- *Written narrative*, which is story telling in written form (see below).

Written narrative and study skills

As children proceed from primary to secondary school, there is an increasing emphasis in the classroom on children being able to express themselves well in written form (written narrative), and on developing improved higher order skills that are important to exam taking success (study and organization skills).

Karen Harris and her colleagues (Harris *et al.* 2008) in the US have developed a structured and systematic teaching programme to improve students' *written narrative skills*. They describe five areas of competence that the student needs to achieve for the development of effective writing skills: generation of content, creation of an organizational structure, formulation of goals and higher level plans, quick and efficient execution of mechanical aspects of writing (including handwriting, spelling and punctuation), and revision of text and reformulation of goals. The authors then go on to describe specific strategies and plans – using key words, scaffolds and prompts – for developing particular types of narrative such as creative writing, persuasive writing and report writing. Teaching instruction is in six stages:

- developing *background knowledge* through direct instruction or giving reading assignments
- discussion of *strategies and plans* for how the essay is to be structured; teacher modelling of the strategies through 'thinking out loud' as the essay is worked through
- *memorizing the strategies and steps* through repetition and practice
- supporting the student while they compose their essays through *scaffolding*: providing direct assistance, feedback and reinforcement, and finally
- achieving student *independence* by gradually fading out the scaffolding as the student becomes more competent
- strategies for *re-reading and revising essays* and on using sophisticated vocabulary are also included.

Studies in the US have shown improvements in students' writing skills using this strategic approach to writing. The method can be adopted in one-to-one teaching sessions, in small tutorial groups and even the larger classroom. There is a strong emphasis on the child as an active collaborator within the context of the teacher providing lots of modelling of techniques, together with positive feedback and reinforcement.

Study skills are competencies associated with acquiring, recording, organizing, synthesizing, remembering and using information and ideas learned in school. While these skills come naturally to many students, children with dyslexia and other specific learning difficulties appear to find acquiring these a considerable challenge; however, there is no doubt that these skills that are so important to higher level studies are teachable. A classic book by Thomas Devine (1981) provides a detailed guide to teachers on how they should develop their students' competencies in study skills through teaching them how to:

- gather new information and ideas (through listening and reading)
- record information gathered and make sense of it (through note-taking, outlining and summarizing)
- think through the information by discussing, exploring and organizing it to develop possible hypotheses or conclusions appropriate to the topic
- remember the information through memory devices and recall techniques
- use the new information in report writing and test taking.

Devine goes on to discuss how these processes can be taught in the context of carrying out topic research, using the library, doing homework, studying for and taking exams, and developing skills specific to curriculum-based subjects like maths, science and literature (as well as in relation to enhancing vocabulary, improving comprehension skills and achieving good written narrative, covered earlier in this chapter).

Sylvia Moody's *Dyslexia: A Teenager's Guide* (2004) was written to inform adolescents and older students on how they might self-improve their higher order skills. The components she covers are:

- *organization*, through the use of labelled stacking trays and files, calendars and wall charts
- *note-taking*, through using headings, abbreviations, key words and voice recorders
- *studying*, by organizing files, creating study timetables, using mind maps and charts, doing verbal rehearsal, and talking through topics with a friend or family member
- in *exam taking*, time management, re-reading questions and underlining key words are emphasized.

Does reading intervention change brain structure and function?

There is some preliminary but exciting evidence that suggests that successful intervention in children with dyslexia results in behavioural (i.e. literacy) improvements that are also accompanied by changes in brain structure and function. For instance, in a voxel-based morphometry study of 11 children with dyslexia (Krafnik *et al.* 2011), grey matter volume in four specific brain regions increased during an eight-week structured intervention in which the children made progress in learning to read. However, to date, studies are small scale and in need of replication.

Interventions at the biological level

Interventions at the biological level have been notoriously controversial and have generated a lot of debate amongst academics, practitioners and even in the media. The logic of these therapies is that a disorder of a higher aspect of cognition such as reading or language is caused by a lower biological-level deficit, most usually in a modality of perception or in some aspect of motor skills. It is hypothesized therefore that treating the lower level perceptual or motor deficit will eventually 'filter through' to the higher cognitive/educational function, thus remediating it. Many of these interventions claim to be grounded in neuroscience research which makes them appear very seductive. Bruce

Pennington (2009) has suggested that for a biological-based intervention to be considered plausible for addressing a higher order skill like reading, it needs to demonstrate:

- first, that the lower level deficit is present in children with reading difficulties
- second, that the treatment can ameliorate the biological deficit
- third, that ameliorating the deficit also remediates the reading disorder and
- finally, that this therapy does so as efficiently and as cost effectively as other available treatments.

This is a tall order and as we shall see, there is little evidence for such biologically based interventions meeting Pennington's stringent criteria. We will look briefly at three types of interventions: tinted lenses which aim to remediate a reading difficulty at the visual perceptual level; FastForWord, a computer-based programme that claims to improve the child's reading and language skills through auditory perception training; Dyslexia, Dyspraxia Attention Treatment (DDAT, also known as Dore Therapy) and primitive motor reflex resolution, which are both motor-based training methodologies.

The use of *tinted lenses* or coloured overlays for printed text was first advocated by Helen Irlen who claimed that some poor readers suffered from 'scotopic sensitivity', now more usually referred to as 'visual stress'. This describes the uncomfortable glare and distortion effect which some individuals experience when confronted by black print on a white page. Great claims have been made in the popular press for the instant curative effect of coloured lenses (although these are largely based on anecdotes), while research studies carried out by Helen Irlen and her associates have resulted in accusations of bias, together with criticisms of the methodology that was used. Indeed, independent studies (Hoyt 1990; Solan 1990) have failed to provide support for the use of tinted lenses in promoting improved reading skill, though one randomized controlled trial conducted by Wilkins *et al.* (1994) produced more positive results. In the Wilkins' study, fifty-one nine- to 14-year-old children were prescribed lenses using an assessment instrument called a colorimeter which allowed the child to select a colour filter that gives maximum reduction of distortion of print under controlled conditions. Each child was then prescribed two different sets of lenses: the experimental lens significantly reduced the level of print distortion for the child while the control lens did not significantly reduce distortion. Of the 51 children who participated in the study, 48 claimed that the experimental tint, but not the control tint, reduced their perception of distortion and of discomfort when reading. On a standardized test of reading, the improvements were greater for the period during which the children wore the experimental lens than for the period when the children wore the control lens – but the difference did not quite achieve statistical significance. The authors suggested that coloured lenses might have a role to play alongside systematic teaching in the management of some children with dyslexia who appear to experience visual stress. However, in my own clinical experience, I find that many children initially show great enthusiasm for their prescribed tinted lenses but this does tend to wane quite quickly, and they are often eventually abandoned; this calls into question the lenses having little more than an initial novelty value but ultimately a failure to be useful in the medium- to long-term.

FastForWord[2] is a computer-based intervention programme based on the temporal auditory processing theory of Paula Tallal and her colleagues which claims that children with language and literacy disorders show inefficient auditory processing at short inter-stimulus intervals, that is, when auditory information is presented rapidly. These authors conducted two small-scale intervention studies that demonstrated that children with language disorders could be trained to process auditory information at increasingly faster rates that in turn led to improvements in their language skills. Following on from these studies, the authors developed FastForWord, a commercially available set of computer games that they claimed improved not only language but also literacy skills. However, a subsequent meta-analysis of randomized controlled

2   www.fastforword.com

trials of FastForWord showed that there was no significant effect of FastForWord on any (language- or literacy-based) outcome measure when compared to active or untreated control groups (Strong *et al.* 2011). These authors went on to provide evidence for conventional therapies having far greater effects on key language and literacy outcomes than FastForWord.

DDAT is a motor-based therapy which again has attracted much interest in the media. It is based on a hypothesis developed by Nicolson, Fawcett and Dean (2011) which stated that complex skills such as reading require automatized skill learning which depends upon efficient functioning within an important motor region of the brain, the cerebellum. They proposed that carrying out a series of motor, balance and posture exercises would improve cerebellar function and subsequently also reading. A treatment trial conducted by proponents of the theory (who were therefore not independent researchers) claimed that the intervention resulted in 300 per cent improvements in reading in the experimental group (Reynolds, Nicolson and Hambly 2003). However, no such data were available for the control group which makes it impossible to control for placebo and 'regression towards the mean' effects and to therefore unequivocally demonstrate that the gains were due to the intervention specifically. (Regression towards the mean is a statistical artefact whereby a low score on a given measure at one point in time will invariably result in a higher score on that same measure taken at a second point, which has the effect of over-inflating the apparent impact of the intervention.) Other criticisms were levelled at this study (including the use of inappropriate statistics) which rendered the results both unreliable and uninterpretable. The DDAT programme has now been withdrawn, though a strikingly similar scheme called the STEP Physical Literacy Programme emerged in 2017. This employs cerebellar based exercises that promote balance and eye-hand co-ordination; it is claimed that children who carry out two 10-minute exercise sessions per day will show improvements in their academic performance. Professor Dorothy Bishop in her 2017 blog has called into question the scientific plausibility of motor programmes to address academic problems, and points to there as yet being no independently conducted RCTs to support the implementation of the STEP programme.

A further motor-based therapy, *Primitive Reflex Therapy*, draws on a neurological theory that hypothesizes that children with learning difficulties have failed to replace their early primitive reflexes (like the Moro or palmar reflex) with more mature postural reflexes. It is proposed that these primitive reflexes need to be revisited before the child can 'move on' in their learning; essentially, the reflexes need to be replicated and resolved so that eventually they disappear and as they do, the child's reading improves. Studies by proponents of this intervention have been heavily criticized on methodological grounds, most usually the lack of a control group, though one randomized double-blind controlled trial exists (McPhillips, Hepper and Mulhern 2000). Sixty-six children who obtained a low score on a standardized reading test and who also showed evidence of having an unresolved asymmetric tonic neck reflex were randomly allocated to three groups. The children in the experimental group were requested to engage in a specific movement sequence (aimed at replicating and ultimately resolving their neck reflex) for ten minutes per day for a period of 12 months. Children in the placebo group performed non-specific movement sequences that were not based on the replication of primitive reflexes, while the third (control) group received no intervention. On the completion of the trial, the children in the experimental group showed a significant decrease in the level of their neck reflex while the children in the placebo and control groups showed no change. More importantly, although all the children in the study showed improvements in their reading over the course of the study, the increase in reading score was substantially greater for those children in the experimental group. While this study seems impressive in terms of its design methodology and its findings, it is not without its problems. It is hard to determine from the authors' description whether the children received direct reading instruction during the study and whether this differed between groups. Nor could it be validated whether the children carried out the exercises on the prescribed basis since there were no trainers or independent observers present during the exercise sessions. Finally, the children's neck reflexes were assessed using a rating scale which cannot be subjected to the same (parametric) statistical procedures as for analyzing children's test scores; yet the authors used the same method of analyses for all their data. Uta Frith has queried whether a failure to resolve reflexes is nothing more than a 'marker' of an immature nervous system which might be expected in children with learning difficulties, but which is unrelated to their cognitive and behavioural presentation.

Biological therapies suffer from a number of general criticisms. First, their claimed efficacy is largely based on anecdotes or testimonials taken from so-called satisfied parents or clients who have 'witnessed great improvements' in their child's functioning. Anecdotes are fine as a means of illustration but they do not constitute proof. The only way to unequivocally prove that an intervention works is through the conducting of RCTs by independent researchers; as we have seen, these are sadly lacking in the case of biological therapies and the few that have been conducted are rife with methodological errors. A further problem for biological therapies is that it is difficult to generalize the measured improvements from the perceptual/motor levels through to the cognitive/educational level whereby gains in reading and language are demonstrable; recall that this was a problem for CogMed discussed earlier in this chapter. Moreover, a number of biological approaches have been criticized because other researchers have been unable to replicate the results; this has certainly been the case for tinted lenses and FastForWord. Furthermore, many biological therapies fail to compare the performance of children receiving the treatment to a suitable control group, which makes them vulnerable to distorting placebo effects and 'regression towards the mean statistical artefact'. Finally, there is the issue of 'value for money'. The theoretically sound and empirically validated intervention package Sound Linkage costs around £50 while heavily criticized programmes like DDAT and FastForWord can cost upwards of £2000.

Planning an intervention programme

In this chapter we have reviewed critically the evidence for cognitive, behavioural and biological interventions that purport to ameliorate the learning and educational difficulties experienced by children with literacy disorders. Good practice dictates that the practitioner should recommend and employ cognitive and behavioural interventions that are individually tailored to the child's difficulties and needs, while biological approaches (that might attract parents) should be viewed with caution and scepticism. Tailoring an intervention programme and methodology to a child's needs requires 'matching' the assessment formulation with a series of intervention and management strategies and accommodations. Indeed, the primary goal of an assessment and formulation should be to develop and design a prescription for intervention and management, which in school settings usually takes the form of an *Individual Education Plan* (though sometimes alternative terminology like *Individual Learner Profile* might be used). Such plans will typically cover the following key elements:

- *targets* that the child needs help to achieve
- *learning support strategies* that need to be put in place for the child to reach their targets
- *criteria* for successful achievement of the targets, and
- *a record* of the date on which each criterion was met.

Some plans might contain additional information such as test results, profiles of the child's strengths and weaknesses, a specification of needs, and possible barriers to learning such as not having English as a first language.

Most children with dyslexia have underlying phonological difficulties which will require a cognitive intervention that takes the form of phonological awareness training (such as that provided by Sound Linkage). At the behavioural level of intervention, a phonic-based programme delivered within a multisensory teaching framework will invariably be needed. Additionally, children with literacy difficulties occurring in the context of co-occurring language problems will also require interventions that specifically target key language skills (including vocabulary and oral narrative) and possibly also auditory/verbal memory. Children with such co-occurring language difficulties are at risk for reading comprehension problems that require not only text-based comprehension interventions but also methodologies that target important oral language skills that are typically deficient in children who fail to comprehend what they read.

Recommendations for addressing a child's literacy difficulties should go beyond the cognitive and behavioural interventions and extend to a consideration of the child's strengths and how these might be capitalized upon to improve outcome. Encouraging the verbally able child to maximize the use of context cues in text made possible by their good verbal reasoning and well-developed vocabulary would be an example of this. It is also important to recognize additional risk factors that need to be incorporated into an intervention plan. Targeting for intervention co-occurring difficulties such as maths or attention problems would be an example of this; specific interventions for these will be described in the next chapter. Another example would be recognizing that a child of lower ability might need a differing level of explanation of newly introduced concepts, slower presentation of new material and the opportunity for repetition and reinforcement to ensure that knowledge and skills are properly consolidated. Finally, broader management issues need to be addressed when making specific recommendations; these could include involving parents in the intervention programme, encouraging the child to take advantage of technological aids, applying for accommodations in formal tests and examinations, and making curricula adaptations within the classroom; again, these will be discussed more comprehensively in the next chapter.

A summary of evidence-based interventions for the individual child presenting with dyslexia, language and/or reading comprehension disorders is provided in Box 7.3.

Box 7.3: Literacy Difficulties: evidence-based interventions for the child presenting with the following difficulties

Phonological processing difficulties: Exercises that *train phonological awareness skills* such as blending and segmenting sounds in spoken words are needed, for example Sound Linkage.

Auditory/verbal working memory difficulties: Computer-based programmes such as CogMed have been met with criticisms. Strategies for *adapting the child's learning environment* and emphasizing the importance of *reducing memory load* and providing opportunities for *practice and reinforcement* may be more effective.

Decoding difficulties: Systematic *phonic-based* programmes delivered within a structured *multisensory* teaching framework are recommended. Useful additional metacognitive-based teaching approaches include *set for variability* strategies that help the child decode irregularly constructed words.

Reading speed/fluency difficulties: Encouraging *regular reading practice* is vital, though more specific strategies such as *repeated reading intervention* may be employed.

Spelling difficulties: *Phonic-based* spelling programmes emphasizing learning about spelling-to-sound correspondences are needed initially, though as children reach more advanced levels of spelling additional approaches such as teaching by *analogy* and through *morphemes* assume increasing importance.

Oral language difficulties: Direct interventions include *vocabulary enrichment*, developing *listening skills* and improving *oral narrative*.

Reading comprehension difficulties: The critical components of a reading comprehension intervention programme are *vocabulary enrichment*, teaching *metacognitive strategies* (e.g. re-reading, scaffolding, mental imagery and comprehension monitoring, reflecting and summarizing), *reciprocal teaching* and *inferencing from text*.

Written narrative and study skills difficulties: For older children, the teaching of higher order skills is needed, utilizing structured teaching approaches for developing *written narrative*, improving *study skills*, teaching students how to *note-take* and better *organize* their work, and *exam taking* skills.

A cautionary note: The evidence for biological-based therapies such as motor training, tinted lenses, auditory training and reflex therapy is very limited; while seemingly attractive, these have a limited theoretical validity, have not been subjected to rigorous randomized controlled trials and are often very expensive.

In this and the next chapter, our case studies will be revisited to provide examples of intervention planning, specific recommendations needed to target each child's individual problems and a comment on likely prognosis and outcome.

Case Study 1: intervention for Alex, a child with dyslexia and developmental language disorder

The first case study for intervention is that of Alex, our 12-year-old with severe dyslexia occurring in the context of a developmental language disorder (Box 7.4).

Box 7.4: Alex's intervention plan

Alex has very severe dyslexia with accompanying milder (and improved) oral language difficulties, both of which need to be addressed and accommodated so his educational needs are able to be met over the remaining years of his secondary schooling. Regular and frequent one-to-one instruction in literacy which is also integrated with interventions that target his vocabulary knowledge, oral and reading comprehension and written narrative will be needed. Accommodations in the classroom and for exams, together with some subject differentiation, will also be required to ensure that he is able to access his curriculum.

Specific recommendations for intervention and management of Alex's language and literacy difficulties should include:

- access to a structured multisensory phonological/ phonic-based literacy intervention scheme that targets the specific skills of phonological awareness, phonic decoding and spelling conventions within a flexible teaching framework that includes real book experience
- provision of an integrated language and reading comprehension programme that promotes vocabulary and higher order language skills, together with specific text-based strategies such as comprehension monitoring, re-reading and highlighting key points, questioning and summarizing
- encouragement to take advantage of the voice-activated, editing and spellcheck facilities that technology offers, while being permitted to submit a significant proportion of his coursework in word-processed form
- being permitted time accommodations, access to a reader and provision of either a scribe or use of a laptop computer in formal written examinations
- curricula and classroom accommodations such as exemption from taking a foreign language, being provided with photocopied notes and having access to a mentor who can support the development of improved study and organizational skills
- ensuring that he is not overloaded with too many subjects at GCSE, and encouraging him to select option subjects that capitalize on his relative strength in maths and his good nonverbal skills (art, design and technology).

Prognosis and outcome

Alex's outcome will undoubtedly be impacted by having very severe dyslexia occurring in the context of language delay and disorder. While this might be considered predictive of a generally poor long-term outcome in many individuals, Alex has experienced a significant number of positive moderators which would be expected to substantially improve his outcome – including early identification and intensive intervention for his language disorder, having good nonverbal skills which might provide some compensatory resources and contribute to his stronger maths ability, a supportive home environment, and good levels of psychological adjustment and motivation. With continued targeted intervention, curricula and examination accommodations, access to technology and high levels of teacher and parent support, it would be well within the realms of possibility for Alex to obtain school-based qualifications and to then proceed to further education courses which reflect his relative strengths within the nonverbal and mathematical domains of ability.

Summary

- New interventions to address reading and related difficulties need to be validated through randomized controlled research trials that demonstrate unequivocally that improvements observed after training are a direct result of the intervention.
- Children with word level reading and fluency difficulties require an intervention that targets their phonological and decoding deficits, and which is delivered within a structured multisensory teaching framework that also provides the opportunity for frequent reading practice.
- Children who have co-occurring language difficulties and those with reading comprehension problems require an intervention that promotes comprehension, narrative and, in particular, vocabulary skills, both within oral- and text-based contexts.
- Spelling presents an especial challenge for children with dyslexia, requiring the adoption of intervention strate-gies that go beyond teaching phoneme-grapheme corre-spondence and which exploit the greater orthographic regularity evident in larger units such as morphemes.

- Biological interventions that target skills at the perceptual and motor levels need to be approached with caution, as most are based on theories that are not well validated scientifically and have not been subjected to randomized controlled trials to demonstrate their effectiveness.

Chapter 8

Beyond Literacy Intervention

In the previous chapter, we looked in depth at interventions that are specific to the literacy challenges experienced by children with dyslexia, including those with accompanying language delay or disorder. In this chapter, we will address the management of simultaneous co-occurring difficulties that complicate the educational presentation for a very substantial number of children. Maths, attention and visual motor difficulties will be considered in turn and the case studies that exemplify these revisited in the context of intervention. Finally, we will look more generally at management strategies that extend beyond specific interventions, but which are important in enabling children to accommodate for their difficulties within the classroom and in exam-oriented settings.

Interventions for co-occurring specific arithmetic difficulty/dyscalculia

Many children with dyslexia will experience maths problems that are as severe as their literacy difficulties. It is as important to recognize, assess and of course to provide intervention for these difficulties as it is for their literacy problems. However, we have far less evidence-based knowledge of how to intervene when a child has a maths problem as opposed to a literacy difficulty.

We saw in Chapters 4 and 6 that many children with maths problems have a deficit in numerosity, in other words in their understanding of the magnitude of number. This can be assessed symbolically by having children compare digit size or non-symbolically by for instance having them count dots. An obvious question to ask would be: is it possible to train up numerosity in a child presenting with a maths problem? There is little research that directly answers this question. However, one example of such an approach would be the Number Race programme, a computer-based tool that aims to improve numerosity. This is a graded game that uses arrays of dots to improve children's number magnitude awareness. The programme clearly targets a cognitive process critical to mathematical development and which is deficient in many children with maths problems. However, although it has been demonstrated that the programme results in improvements in number-comparison performance, there is little evidence of generalizing to counting ability or arithmetic (Rasanen *et al.* 2009). Price and Ansari (2013) have suggested programmes that use symbolic (number-based) materials are likely to be more effective in boosting maths performance than those that adopt non-symbolic materials (e.g. dots).

It may be of greater relevance and indeed prove far more effective to directly teach the specific mathematical weaknesses experienced by children with dyscalculia or arithmetic disorders. Gersten *et al.* (2009) conducted a meta-analysis of RCTs or experimental studies that provided maths interventions for children with arithmetic disorders. The largest effect sizes were obtained for studies that contained explicit instruction in specific maths skills, instruction in a general strategy for solving problems, teaching children to give explicit verbal descriptions of maths processes and learning a specific strategy with a range of examples. Interestingly, interventions that focused on using visual representations were less effective.

Of course, some children with maths problems experience underlying difficulties that have their source not in a deficit of numerosity but in visual spatial or working memory difficulties. Children with visual spatial problems are likely to have difficulty with maths concepts that have a strong visual basis, such as geometry and symmetry, number lines, abstract measurement, fractions, interpreting and drawing graphs, and understanding principles related to time. These children need to have access to interventions that specifically target these visually based aspects of their maths curriculum, perhaps encouraging them to develop verbal descriptors of the processes involved (which showed promising results in the Gersten *et al.* study). For children with working memory difficulties, programmes that have inbuilt procedures for practice and reinforcement of maths skills and concepts are important: so, Kumon and related schemes, which strongly emphasize repetition through regular and frequent worksheet practice, can be especially helpful for children whose working memory is deficient.

Examples of specific systematic maths programmes that are used in the UK to support children with maths problems are *Numicon*, *Addacus* and *Dynamo Maths:*

- *Numicon* is published by Oxford University Press and has particular relevance for children in the early stages of a maths curriculum. It follows Jerome Bruner's sequence of teaching that begins by the child working with structured concrete materials and then developing imagery with pictures and lastly developing abstract maths concepts. Flat plastic shapes with holes represent numbers from one to ten, with each number having its own colour. The aim of Numicon is to make numbers (that are essentially abstract representations) real for children through being able to see and touch them. The teaching approach is multisensory-based and progresses through four stages: finding patterns, sequencing and ordering shapes, counting the holes to concretize number representation and early calculating to solve simple number problems. Teacher surveys conducted by Numicon from 2008 to 2011 have shown a 47 per cent increase in students achieving (above average) Level 3 at Key Stage 1 after using Numicon and a 72 per cent increase in students achieving (above average) level 5 at Key Stage 2, having used Numicon in Key Stage 1. Teacher customer satisfaction ratings as high as 99 per cent are reported, with also high ratings for children's improved mathematical self-confidence. It is important to appreciate that these findings, while positive, are not based on studies by independent researchers and nor are they drawn from experimental studies or RCTs.

- *Addacus* is a multisensory-based and systematic maths programme that uses materials that are either visual (cubes, number strips, colour-coded number cards) or auditory (CDs of stories, songs and poems) to help develop children's grasp of a wide range of maths-related concepts and abilities – including number facts and values, the four operators, place values, number conservation and the language of maths. While testimonials to the effectiveness of Addacus are positive, there are as yet no independent studies to back these.
- *Dynamo Maths* is a multisensory programme for 4- to 11-year-olds that employs three pathways to learning (lesson plans, online activities and worksheets), with each structured in small cumulative steps aimed at building number knowledge. A study conducted by Ann Dowker (2016) looked at the effectiveness of Dynamo Maths for 50 students aged 6–15 years. Following pre-testing with the Dynamo Number Sense Developmental Profile, the students received 12 weeks of intervention. At post-test, there was an 11.7 per cent improvement in the students' scores. Even when small improvements in the children's understanding of number meaning and magnitude were recorded, this led to a large improvement (of 32%) in the children's grasp of number relationships (for instance, the ability to carry out the four numerical operators).

Ever more maths intervention programmes are entering the educational market, though it needs to be borne in mind that the efficacy of these is not as well established through RCTs as it is for literacy programmes.

Dr Steve Chinn is a leading authority on teaching maths to students with specific learning difficulties. He has written excellent books that guide both specialist and class teachers in hands-on approaches to teaching and reinforcing maths principles and procedures for children who find maths both challenging and daunting. His best-known general book is *The Trouble with Maths*

(Chinn 2016), with other useful books targeting more specific mathematical domains like learning multiplication tables (Chinn 2009); the latter is often a major chore for children with literacy and maths difficulties, many of whom have auditory working memory difficulties that mean they cannot easily retain number facts like tables.

Case Study 2: intervention for Jyoti, a child with dyslexia and dyscalculia

Let us now revisit the case of Jyoti, a verbally able nine-year-old who had both dyslexia and co-occurring dyscalculia. An assessment had shown that the literacy difficulties she experienced (mainly regarding spelling) were a consequence of her phonological processing and auditory working memory weaknesses. It was also revealed that she had visual spatial difficulties that impacted visual subitizing, together with auditory working memory difficulties that made mental maths and the retention of number facts very challenging for her. Her intervention programme is shown in Box 8.1.

Box 8.1: Jyoti's intervention plan

Jyoti clearly has a dyslexic difficulty which has its origin in her weak short-term auditory working memory and her phonological deficits. It is evident that she has had very good phonic decoding instruction which has enabled her to resolve her reading problems, though it may be that her persisting phonological difficulties are behind her more intractable spelling problems. She will clearly need continuing literacy support aimed at improving her spelling both at the word level and in continuous prose writing contexts. Jyoti also needs maths intervention that takes account of her difficulties with number magnitude and her visual spatial and working memory difficulties. Accommodations in the classroom and for exams, that include time allowances and laptop usage, are also needed.

Specific recommendations for intervention and management of Jyoti's learning difficulties should include:

- access to a structured multisensory delivered phonological awareness training programme that includes auditory based exercises covering phoneme discrimination and blending, manipulation of phonemes and most critically 'linkage' exercises that help to bind sounds to letters (e.g. Sound Linkage)
- provision of a systematic programme that includes learning about spelling-to-sound consistencies and rules of English spelling, developing a strong key word spelling vocabulary and in the near future beginning to introduce her to more complex orthographic units like morphemes
- working towards improving Jyoti's spelling in broader writing contexts (i.e. written narrative) and also developing better writing structures
- encouragement to take advantage of the editing and spellcheck facilities that technology offers alongside permitting her to submit a significant proportion of her coursework in word-processed form
- access to a maths intervention programme that provides the opportunity for revisiting, reinforcing and practising (using regular worksheets) standard numerical operational procedures that she is finding hard to retain and recall; she will also need to address visual concepts within maths, including working with fractions, understanding charts, diagrams, calendars and graphs, working with decimal point placement and later on targeting other visually based principles in maths such as geometry and symmetry, understanding areas, perimeters and volumes, and so on
- recognition of the impact that Jyoti's short-term auditory/verbal working memory difficulty has on her classroom learning; she will need quite a lot of repetition and reinforcement of new concepts and facts, together with chunking of presented

information, and the provision of scaffolds and
memory aids to support learning and retention
- being permitted time accommodations and use of a
laptop computer in formal written examinations
- future monitoring into Jyoti's senior school years, with
a view to reassessing her difficulties and needs prior to
her commencing her GCSE programme.

Prognosis and outcome

While Jyoti is likely to experience continuing difficulties in maths
and spelling into her senior school years (which will require
further targeted intervention), we would nonetheless expect
a good overall educational outcome for her in the medium- to
long-term. Positive moderators, which would be expected to
contribute to this expected outcome, include her high verbal
IQ (which provides a substantial compensatory resource), an
already good response to early reading intervention, her high
levels of motivation and engagement, and finally, exemplary
teacher and parent support.

Interventions for co-occurring attention deficit disorders

There are a number of approaches to the treatment of attention
deficit with hyperactivity disorder, ADHD, and its often-
associated behavioural problems. While prescription medication
and psychological interventions are the most commonly used,
there has been a recent increasing interest in the use of dietary
approaches.

Prescription medication and ADHD: Medications (such as
Methyphenidate/Ritalin and Concerta) are recommended for
children who have severe attention problems which are most
usually accompanied by significant hyperactivity, impulsivity and
behaviour problems (especially oppositional defiant disorder).
The Cochrane meta-analysis of the effects of Methylphenidate
(Storebø et al. 2015) showed treatment effect sizes as large as
0.8, with notable improvements in attention and decreases in
hyperactivity and the incidence of behaviour problems. There was

also some evidence that Methylphenidate improved teacher-reported ADHD symptoms and general behaviour and even parent-reported quality of life. Because ADHD medication has a short half-life (i.e. it enters the body's system quickly and is also dispersed and eliminated rapidly), it can be used strategically or on an as-needs basis, for example on school days, during study periods and so on. The Cochrane review found no evidence that ADHD medication has serious side effects though there is a relatively high risk of minor side effects such as lessening of appetite and sleep problems. There is evidence from a long-term follow-up of children treated with Methylphenidate that the medication can lose its effectiveness with prolonged use (Jensen *et al.* 2007); this points to the need for ongoing monitoring and careful titration of dosage. Many families elect not to take up offers of medication because of concerns about side effects and long-term efficacy. It is important, therefore, to be able to offer alternative psychological and dietary interventions which might prove more acceptable to many families.

Parent/teacher training and behaviour modification are psychological interventions for ADHD. Used alongside structured educational interventions, these might include training parents and teachers in effective behavioural-based strategies such as:

- *providing information to parents and teachers* about the nature and impact of attention deficits. This helps them better understand and more sympathetically manage the child's difficulties.
- *behaviour modification approaches* such as using rewards for 'on-task' behaviour, task completion and behavioural compliance; setting clear boundaries and expectations; reducing parent-child conflict; modelling socially appropriate behaviour; restructuring the child's environment as a means of improving attention and behaviour; and reducing family hostility levels. A meta-analysis of behavioural interventions for children with ADHD (Daley *et al.* 2014) demonstrated improvements in parenting behaviours and children's conduct problems, social skills and academic performance, with moderate effect sizes of 0.3–0.5; while these are not

as high as for prescription medication they are nonetheless very respectable, with behavioural approaches to be recommended because of the broad effects on the family.

- *coaching interventions* for older children with ADHD. These concentrate largely on improving executive skills such as organization, task initiation and time management. A UK programme 'Connections in Mind' provides face-to-face and skype training, mentoring and support to help children improve their executive skills that should potentially lead to improvements in their academic performance.

Dietary approaches to ADHD: Many parents of children with concentration difficulties, hyperactivity and difficult behaviours attribute their problems to 'junk food', claiming that certain foods in their children's diet appear to trigger worsening behaviour. However, we do need to caution against this belief becoming a dogmatic adherence to the idea that dietary factors are the exclusive and sufficient explanation for children's attention problems and difficult behaviour. As Edmund Sonuga-Barke (2015) has pointed out, such views may place a barrier in the way of access to appropriate evidence-based assessment and pharmacological and psychological treatments. I have in the past been very sceptical about the dietary approach to treating ADHD; however, the findings from recent research studies have prompted me to reconsider my stance on diet modification and nutritional supplements. Of course, the dietary approach to treating attention and behaviour problems is a perfectly testable hypothesis, and indeed some recent RCTs have demonstrated that diet modifications and nutritional supplements have a role to play in the management of children with mild-to-moderate attention deficits. The best validated dietary approaches to the management of ADHD are as follows:

- *Restricted elimination diets* involve either the removal from the diet of specific food stuffs to which the child has an allergy or a hypersensitivity, or more generally the removal of foods containing high levels of artificial flavourings and colourings; restriction or removal of food stuffs is done when it is suspected that the consumption of these triggers hyperactive behaviours. Meta-analyses of the effects of specific food restriction on attention and behaviour show moderate effect sizes of about 0.4, and for the general elimination of artificial flavourings and colourings of about 0.35 (Stevenson *et al.* 2014). Specific food restriction diets and elimination of artificial flavourings/colourings may be especially beneficial for children with ADHD who have a history of adverse reactions to certain foods.

- *Omega 3 supplements* have been shown in most RCTs to achieve effect sizes of between 0.2–0.3 for improving attention and reducing impulsivity/overactivity, in other words fairly small effects which are nonetheless statistically significant (Stevenson *et al.* 2014). In this meta-analysis, there were no beneficial effects of omega 3 on conduct disorder or oppositional defiant disorder. However, a recent randomized, double-blind, placebo-controlled trial of omega 3 supplements given over a six-month period found a 40–60 per cent improvement in children's behaviour which was sustained long-term (Raine *et al.* 2015). The positive effects were evident for both externalizing behaviours (such as aggression, oppositional behaviour, rule-breaking behaviours) and internalizing behaviours (such as anxiety, depression, somatizing behaviours).

- *Micronutrients* which are thought to be necessary for optimal brain functioning have generated recent interest in the ADHD domain. In a study by Rucklidge *et al.* (2018), a micronutrient formula consisting of 13 vitamins, 17 minerals and four amino acids (supplied by Hardy Nutritionals) was used to treat symptoms of children with ADHD in a triple-blind, randomized placebo-controlled trial. It was found that micronutrients improved overall clinical function, and reduced inattention, behavioural dysregulation and aggression (though not hyperactive/impulsive symptoms). Overall effect sizes were between 0.35 and 0.6 (i.e. moderate effects). Many parents commented that while the symptoms may still have been present, their child was nonetheless calmer, more able to be reasoned with and generally happier.

Note that micronutrients of the type used in this study are not available over the counter in the UK, though they may be obtained through the Hardy Nutritionals website.[1] The producers of micronutrients advise parents to seek approval from their GP before use.

The general consensus is that prescription medications are the treatment of choice for children who have severe ADHD, especially when their attention problems are accompanied by very high levels of overactivity and significant behavioural problems (in particular aggression and oppositional-defiant behaviours). However, for children with mild-to-moderate ADHD whose overactivity is not overly excessive and where behaviour problems are comparatively minor, a combination of psychological/behavioural interventions and dietary approaches may well suffice to address their difficulties.

Case Study 3: intervention for Billy, a child with dyslexia and attention deficit disorder

Let us now look at the intervention programme for Billy, a bright seven-year-old with mild dyslexia (mainly affecting his spelling) and co-occurring attention problems that affect his ability to stay on task, to sustain his focus long-term and to process information quickly and efficiently. His intervention is described in Box 8.2.

Box 8.2: Billy's intervention plan

Billy's mild dyslexia is showing signs of resolving, at least in respect of reading which is responding well to intervention. He also appears to be developing effective compensatory strategies through drawing on his good language skills to support accurate word identification and reading comprehension. He will, however, need targeted intervention to address his spelling and associated writing problems. Given that Billy is only seven,

1   www.hardynutritionals.com

it is possible that his attention problems will improve with increasing age and maturity, though it would be facilitative to set in place appropriate behavioural supports at home and school and to consider whether a dietary intervention might be appropriate. Billy's attention problems and slow processing speed indicate that extra time to complete prescribed activities together with rest breaks might be needed.

Specific recommendations for intervention and management of Billy's difficulties should include:

- access to a systematic multisensory based spelling programme that incorporates structured phonics, learning about spelling-to-sound consistencies and acquiring a secure key word spelling vocabulary
- home-based support that provides opportunities for regular reading (so that Billy can practise his decoding skills and build up his word-specific reading vocabulary), reinforcing key word spellings and specific phoneme-grapheme pairings being worked on at school, and using fun-based literacy-oriented computer games
- giving Billy access to technology from age eight to nine onwards to that he can take advantage of the spell checker and editing facilities that word processing offers
- exploring whether a dietary approach to improving Billy's attention would prove efficacious, using a combination of an additive-free diet, and the regular taking of omega 3 capsules and possibly also micronutrients
- providing strategies for Billy's parents and teachers to use to help develop his attention span and reduce the negative impact of his distractibility – these might include breaking tasks into smaller chunks, providing rest breaks, setting clear goals and expectations, using rewards (e.g. sticker charts) for staying 'on task' and

completing activities, creating a quiet work corner, helping him become more time aware and efficient by using timers and feedback charts, alerting him to changes in task or routines with a one-minute warning, and using a soft squeezy ball for non-intrusive fiddling
- providing Billy with suitable rest breaks and extra time in written tests in order to compensate for his attention problems and his slow rate of processing.

Prognosis and outcome

While Billy is likely to experience continuing difficulties in spelling and associated writing skills, it is hoped that these can be readily managed through 'booster' spelling interventions and use of technology. Indeed, we would expect an overall good educational outcome for Billy, bearing in mind the positive moderators of high IQ and good verbal skills (which together provide a substantial compensatory resource), his already good response to early reading intervention, his strengths in maths and high levels of teacher and parental support. However, it will be important to monitor Billy's attention development. If his concentration does not significantly improve as he gets older, and in response to behavioural and dietary interventions, it may be appropriate to refer him to a paediatrician or psychiatrist for a consideration of prescription medication.

Interventions for co-occurring developmental co-ordination disorders, DCD/dyspraxia

There are essentially three approaches to addressing motor difficulties which accompany literacy disorders in some children – *process* and *functional/performance* approaches are usually the province of occupational therapists and physiotherapists, while treating the *educational consequences* of the motor problem would be typically conducted by a teacher.

The process approach identifies the underlying sensorimotor deficit and then targets its remediation with the expected result that the child will improve in their motor organization in general and their handwriting and written presentation in particular. The most widely adopted process approach is sensory integration therapy, developed by Ayres (1972), which provides proprioceptive, kinaesthetic and vestibular stimulation to improve the sensory and sensory integration deficits thought to underlie the child's motor problems; suggested activities that 'enrich' the sensory systems and promote their integration include swinging, rolling and jumping, joint manipulation, brushing the body and playing with textured toys. A review of sensory integration training studies by Wilson (2005) found poor treatment effects which calls into question the conceptual and theoretical validity of this approach. Rather more dangerously, it has been proposed that sensory integration therapy can effectively treat broader difficulties, including reading and arithmetic problems; however, there is no convincing evidence that supports this.

The functional or performance approach to treating DCD concentrates on skill acquisition, task modification and environmental modification. An example of this approach is the Cognitive Orientation to daily Occupational Performance programme, CO-OP, whose main proponents are Polatajko and Mandich (2004). The child and therapist select jointly a motor skill to be mastered which is then broken down into steps, with each addressed using strategy-based and problem-solving methodologies. This is a task-oriented approach, with the therapist (or indeed a parent) functioning as a mediator who provides verbal prompts while the child carries out each step of the task.

There has been little evidence-based research into occupational therapy approaches to the treatment of motor disorders. However, some important issues were raised by one systematic review of 21 studies of process and functional intervention approaches to motor disorder conducted by Polatajko and Cantin (2010). They acknowledged the difficulties created by the heterogeneous populations of the studies and the very small number of even quasi-experimental studies, though they were able to draw the cautious conclusion that there is some positive evidence supporting the use of functional approaches such as CO-OP. They went on to highlight the urgent need for well-controlled studies looking at the effectiveness of occupational therapy interventions in paediatric populations.

Of course, many children with mild motor disorders do not have access to sensory or motor programmes such as those described above. Rather, it is left to teachers to address the educational consequences of the child's motor problems, most usually their handwriting and written presentation and organization. Children with handwriting problems require a systematic teaching approach that begins with pre-writing activities in the context of developing a good posture for handwriting and a correct (tripod) pencil grip. A suggested methodology for teaching letter formation and the order in which letters should be taught is given in Taylor (2002). Many children with handwriting difficulties appear to benefit from an early transition from a printing to a cursive script which can overcome the often-seen problems of uneven letter sizing and spacing. As with most motor skills, frequent practice is needed to develop improved neatness and speed. Many older children with motor difficulties need support to develop improved written presentation and organization as these skills assume increasing importance as the child is required to produce longer scripts. Executing written work to speed is a long-term challenge for many children with motor disorders; providing extra time to complete written assignments and in particular tests and examinations is likely to be an important accommodation that needs to be set in place for them. Finally, most children with motor problems benefit from being provided with an alternative means of expressing themselves in written form, for example through executing written assignments and even selected written exams in word-processed form.

Case Study 4: intervention for Freddie, a child with dyslexia and DCD

Recall that Freddie is a 12-year-old boy, generally able, with strengths in his verbal abilities and his maths, but with a specific learning difficulty that comprises dyslexia and co-occurring nonverbal difficulties (including significant motor problems). His dyslexia is characterized by gaps in his word recognition vocabulary, slow reading speed, very weak spelling and poor phonic decoding. His phonological processing and short-term verbal working memory are also weak. Freddie has visual perceptual, spatial and motor problems that significantly impair his handwriting, speed of writing and general written presentation/ organization. Freddie has shown signs of increased disengagement in the classroom context and there have been frustration-based behaviour problems evident at home. Freddie's recommendations for intervention are given in Box 8.3.

Box 8.3: Freddie's intervention plan

Although Freddie's functional reading skills (reading compre-hension and silent reading speed) are of an acceptable standard, there are gaps in his word recognition, he reads out loud inordinately slowly and he is a reluctant reader. Alongside addressing these residual reading problems, Freddie requires intervention that targets his spelling and poor structural written narrative skills. Whether improving his handwriting is a realistic goal at his age is debatable, given that his incorrect pencil grip and poor letter formation may be difficult to modify. It may be more realistic to focus on Freddie taking advantage of technological aids through making the transition to laptop-executed written output in both home and classroom contexts. Accommodations in written examinations will almost certainly be necessitated. Finally, Freddie's behavioural difficulties need to be addressed.

Specific recommendations for the intervention and management of Freddie's difficulties should include:

- encouraging him to read as much and as broadly as possible in order to give him the opportunity to practise decoding-based word attack strategies, to broaden his reading vocabulary and increase his reading speed

- giving him access to curriculum-based texts in auditory format, thus capitalizing on his long-standing keenness for listening to stories
- implementing a *repeated reading intervention* strategy as a systematic means to increasing his reading speed and fluency
- providing access to a structured literacy intervention programme that targets spelling and the development of improved written narrative skills; as well as adopting a systematic phonic-based approach to spelling, Freddie is likely to benefit from learning about larger orthographic units such as morphemes
- in the unlikely event that Freddie's pencil grip and letter formation in handwriting will be readily improvable at his age, encouraging him to develop touch typing, keyboarding and word-processing skills that will enable him to submit most of his coursework and projects in laptop-executed format; after sufficient touch typing practice and experience, he may well achieve faster speeds of typing than writing and he will also be able to take advantage of the editing and spellcheck facilities available
- permitting time allowances in formal examinations (in order to accommodate for his slow processing speeds), and also providing access to either a scribe or a laptop computer as appropriate
- applying classroom-based accommodations such as having text-based materials photocopied for him and dropping one of his two foreign languages
- setting in place incentive programmes at school to address his disengagement, together with assigning a mentor to play a generally supportive role and more specifically to ensure he completes and hands in work projects and homework on time
- referral to a clinical psychologist for anger management and cognitive-behaviour therapy for Freddie, and for advice to his parents on behavioural management.

Prognosis and outcome

With the implementation of the above literacy interventions and class-based management strategies, it is anticipated that Freddie will make a positive response and demonstrate improvements in his written language skills. He is likely to have long-standing handwritten output challenges, but with the provision of exam accommodations and increased access to technology, these might be significantly reduced. Freddie has shown good capacity to compensate for his dyslexia in terms of his functional reading skills and will hopefully be able to generalize similar verbally based strategies to other aspects of literacy. Negative moderators include Freddie's disengagement and his frustration-based anger outbursts, though hopefully these might be ameliorated through a combination of school-based mentoring and incentive programmes, together with psychological therapies.

A summary of evidence-based interventions for the individual child presenting with co-occurring learning difficulties is provided in Box 8.4.

Box 8.4: Interventions for simultaneous co-occurring learning difficulties

When the Child Presents with Maths Disorder/Dyscalculia

Deficit in numerosity: Numerosity training using programmes like Number Race show poor generalization to broader arithmetic skills; the evidence suggests that direct number-based teaching programmes are more effective, with examples including Addacus, Numicon and Dynamo maths (Steve Chinn's books are also an excellent resource).

Short-term auditory working memory difficulties: Supplementing maths programmes with regular worksheet practice to reinforce, consolidate and automatize number facts and numerical operational procedures is essential for the child with working memory limitations.

Spatial/perceptual difficulties: There is little convincing evidence for visual perceptual or spatial training improving the child's understanding of visual concepts in maths (e.g. fractions, geometry, symmetry). These concepts need to be taught individually and directly, with accompanying explicit verbal descriptions.

When the child presents with an attention deficit disorder

For children with *severe attention disorders*, especially when these are accompanied by hyperactivity and behavioural problems, the evidence-based intervention of choice is usually *prescription medication*.

For children with *mild-to-moderate* attention disorders, *behaviour modification* (setting up reward schemes, establishing clear boundaries, modelling good behaviour), *parent training/support* and *individual coaching* have been demonstrated to improve concentration and especially the behavioural difficulties experienced by these children.

There is increasing evidence from randomized controlled trials for the effectiveness of *dietary controls* for children with mild-to-moderate attention deficit disorders; these include *restricted elimination diets*, and the taking of *omega 3 supplements* and/or *micronutrients*. These appear to reduce inattention and aggression while helping the child remain calmer, though hyperactivity and impulsivity usually remain unchanged.

When the child presents with developmental co-ordination disorder – DCD/dyspraxia

There is no convincing evidence that *occupational therapy* (including sensory integration therapy) is effective in the treatment of DCD/dyspraxia. However, *task-oriented* approaches that incorporate verbal direction and prompts can be helpful in targeting specific motor skills. A more direct approach to addressing the child's motor-related handwriting difficulties is to work on correcting (if needed) the child's *pencil grip*, teaching them *systematic letter formation* and in the long-term encouraging the increasing *transition to word-processed written output.*

Broader management issues
Empowering parents

A parent's role in supporting their child with a learning difficulty is crucial; parents know their child better than anybody else and they are a permanent fixture throughout their childhood. The knowledgeable and supportive parent who creates a positive home-based learning environment for their child critically affects their long-term educational outcome, alongside their motivation, self-esteem and confidence. My colleague, Dr Helen Likierman, and I felt that parents had such an important role to play in influencing their child's progress and academic outcome that we together wrote a book specifically for parents: *Dyslexia: A Parent's Guide to Dyslexia, Dyspraxia and Other Learning Difficulties* (Muter and Likierman 2008). The aim of this book is to provide information to parents about their child's learning difficulties, which will in turn empower them to create a positive partnership with teachers to address the child's problems, even ensuring in some instances that intervention programmes are delivered and maintained. Furthermore, we wanted to give practical strategies for parents to adopt in the home environment that would reinforce the child's learning and support their progress. Areas that we cover in our book include:

- *reading regularly at home* (to increase print exposure)
- practising key word spellings
- providing access to *computer games* that reinforce literacy and numeracy skills (e.g Word Shark and Number Shark)
- *supporting homework*
- helping *develop improved study and organization skills*
- *encouraging extra-curricular activities and non-academic strengths* that help promote self-esteem and resilience.

In line with the view that pre-school learning experiences have

226

an important preparatory role to play in developing language and educationally related skills, Helen Likierman and I have also published companion books aimed at parents of pre-schoolers (Likierman and Muter 2006; Likierman and Muter 2008).

Use of technology

Children with disorders of literacy and handwriting are greatly aided by having access to technology. The priority in early years education is of course to develop the child's basic reading, handwriting and spelling skills, but there is an increasing role for computers, laptops and iPads as children progress during their middle and later school years. Disorders of literacy and motor organization are lifelong challenges for many children, and certainly difficulties in spelling and handwriting are likely to persist into adolescence and even adulthood, with intervention by then sometimes having a diminishing return. It follows therefore that the child needs to be provided with alternative means of accessing print and producing accurate and legible written output – which is where computers come in. For children with unusually severe and persisting reading problems, it may be necessary to provide access to, and training in, voice activated programmes. Even children with relatively mild spelling and writing problems benefit from submitting coursework, projects and essays in word-processed form; not only does this overcome the problem of difficult-to-read handwriting but also improves the child's technical accuracy through the use of editing and spellcheckers that computers provide. Critically, children should be introduced to touch typing early on as a foundation skill which enables them, with practice, to achieve faster and more accurate written output than all-too-common 'hunt-and-peck' techniques. Instruction in word processing, and in particular encouragement to take maximum advantage of the spellcheck, is critical to ensure that children make the most of technology. Senior school-age children who have become increasingly keyboarding speedy and confident may be permitted to take a laptop into the classroom for the execution of ongoing coursework and note-taking in relevant subjects like English and history. It is usual for students for whom the laptop has become their 'normal mode of working' to be permitted to use it in selected formal written examinations.

Of course, some parents worry that allowing their child to use technology (including the internet) on a frequent and regular basis might have negative as well as positive consequences. While the benefits of screens and new technologies are evident in relation to social connectivity and educational opportunities, there are understandable worries about screen addiction and sexual and other inappropriate content. A recent editorial published in the *Association of Child and Adolescent Mental Health Journal* reviewed the evidence for this (Dubicka, Martin and Frith 2019). These authors point to there being minimal evidence of harm from screen usage at the general population level. However, concerns remain about a range of potential harms in vulnerable youngsters, including those with learning difficulties. Dubicka and colleagues describe a 'digital divide' between those children who can healthily engage in and therefore benefit from internet usage and those at the opposite end of the scale who are likely to engage in and experience negative screen and online interactions. There is also some evidence that even short-term engagement with online activities can result in usually temporary but nonetheless significant reductions in attentional capacities, an important consideration for children with learning difficulties. Parents of such vulnerable children need to be encouraged to monitor and supervise their children's screen usage, limiting the time spent on activities that are not educationally related and modelling appropriate usage themselves.

Classroom, curricula and exam accommodations

While intervention programmes are essential to improving specific educational skills, there is an important part to be played by providing accommodations to the child with a learning difficulty, in order to create for them an 'even playing field' that means that they are not unfairly disadvantaged relative to their peers. The specific accommodations to be set in place will of course be dictated by the child's presenting difficulties and their own individual needs.

These should be explicitly stated in the child's IEP alongside the intervention programmes that are being implemented.

Classroom-based accommodations might include:

- sitting the child at the front of the class
- providing quiet study spaces
- allocating a competent peer mentor (to check on missed instructions or homework requirements)
- providing photocopied notes instead of requiring the child to copy from the blackboard
- setting up a school-to-home-to-school diary to create a liaison between parents and teachers (so ensuring that key skills are practised and reinforced at home and homework completed)
- providing timetables and homework charts that help with time management and planning, and
- using visual aids like spider diagrams and bullet point checklists that provide scaffolds to improve essay and project technique.

Curricula-based accommodations could include:

- exemption from studying a foreign language (particularly for children who have unusually severe language and literacy difficulties)
- reducing the number of subjects taken at for instance GCSE (this being especially relevant for children who have severe difficulties that are likely to include marked processing speed problems), and
- curriculum differentiation in subjects where the child is unlikely to be able to function at other than a very basic foundation level.

Many children with learning difficulties are able to have access to *accommodations in formal written examinations*. Two concepts are of relevance here. The first is that in order to be eligible for such accommodations, it is essential that there is clear 'evidence of need' which is then used to determine what specific accommodations should be made; this entails documenting a 'history of need' and also demonstrating (in quantitative terms) a 'substantial impairment'. The second concept is that a 'reasonable adjustment' should be made for the 'disabled' student such that they are not substantially disadvantaged in comparison to someone who is not disabled. In the UK, the Joint Councils for Qualifications (JCQ) annually publishes an Access Arrangements document which outlines procedures and criteria needed for an individual student to apply for accommodations in examinations such as GCSE and A levels. Assessments for access arrangements must be carried out by an assessor approved by the school or exam centre. Available accommodations include:

- *Extra time in exams:* In order to obtain 25 per cent extra time in examinations, the student must obtain on testing at least one standard score of 84 or below on a measure of speed of reading or speed of writing or speed of processing. To be permitted up to 50 per cent extra time, a more stringent criterion is applied, specifically that the student obtains standard scores of 69 or below on testing in at least two different areas of speed of working. Many students will need considerable practice to ensure that they make full and effective use of allocated extra time.
- *Allocation of a reader:* For a student to be permitted a reader (or computer reader), they must obtain a standard score of 84 or below on a measure of reading accuracy, reading speed or reading comprehension.
- *Laptop usage:* Formal testing is not necessitated for the student applying for laptop usage in exams, but they must be able to demonstrate that the laptop has become their 'normal mode of working'; the spellcheck is usually disengaged in exams, but a request for spellcheck engagement may be made if the student has especially poor spelling (obtaining a standard score of 84 or below on a standardized spelling test).
- *Provision of a scribe:* A scribe may be permitted if the student has demonstrably illegible handwriting (usually

accompanied by poor spelling) and is not sufficiently confident or competent to use a word processor.

- *Supervised rest breaks*: These may be available for students with diagnosed attention deficit disorders.

Motivating disengaged students

Many children with specific learning difficulties experience strong feelings of failure, low self-worth and frustration because (as it seems to them), in spite of their efforts they do not progress as do their peers. Not surprisingly, they lose the motivation to learn which may present as 'giving up', avoiding work, saying they have no homework, making excuses for not settling to work and so on. Parents and teachers often find themselves expending a lot of effort aimed at restoring and then maintaining the child's lost motivation. Some general techniques to engage and motivate students include:

- encouraging areas of competence even if these are not academic
- using praise for 'on-task' behaviour, completing tasks and meeting deadlines
- providing the student with a *mentor* (e.g. a teaching assistant or even an older mature student) who meets with them regularly to provide non-judgemental advice, support, praise and encouragement
- setting goals in graded, realistic and achievable steps and presenting work in small manageable 'chunks', and
- using 'positive language' to describe what the student needs to do (as opposed to criticizing them for not doing it).

A more targeted approached to motivating students is that of using specific *rewards* or *reinforcers* applied contingently for being 'on-task' and for completing prescribed activities. Younger children will usually respond to a simple sticker or star chart which is backed by more concrete rewards such as having access to a favourite computer game, earning a small toy, choosing a favourite pudding for dessert or having a special outing. Older children will require a more sophisticated reward programme such as a points system which might be sold to them as a form of *performance-related pay*; points can be added up to earn more teenage-appropriate concrete rewards such as having a sleep-over or earning pocket money.

Summary

- For children with maths difficulties, there is emerging evidence to suggest that programmes should target the child's numerosity difficulties at the symbolic (number-based) level and which also recognize the need for teaching and consolidating basic number concepts and arithmetic procedures.
- Children with mild-to-moderate attention deficit disorders may show improvements in concentration in response to dietary modification and nutritional supplements, structuring the child's learning environment and using behaviour modification programmes to promote on-task and task-completion behaviours, though it is likely that children with severe ADHD will need prescription medication.
- Children with motor co-ordination/organization difficulties require systematic handwriting intervention in their early years, but in the long-term will most likely improve their written output mainly through access to technology.
- Broader management issues of relevance to almost all children with specific learning difficulties include empowering parents to support their child, promoting the use of technology to improve written output, setting in place appropriate accommodations in the classroom and in formal examinations, and finding means of engaging and maintaining the child's motivation.

Chapter 9

Bilingualism
A Sociocultural Risk Factor

Bilingualism (or indeed even multilingualism) is a cultural and educational reality for many children, whether due to immigration, greater global mobility or multi-culturalism. It has been estimated that around 13 per cent of the UK population is foreign born, with understandably significant numbers of individuals not having English as their language of origin. It thus follows that learning to read in a language that is not their mother tongue is a common experience for children the world over. Bilingual children have two main challenges in the classroom: first, coping with speaking two languages while being educated in what is usually their second language; and second, for some (though not all) children, learning to read in more than one language. Bilingualism can present a challenge for psychologists and teachers too, bearing in mind that virtually all research into assessing and teaching reading is with monolingual English speakers. Do bilingual children learn to read in the same way as monolingual learners, and does it present them with an additional challenge beyond that experienced by monolingual learners? Perhaps most importantly for the purposes of this book, if a bilingual child is struggling to learn to read, should we attribute this to their having to cope with two languages, or could it be due to their having an underlying learning difficulty – and how would we know which it is?

For a given child, there are a number of ways in which two languages may be acquired. For the child who grows up in a family where one parent's mother tongue is different from that of the other parent, both languages may be being learned at the same time. For other children, where both parents speak the same foreign language, the child learns to speak this language first and the second language is introduced later, usually at nursery school or the commencement of formal schooling. For most children, learning two languages presents them with no especial difficulty, though it is recognized that their vocabularies in each language may be smaller than for the monolingual learner; this is because the bilingual child is having to 'spread' their vocabulary knowledge across two languages. Gradually, as the child proceeds through school, the language of education becomes the dominant language, with the growth of its vocabulary accelerating to the point where it will eventually outstrip the vocabulary of the child's other language(s).

While many people might expect classroom learning to be a challenge for children who have to cope with two languages, there is in fact considerable evidence for there being certain educational advantages of bilingualism. First, there is the phenomenon of positive *cross-linguistic* transfer which means that acquiring a second language is facilitated by having already learned one language, especially if the two languages share common features of structure, phonology and word roots; so for instance, we would expect more positive cross-linguistic transfer between two European languages like English and German than between languages that have very different orthographic structures such as English and Mandarin. Second, it has been found that children with two languages often have enhanced phonological sensitivity. Rubin and Turner (1989) demonstrated that English-speaking children learning to read in French had better phonological awareness skills than English-speaking children being educated only in English. It seems that exposure to two languages draws children's attention to the sound structure of words, which in turn facilitates their development of phonological awareness.

Could there be disadvantages of being bilingual? There is a strong traditionally held view that children with speech and language impairment may be disadvantaged by exposure to more than one language. Indeed, it is common practice for speech and language therapists to recommend that the parents of a bilingual child who has a diagnosed developmental language disorder restrict themselves to speaking to the child in just one language. However, a recent review paper (Uljarević *et al.* 2016) found no systematic negative effects of multilingualism on language development in children with neurodevelopmental disorders; they argued that there was no evidence to support the recommendation of single language exposure for children with neurodevelopmental disorders who are from multilingual backgrounds. However, whether this conclusion can also be applied to children who are learning to read is unclear.

A further issue is whether bilingual children should learn to read in their two languages concurrently, or whether they should be taught to read in one language first, with the other brought in later once the first is well established. This question generated a professional debate on the website of the Society for the Scientific Study of Reading, SSSR, in 2018. Professor David Share presented the case for the child learning to read in their native language first, with this needing to become firmly established before a second orthography is introduced later on. However, Professor Esther Geva challenged this view, arguing that children can learn to read in two languages concurrently, even when the writing systems are very different from each other. She acknowledged that specific elements may be slower to develop due to 'negative transfer' (possibly initial confusion between the two orthographies), but typically developing children usually overcome these challenges. We shall see later in this chapter that Geva is strongly of the view that bilingualism should not present challenges for *most* children in respect of their written language development – unless they experience difficulties in underlying cognitive and language processes.

Vocabulary, phonology and learning to read in bilingual children

Throughout this book we have explored evidence that clearly demonstrates a strong causal connection between early phonological skills and later ease of learning to read. And we also saw in Chapter 1 that common cognitive processes, in particular phonological skills, underly the development of literacy irrespective of the language in which the child is learning to read. Caravolas *et al.* (2012) demonstrated that phonological awareness, emerging letter knowledge and rapid automatized naming predicted later reading development in *all* of the European languages they studied. But, does this connection also hold for children who are bilingual and who are being educated in their second language, for our purposes English? (This is typically the case for children who are from immigrant families or who experience global relocation due to their parents' work lives.) Furthermore, of practical relevance, can assessment measures developed for English-speaking children be used confidently to assess reading difficulties in bilingual children?

Kay Diethelm and I attempted to address these issues in a study of 55 children attending an international school in Geneva who were being educated in English; 40 per cent of the children were English mother tongue while 60 per cent were non-English speakers (Muter and Diethelm 2001). They were aged five years at the outset of the study and had received approximately one full term of exposure to English as their primary language of instruction. The children were administered tests of phonological skill, letter knowledge, nonverbal cognition and receptive vocabulary. They were then followed up a year later, age six years, and given tests of phonological skill, vocabulary, letter knowledge and importantly single word reading. We found that at ages five and six years, the English speakers were superior to the non-English speakers on the measures of letter knowledge and vocabulary, but not on nonverbal cognition or phonological skill. In keeping with the findings of our earlier research (Muter *et al.* 2004), phonological segmentation (but not rhyming) skills at five years predicted reading ability at age six, and this was the case for *both* groups of children. As expected, letter knowledge at age five predicted reading ability at age six, again for *both* groups. However, vocabulary was *not* a predictor of reading ability in this sample. These findings have important implications for assessing and teaching reading to bilingual children. First, we can see that the same skills (phonological awareness and letter knowledge) contribute to children's ease of learning to read, *irrespective of* their language of origin or indeed their oral vocabulary level. It follows therefore that administering tests of phonological skill and letter knowledge can be a reliable means of assessing and identifying multilingual children at risk of reading problems, even after they have had minimal exposure to their language of education. Second, because vocabulary was not a predictor of word level reading in this sample, it is not necessary for the bilingual child to have a well-established spoken vocabulary before they start to learn to read.

The literacy profile of second language learners

There are numerous myths about second language (or L2) learners (i.e. children who are learning to read in a language that is not their mother tongue) and especially about those children who are proving slow to acquire literacy skills. The first and the most obvious myth is that inadequate oral language proficiency in the language of instruction is the cause of slow progress in literacy; however, as the Muter and Diethelm (2001) study demonstrated, vocabulary is not a predictor of progress in word level reading. Related to this is the second myth, namely that we should wait until oral language proficiency in the language of instruction is well developed before beginning to teach the child to read. However again, our study showed that it is not necessary for a bilingual child to have a well-established oral vocabulary before they start to learn to read in that language. The third myth is that L2 learners show confusion between their two languages and the fourth is that we should assess the child in their home language. At an informal level, we found no evidence from our study to support these views. However, there is extensive research by Esther Geva and her colleagues which has addressed these issues more specifically and we shall look at this in some depth; for a fuller description of these studies, see Geva and Wiener (2015).

Geva and her colleagues have studied large cohorts of Canadian L2 learners from a wide range of home languages but who were being educated in English. The majority of these studies have been long-term longitudinal designs that have allowed detailed analyses of the children's trajectories of learning over periods as long as six years. The emphasis has been on exploring and contrasting the cognitive, linguistic, oral language, word level and text level skills of L2 learners with those of L1 (monolingual) children as they acquire literacy related skills in English. The key findings from the Geva longitudinal studies were as follows:

- The study of the children's English vocabulary trajectories showed that the monolingual speakers had bigger oral vocabularies than the L2 learners, with the gap failing to close over time (though it narrows a little); indeed, in general, the L2 learners did not achieve the vocabulary, syntactic, morphological and listening comprehension levels of their L1 peers.
- However, there was no difference in the trajectories of L2 learners and monolinguals in reading real and nonwords; the L2 learners achieved word and text level reading skills at the same rate as their monolingual peers, and it seemed that they could learn to decode words without knowing their meanings.
- There were also no differences in phonological awareness and rapid naming skills between the L2 learners and monolinguals.
- A similar situation existed in respect of spelling, where Geva and her colleagues were able to demonstrate that the spelling skills of L2 learners usually develop at much the same rate as L1 learners.

Geva and her colleagues concluded that first, the L2 learner does not need to be oral language proficient to learn to decode and therefore to read, and that second, in keeping with the findings of the Muter and Diethelm study, it is possible to assess phonological abilities in L2 learners who are not proficient in English.

While L2 learners appear to progress well in developing accurate word level reading and spelling skills, there is evidence for them having far greater difficulty in acquiring literacy skills that are more heavily dependent on oral language proficiency. Most importantly, there are significant differences in reading comprehension skills in L1 and L2 learners, with the gap widening over time. Of course, reading comprehension is more strongly related to oral language skill (especially vocabulary knowledge) than is reading accuracy, and this is especially true in older children. Given that L2 learners show a long-term disadvantage in their oral language skills, it is not surprising that they are often compromised in their reading comprehension. There is also some evidence that reading fluency may be compromised in L2 learners because it is more influenced by oral language proficiency than is word level reading. Finally, written expression presents a greater challenge for L2 learners because of its dependence on language factors like vocabulary, sentence construction, grammar and so on. These findings in relation to language-related literacy skills in L2 learners point to the importance of ensuring that such children have access to additional lessons that specifically target the development of their vocabulary and other language abilities.

Literacy disorder and second language learners

A question asked by many psychologists and teachers who work with children from bilingual or multilingual backgrounds is: how do we disentangle whether a bilingual (or multilingual) child is struggling with literacy because they are having to cope with two languages, or alternatively could they have an underlying learning difficulty?

We have seen that most L2 learners acquire word and text level reading skills (and indeed also phonological awareness and decoding abilities) as easily as their L1 peers. We can confidently conclude, therefore, that if an L2 learner is having persisting difficulties with word level reading and spelling skills, phonological awareness, rapid naming and working memory, there is a strong likelihood that they have a dyslexic learning difficulty (which would be evident even if they were exposed to only one language). The obvious message here is that we should not delay assessment and intervention for L2 learners who are proving slow to acquire word level reading and spelling skills.

The situation for L2 learners presenting with reading comprehension, fluency and written expression difficulties is rather more complicated. There is a need to differentiate whether poor reading comprehension in L2 learner is a consequence of insufficient oral language exposure or other factors like poor verbal working memory and phonological skills which are typically observed in children with language and literacy difficulties. The problem is that their overall profiles can look remarkably similar. Questions that can be asked that enable us to decide whether poor reading comprehension is a consequence of inadequate oral skills related to second language acquisition or whether it reflects an underlying learning difficulty (possibly even a developmental language disorder) might include:

- Did the child have difficulty acquiring language in their mother tongue?
- Has the child had sufficient opportunity to develop language and literacy skills in their second language?
- To what extent is the L2 learner's development typical in relation to an appropriate reference group (most usually children with the same mother tongue)?

Moving forward from this, it is important on assessment to look at literacy components which are less dependent on L2 proficiency (word level skills) and compare those to skills that are more language dependent (reading comprehension), and to (if possible) even assess the child in both languages to provide the fullest picture of their linguistic abilities. Including 'marker' tests for developmental language disorder (for instance, nonword repetition, auditory working memory, sentence repetition tests) can be useful in determining whether the child's difficulties are related to restricted opportunities to acquire sufficiently good oral language skills or whether they are due to a developmental language disorder; we would expect the latter to have adverse consequences even if the child had only one language but these are likely to be exacerbated when the child is learning in two languages.

Interventions for second language learners

There are few controlled research trials that have addressed teaching language skills to L2 learners, though this is clearly an important issue, bearing in mind the findings of the Geva studies in relation to the disadvantages experienced by L2 learners in respect of language dependent literacy skills. A promising series of studies by Bowyer-Crane *et al.* (unpublished manuscript) aimed to train language skills (especially vocabulary) in Reception class L2 learners. The programmes were conducted in one-to-one and small group lessons and included the teaching of vocabulary (in multi-contexts), listening comprehension, oral narrative, phonological awareness and letter sound knowledge. The lessons were delivered by trained teaching assistants over a nine-week period and the impact on the L2 learner's language was compared with that of an L1 control group at the end of the study and at follow-up. The programme led to improvements in taught vocabulary (though not other language abilities) in the L2 learners at the end of the study, and these were sustained at follow-up. These results, while showing some positive effects over an admittedly very short period, point to the need for *sustained* language interventions for children from L2 backgrounds.

We conclude the chapter by looking at a bilingual child, Samira, who has both underlying specific language impairment and developmental dyslexia (see Box 9.1).

Box 9.1: Samira

Introduction

Samira is a nine-year-old girl who was referred for assessment by her parents and her teachers because of concerns about her slow academic progress. She was born in France and both parents are French speaking. She attended local French schools up until the age of seven years when her family relocated to the UK because of her father's job. Samira found the transition to a country with a different language, culture and educational system very challenging. She started in Year 2 at her local state primary school and has had EAL (English as an additional language) instruction for the last two years. Her progress in developing spoken English has not been as rapid as expected and she struggles to express herself in grammatically complete sentences, though her comprehension of English seems to be more secure. French continues to be the primary language spoken at home and Samira attends French lessons on Saturday mornings. Her teachers in French school have commented on her lack of vocabulary breadth in her mother tongue and her difficulty in learning to read and write in French. At her English school, Samira is observed to concentrate well and she is a hard worker. She appears quite confident in maths (apart from some difficulty in understanding word problems), and her handwriting is neat. She is however struggling to learn to read and spell in English, so, now in Year 4, she has recently commenced targeted literacy intervention which includes phonic instruction.

Samira's parents recall that her speech and language was slow to develop during her pre-school years; she was assessed at age three by a speech and language therapist who acknowledged her delay but did not think that therapy was indicated. Samira is a healthy girl. There is a family history on father's side of poor spelling.

Samira's test scores at nine years three months
Wechsler Intelligence Scale for Children V (WISC V)

Verbal Comprehension
Index = 86 (75–95)
Similarities = 9
Vocabulary = 6

Visual Spatial
Index = 119 (109–125)
Block Design = 12
Visual Puzzles = 13

Fluid Reasoning
Index = 118 (110–116)
Matrix Reasoning = 12
Figure Weights = 14

Auditory Working
Memory Index = 84 (77–94)
Digit Span = 6
Letter Number Sequencing = 8

Processing Speed
Index = 111 (101–119)
Coding = 13
Symbol Search = 11

WECHSLER INDIVIDUAL ATTAINMENT TEST (WIAT III)
1. Single Word Reading – Standard score = 85
2. Pseudoword Decoding – Standard score = 75

3. Spelling – Standard score = 72
4. Numeracy – Standard score = 110
5. Maths Problem Solving – Standard score = 90
6. Sentence Repetition – Standard score = 84

YORK ASSESSMENT OF READING FOR COMPREHENSION (YARC)
1. Reading Accuracy Standard score = 90
2. Reading Comprehension Standard score = 75
3. Reading Speed Standard score = 85

DETAILED ASSESSMENT OF SPEED OF HANDWRITING (DASH)
Free Writing Standard score = 80; content poor, with grammatical errors evident and limited range of vocabulary used.

COMPREHENSIVE TEST OF PHONOLOGICAL PROCESSING II (CTOPP II)
1. Phoneme Elision – Standard score = 85
2. Rapid Letter Naming – Standard score = 80
3. Nonword Repetition – Standard score = 85

Samira's formulation

Samira is a little girl of above average intelligence, assessed nonverbally. Her lower scores on the WISC V Verbal Comprehension subtests reflect her relative weakness in her oral language development, with her vocabulary knowledge being especially poor. Samira is making good progress in her numeracy development; her slightly lower score on Maths Problem Solving is likely to be attributable to her weak word problem solving (reflecting struggles with the language of maths). Samira is making slow progress in developing word level reading and spelling skills and she reads and writes slowly. Her reading comprehension is especially poor.

Samira is an able little girl whose cognitive profile is consistent with her having a developmental language disorder together with co-occurring dyslexia. Samira struggled with acquiring her mother tongue of French as a pre-schooler and even now shows some limitations in her ability to express herself in this language. She has made slower than expected progress in acquiring English as a second language in spite of receiving EAL for two years. Samira recorded low-average to below average scores on tests known to be 'markers' for language impairment (Nonword Repetition and Sentence Repetition). Co-occurring alongside the language disorder is developmental dyslexia. In contrast to most bilingual children, Samira has made slow progress in acquiring word and text level reading and spelling skills (and also phonological awareness). Indeed, she exhibits phonological processing, short-term verbal working memory and decoding problems characteristic of the child with dyslexia. It is of interest to note the positive family history of literacy problems. Samira's reading comprehension difficulties are most likely attributable to her poor oral language skills, in particular her limited vocabulary knowledge. Language disorders and dyslexia commonly co-occur and of course in Samira's case the educational expression of her learning difficulty is likely to be exacerbated by (though not causally related to) her French-English bilingualism.

Samira's intervention plan

Samira will clearly need to continue with EAL and targeted literacy support. However, in addition, it will be advisable to seek further assessment of her language skills by a speech and language therapist.

Specific recommendations for intervention and management

- Referral to a speech and language therapist for a more detailed evaluation of Samira's language skills in English; face-to-face therapy may be indicated but the therapist should also recommend programmes to be adopted at home and school that especially facilitate vocabulary growth in multi-contexts and improvements in grammar and syntax.
- Samira will continue to require access to a systematic

literacy programme that includes phonological awareness training, phonic decoding and learning about spelling-to-sound consistencies, delivered within a structured multisensory framework.

- Samira's reading comprehension should improve as her oral English develops though some specific teaching of reading comprehension strategies such as comprehension monitoring may be needed.
- Samira's parents will need to encourage her to read English books and watch English TV and videos (especially during lengthy holidays likely to be spent in France) in order to ensure that she has sufficient exposure to English oral and print environments.
- Samira may need teaching assistant support from time to time in the classroom in order to enable her to access the curriculum, especially in terms of the comprehension demands placed on her in an oral instruction environment.

Summary

- Bilingualism is a cultural and educational reality for increasing numbers of children, though fortunately most children who have experience of more than one language have no difficulty in acquiring at least word level reading and spelling skills in their second language.
- If a bilingual child does not acquire word and text level reading skills relatively quickly, it raises the possibility that they have an underlying dyslexic difficulty; administering tests of phonological processing and letter knowledge is a reliable means of assessing for dyslexia, even if the child has had minimal exposure to their new language.
- Many bilingual children have persisting oral language (especially vocabulary) limitations, though the gap may narrow over time; this has a 'knock-on' effect on educational skills which are strongly related to oral language skills, in particular reading comprehension and written narrative.

- Assessment and intervention for bilingual children who are slow to acquire oral and written language skills should not be delayed, as research has shown us that a significant proportion of these children are likely to have underlying learning difficulties, most usually developmental language disorder and/or dyslexia.

Chapter 10

Extreme Prematurity
A Neurological Risk Factor

In this book, I have strongly emphasized the importance of 'risk' factors that increase the probability that a given child will develop a learning disorder. The risk factors we have looked at so far have been mostly cognitively based, though Chapter 9 dealt with what might be termed a sociocultural risk factor: bi- or even multilingualism. Another sort of risk factor may be termed 'neurological' which means that the child has a brain injury which impacts learning and educational progress. Most neurological risks arise as consequence of an accident which results in a traumatic brain injury or are due to a medical condition or illness such as epilepsy, encephalitis or a brain tumour. A discussion of these neurological risks is beyond the scope of this book. However, there is one neurological risk factor which is, like bi- and multilingualism, on the dramatic increase and of which learning disability practitioners should be aware. This is extreme prematurity. With advances in medical and clinical research and improved health care practices, many more babies born at extreme prematurity are surviving. However, what we are increasingly realizing is that being born pre-term constitutes a significant risk to cognitive and educational development because it is associated with aberrant brain function.

Studies of cognitive outcome in preterm children

One of the largest-scale studies of babies born prematurely is the Bavarian Longitudinal Study conducted by Professor Dieter Wolke and his colleagues. Two hundred and seventeen babies born in the mid-1980s in Southern Germany who were delivered at less than 32 weeks gestation or who had very low birth weight of under 1500 grams were recruited. Their cognitive and educational development was studied longitudinally through to 26 years of age and compared with that of 197 control children who were born at full term. Somewhat depressingly, across all assessments through to adulthood, the extreme pre-term group recorded significantly lower IQs than the control group, with stability in the IQ scores being evident from infancy through to 26 years. Indeed, the authors found that adult IQ could be predicted with fair certainty from age 20 months onwards (Breeman, Jaekel and Baumann 2015). It thus appears that pre-term individuals do not outgrow their cognitive problems, despite many having received special educational support during childhood. The Bavarian study also looked at executive function in pre-term children (Madzwamuse, Baumann and Jaekel 2014), together with attention skills (Jaekel, Wolke and Bartmann 2013). Higher-level executive skills were impaired, and also the attention (but not the hyperactivity) component of ADHD. Jaekel and colleagues found that attention measures predicted academic achievement in both the pre-term and control children during their adolescent years. The Bavarian study also uncovered elevated levels of language impairment and very high rates of co-occurrence of learning difficulties (Wolke and Meyer 1999). Not only did the pre-term children perform at a significantly lower level on the measures of cognition and language than the controls, but they also demonstrated major cognitive deficits 10–35 times more often than the controls. Deficits in speech articulation and pre-reading (e.g. phonological) skills were three to five times more prevalent in pre-term children. More than 18 per cent of pre-term children showed cognitive deficits in more than five areas of cognitive functioning compared with none of the control children, indicating a very high rate of multiple co-occurrence of learning disorders in pre-terms.

The Bavarian study findings have been replicated by other researchers in the US and UK. For instance, a study by Johnson et al. (2011) in the UK found that children born pre-term had significantly poorer academic attainment and a higher prevalence of learning difficulties than their full-term peers. General cognitive ability and deficits in visual spatial skill at age six were predictive of mathematics attainment at age 11 years, while general cognitive ability and phoneme deletion scores at age six predicted reading attainment at age 11. The pre-term children also had executive and attention problems which were predictive of poor academic outcome.

Some studies have focused on children who are at the very extreme of the prematurity continuum, that is, those born before 26 weeks gestation. Though still a rare phenomenon, increasing numbers of these children are surviving as medical care becomes increasingly sophisticated. A study of UK and Irish children born before 26 weeks found that the rates of severe, moderate and mild learning disability were 22 per cent, 24 per cent and 34 per cent respectively (Marlow et al. 2005). Thus, 80 per cent of the children had a learning difficulty which for some would necessitate special schooling and for the remainder a high level of learning support in mainstream schools for the duration of their education. Disabling cerebral palsy was evident in 12 per cent of this sample. It is also worth noting that children born at less than 26 weeks will be vulnerable to experiencing cerebral haemorrhages or seizures during the peri-natal period which increases their cognitive risk even further. Maths is the educational skill which is most heavily compromised in children born at the very extreme end of the prematurity range; in a study of 11-year-olds born before 26 weeks, Simms et al. (2013) found that these children were weak at number estimation and maths attainment even after controlling for cognitive ability. This means that the children's mathematical difficulties were not totally explicable from their IQ scores, but appeared to be related to a core deficit in numerosity, similar to that observed in children with dyscalculia. Johnson et al. (2016) confirmed these findings, and additionally highlighted that in pre-term children maths problems are far more likely to be present than reading difficulties. Finally, children at this extreme of prematurity are at increased risk of autistic spectrum disorder, as demonstrated in a study by Johnson et al. (2010) who found that children born under 26 weeks obtained lower scores on a social communication checklist when compared to a full-term control group, with further confirmation of an ASD diagnosis through psychiatric evaluation.

What is rather concerning is that even children born just a few weeks early may be at increased risk of cognitive and educational difficulty. A large sample from the UK Millenium Cohort Study was followed longitudinally from three to seven years, with the children administered a range of tests, some cognitive and others related to school readiness and mathematics (Poulsen, Wolke and Kurinczuk 2013). Children born at less than 32 weeks had a 40–140 per cent increased risk on seven tests (compared to the full-term controls), those born at 32–33 weeks had a 60–80 per cent increased risk on three tests, those born at 34–36 weeks had a 30–40 per cent increased risk on three tests and those born at 37–38 weeks had a 20 per cent increased risk on two tests. These findings suggest that cognitive and educational abilities may be at continuous risk across the entire range of gestational age, even for those born just a few weeks early.

What about individual risk?

The above certainly makes rather depressing reading, but it needs to be recognized that not all children born prematurely have learning difficulties. There are many examples of extremely pre-term children going on to progress well, both cognitively and educationally. Indeed, Dieter Wolke and his colleagues make a very strong case for pre-term status being an important risk factor which increases the probability that a given child will have a learning problem, but this does not mean that all children who are born early will have such problems. The authors of the Bavarian study have suggested that children born before 32 weeks or weighing under 1500 grams seem to divide into three groups in terms of cognitive/educational outcome, with roughly equal numbers in each group:

- One third will have learning difficulties sufficiently severe and pervasive to necessitate special schooling.
- One third will exhibit mild-to-moderate specific learning

difficulties which will require sustained and specialist educational provision within a mainstream school setting.
• The remaining third may experience very few or even no learning or educational compromises (and some will even achieve at an above average level).

Not surprisingly, the more extreme the prematurity, particularly if this is accompanied by neurological complications such as seizures or cerebral haemorrhaging, the more likely the child is to have a poor outcome, both cognitively and educationally.

There is evidence from case studies of selected pre-term children that some do develop compensatory processes which can act to improve both cognitive and educational outcome. This chapter's case study, Sadiq, is an example of this. Neuro-psychologists believe that outcome is improved if the brain injury incurred due to prematurity is localized, in other words is within a specific region of the brain as opposed to generalized across a number of brain regions. There is much evidence to support the view that the infant brain is sufficiently plastic (in essence, flexible enough) to enable *functional reorganization* to take place. What this means is that, largely irrespective of the location of the injury, the infant brain will be able to reorganize itself so that the most important functions are preserved, the most critical of all being language function. So, even if the brain injury is to the left-frontal-temporal region of the brain (which typically subserves language function in most adults), other parts of the brain come to take over this function; sometimes, language skills are relocated to another region of the same hemisphere and sometimes to the other hemisphere. However, there is a price to be paid for successful functional reorganization. For language to be preserved in what is now a more limited 'neural space', other cognitive processes may be compromised; this is sometimes referred to as *cognitive crowding*. The skills most usually degraded as they are 'crowded out' (so that language can be preserved) are nonverbal and motor abilities and also usually processing speed.

It is evident that because children who are pre-term are at significant risk of long-term cognitive and educational difficulties, and especially bearing in mind the high rates of co-occurrence of learning disorders in these children, it is essential to set up learning support provision from a very early age – and to sustain this beyond childhood and well into adolescence. For children with complex presentations, a comprehensive neuropsychological evaluation by a paediatric neuropsychologist is likely to be needed. Additionally, professionals should be aware of the need for multi-domain assessments which could include speech and language and occupational therapy assessments and perhaps also psychiatric evaluations. Pre-term children who fall into the third who have severe and pervasive difficulties will almost certainly require a statutory assessment conducted by the local education authority that results in an education, health and care plan (EHC plan); see Box 10.1 for a summary. A fuller description of the EHC process can be found on the website of the Independent Provider of Special Education Advice (IPSEA) which is a registered charity that provides free and independent advice with all kinds of special educational needs and disabilities.[1]

Box 10.1: The education, health and care plan (EHC plan)

The EHC plan is a legal document which describes a child's or young person's special educational needs, the support they need and the outcomes they would like to achieve. The special educational needs described in the EHC plan must be provided by the child's local authority (LA). Not only does the plan provide extra learning support, but it also gives parents more choice about alternative school placements or educational settings. The first step in the process is requesting an EHC Needs Assessment.

Applying for an EHC Needs Assessment

The assessment is requested by a parent (most usually in conjunction with and including the support of the school) for a child who is deemed to be in need of special educational provision. This is in the form of a letter to the LA which must

---

1   www.ipsea.org.uk

reply within six weeks. The LA may or may not agree to the assessment; if they do not, parents have a right to appeal through the Tier 1 tribunal process.

What is involved in the EHC Needs Assessment?

The LA must seek advice from a range of sources as follows:

- the child's parent or the young person
- educational reports from the school
- medical advice and information from a healthcare professional
- psychological advice and information from an educational psychologist
- advice and information in relation to social care
- advice and information from any other person the LA deems appropriate.

Parents may request information from a particular person, for example a speech and language therapist, and recently completed reports from other sources may be submitted. Advice sought should address the child's needs, the specific educational provision required to meet those needs and the outcome this provision aims to achieve. A Plan should be issued within a maximum of 16 weeks from the request for assessment. If the LA decides not to issue a Plan, parents may appeal through the SEND (Special Educational Needs and Disability) Tribunal process.

Appealing against an EHC needs decision

The SEND Tribunal is an independent national tribunal which hears parents' appeals against an LA's decisions in regard to their child's special educational needs. The Tribunal has the power to order the LA to carry out an EHC Needs Assessment, to issue an EHC Plan and to amend existing EHC Plans. The LA must comply with the orders made by the Tribunal. The SEND Tribunal looks at the evidence put before it and decides whether the LA followed the law and the SEN Disability Code of Practice. It then makes a decision based on what is right for the child at the date of the hearing. According to 2011–2017 statistics, 75 per cent of appeals are settled before the hearing through an agreement with the LA. The SEND Tribunal publishes a free booklet *How to Appeal* which can be accessed on their website.

Most parents proceed with an appeal without legal representation though it is possible to apply for legal aid if parents wish to appoint a lawyer to represent them at the hearing. The IPSEA Tribunal Helpline is able to provide advice on how to submit an appeal for parents who have not appointed a lawyer.

The EHC process is not without its criticisms. Department of Education figures reveal that in 2017, 4000 children with approved EHC Plans received little or no additional support. Additionally, the list for students waiting for Plans was over 4000, with many local authorities refusing to issue them. Finally, many parents report that pursuing an appeal causes them stress and often financial hardship, a view with which I would concur, having represented parents as an expert witness at a number of tribunals.

We conclude the chapter with a longitudinal perspective of Sadiq, a child born at 28 weeks weighing 600 grams.

Box 10.2: Sadiq

Introduction

Sadiq had been born very premature, at 28 weeks, weighing just 600 grams; the prematurity was occurring in the context of slow rate of growth in the womb. He was admitted to the Special Care Baby Unit where he suffered a brain haemorrhage; he then continued in this setting on a ventilator while also requiring blood transfusions and oxygen therapy for a total of two months. Sadiq received courses of physiotherapy, occupational therapy and speech and language therapy as a pre-schooler. He was at the time of my first assessment (when aged five) attending a local state school where his teachers expressed concern about his poor oral communication skills, his very slow educational progress and his immature (and at times difficult) behaviour.

Sadiq underwent four cognitive-educational evaluations over a five-year period, with the final assessment taking place when he was ten years old. During his primary schooling, he exhibited difficulties within the domains of language, visual motor skill, educational attainments, attention and also in respect of behaviour and socialization. When he was seven years old, his school applied to the local education authority requesting that a statutory assessment take place. This eventually resulted in an EHC plan which was completed when he was eight years old. This provided funding for a part-time learning support assistant for 15 hours a week to support Sadiq during core lessons. His curriculum was differentiated, most obviously in maths but also to some degree in literacy. Additional funding was provided so that Sadiq could receive one-to-one targeted intervention in maths and literacy, and also speech and language therapy in 'blocks'.

Intellectual functioning

At Sadiq's first two assessments (aged five and seven years), he had recorded WISC IV Verbal Comprehension Index /Verbal IQ scores in the low-average range (80s). However, at the two later assessments (aged nine and ten years), his WISC V Verbal Comprehension Index/Verbal IQ scores had risen to a comfortably average level (104 and 102 respectively). His WISC IV/V Perceptual Reasoning Index/Nonverbal IQ was low at all four assessments, with index scores ranging from 80 to 86. His Processing Speed Index at the age ten years assessment was a low-average 85.

Educational attainments

When Sadiq was first assessed aged five years, he was essentially a non-reader and he was able to demonstrate only very basic concrete number skills. When he was re-assessed at age seven, his literacy and numeracy skills were beginning to develop, albeit slowly. His attainments at the last two assessments are given in the following table:

Educational skill (WIAT II and YARC)	Age 9 standard score (SS) and age equivalency	Age 10 standard score (SS) and age equivalency
Numerical Operations	SS = 82 (6y8m)	SS = 71 (7y0 m)
Mathematics Reasoning	SS = 66 (6y0m)	SS = 60 (6y4 m)
Single Word Reading	SS = 81 (6y8m)	SS = 84 (7y4m)
Prose Reading Accuracy	SS = 87 (6y10m)	SS = 85 (7y6m)
Reading Comprehension	SS = 101 (8y6m)	SS = 100 (9y4m)
Reading Speed	SS = 87 (7y0m)	SS = 87 (7y11m)
Pseudoword Decoding	SS = 83 (6y0m)	SS = 80 (6y0m)
Spelling	SS = 81 (6y8m)	SS = 69 (6y4 m)

Diagnostic tests given at age ten years

1. *Dyslexia-sensitive tests:* Sadiq scored at a comfortably average level (55th centile) on a measure of phonological *awareness* (CTOPP2 Phoneme Elision), having greatly improved since the previous year (16th centile). He did however score at a below average level (5th centile) on a measure of phonological *processing* (CTOPP2 Rapid Letter Naming).
2. *Short-term verbal working memory:* Sadiq has significant short-term verbal working memory limitations, as evidenced by his scaled score of five on WISC V Digit Span.
3. *Dyspraxia-sensitive tests:* Sadiq scored at a low-average level (scaled score of seven) on WISC V Coding, a measure of speed of graphomotor processing, and at a well below average level (5th centile) on the Rey Complex Figure Copy Test, a measure of motor organization.
4. *Dyscalculia-sensitive tests:* Sadiq was administered three subtests from the Test of Basic Arithmetic and Numeracy Skills (TOBANS), specifically the measures of numerosity (i.e. Count the Dots, Dot Comparison and Digit

Comparison) on which he achieved low-average to below-average standard scores of between 68 and 83.

5. *Attention skills:* Sadiq obtained a below average scaled score of four on Score!, a measure of sustained attention from the Test of Everyday Attention for Children (TEA-Ch).

Formulation

Sadiq is a young man of competent verbal ability, which is known to be predictive of good academic attainment. Given the increase in his Verbal IQ over the last five years (to a now average level), contrasted with his relatively weaker nonverbal ability and processing speed, he may have undergone brain-based functional reorganization with accompanying cognitive crowding; this has resulted in good preservation of his language skills but at the cost of diminished nonverbal ability and processing speed.

Sadiq exhibits the underlying cognitive deficits typically seen in children with *dyslexia*, notably selective weaknesses in short-term verbal working memory, phonological processing and phonic decoding. He has nonetheless made steady gains in his single word reading over the last year or so. His phonological awareness, prose reading accuracy, reading speed and his decoding have shown some improvements over the course of the last 15 months in response to targeted intervention. His reading comprehension (being age appropriate) is a relative strength, and is likely to be being supported by his good oral language. Sadiq has made no registrable improvements in his spelling over the last year.

Sadiq has additional (co-occurring) specific learning difficulties beyond his dyslexia. He has a mild-to-moderate *attention deficit disorder (ADD)*, evident on both diagnostic testing and on behavioural observation. He also has *dyspraxia/ developmental co-ordination disorder (DCD)*; his graphomotor and motor organization skills are poor and these impact on his handwriting speed and quality. Finally, Sadiq has severe *dyscalculia*; he has very poor numerosity which explains his inability to progress in maths over the last year or so.

In conclusion, Sadiq has a complex learning disorder of neurological origin which results in a diverse range of cognitive, educational, motor and attentional problems. Although currently presenting as being of normal ability and average verbal intelligence, he has a multi-component specific learning difficulty that comprises several co-occurring disorders, specifically moderate dyslexia, mild-to-moderate dyspraxia, severe dyscalculia and mild-to-moderate ADD. Sadiq exhibited symptoms associated with social communication disorder when younger. However, there is clear and converging evidence of significant improvements in this domain, observable at the present assessment and reinforced by the recent comments of parents, teachers and clinical psychologists working with the family.

Sadiq's intervention plan

Sadiq's senior schooling needs are now under consideration. He will need a revision of his EHC Plan during his last year at primary school in order to determine his current special needs and how these should be met when he proceeds to his next school. It will be important for him to receive a high level of ongoing in-class learning support and accommodations, together with specific interventions for literacy and numeracy, throughout his senior school years.

Specific recommendations for intervention and management

- Sadiq's EHC Plan should continue throughout his senior schooling, with annual reviews taking place as statutorily required.
- Sadiq's access to 15 hours a week of learning support assistance during core (academic) lessons should be maintained at senior school; this is important not just to enable him to access his curriculum but also to support his compromised attention and short-term memory skills.

- Sadiq will need access to an individualized literacy support programme that especially targets his poor decoding, reading fluency and spelling.
- Sadiq will require a differentiated maths curriculum which takes account of his minimal numerical attainments, together with daily one-to-one intervention.
- Sadiq will need access to technological aids and to be given explicit instruction in their application in order to enable him to improve the quality of his written output.
- Sadiq's attention skills to date have been sufficiently supported through in-class provisions though, given the increased attentional and organization demands of senior school, it may be necessary to consider coaching/mentoring support and perhaps also the use of prescription medication.
- Sadiq will require classroom accommodations to be set in place to support, and to compensate for, his poor verbal working memory (to include cueing, repetition, 'chunking' of information, reduced complexity and length of instructions and scaffolding).
- Sadiq will eventually need full accommodations when he takes formal tests and examinations, which could include having questions read to him, extra time, access to a scribe and rest breaks as needed.

Prognosis and outcome

Given the complexity of Sadiq's cognitive/educational profile, his very slow progress in maths and the observation that extreme pre-term children tend to have learning difficulties that persist through to the adult years, statements about prognosis should be guarded and expectations for medium- and long-term outcome kept appropriately conservative. While taking GCSEs is not out of the question for Sadiq, it will be necessary for him to work towards a reduced number of subjects so as not to overload his compromised verbal working memory, attention and processing speed skills. Core subject will need to be taken at 'foundation' level, and options selected according to his emerging strengths and interests. Post-GCSE, Sadiq's EHC Plan should be maintained so that he is able to proceed to a college with high levels of special needs provision.

Summary

- Children born at extreme pre-term are significantly at risk of experiencing a wide range of cognitive and educational difficulties, many of which persist into the adult years.
- Having said that, the outcome for individual children varies a great deal, with one third of extremely premature children having severe and pervasive learning difficulties, one third having mild-to-moderate (and possibly more selective) difficulties, while the remaining third will present with few or even no learning compromises.
- Some pre-term children with localized brain injury show evidence of functional reorganization which results in good language preservation, though other abilities (nonverbal and processing speed in particular) may be diminished through a process of cognitive crowding.
- Many pre-term children require multi-domain assessments and high levels of learning support, specialist interventions and therapeutic input for the duration of their formal schooling.

Closing Comments

The major theme of this book has been to introduce the reader to the concept of multiple deficit models of literacy disorders, though clearly this approach can be applied to a wide range of cognitively based developmental disorders. Over the last twenty years or so, multiple deficit models have taken us a long way from the simplistic single deficit models that have emphasized one-to-one relationships between brain, cognition and behaviour. The difficulty with single deficit models is that they fail to explain why children given the same diagnostic label look very different one from the other. Multiple deficit models enhance our understanding of learning difficulties and offer an explanation for these 'variable profiles' because first, they recognize that literacy disorders (and indeed other developmental disorders too) occur along a continuum of severity, ranging from borderline through mild to moderate and finally to severe. Second, multiple deficit models explain variations in expression and outcome as arising from the interaction of multiple risks; the more risks the child has, the more likely they are to receive a formal diagnosis of literacy disorder. Third, multiple deficit models explain the high incidence of literacy disorders co-occurring alongside other developmental disorders (whether disorders of maths, language, attention or visual motor skill); indeed, co-occurrence with other disorders is the rule rather than the exception. Fourth, multiple deficit models recognize the importance of 'protective factors', some of which may be inherent within the child (for instance, having good language skills or having a resilient temperament) while others may be drawn from the child's learning environment (for instance, having the advantage of a supportive home environment, or access to early high quality intervention); these protective factors increase the probability that the child will have a positive educational outcome. Finally, the 'take away message' from this book is that practitioners need to direct their assessments and interventions in such a way as to take account of dimensionality, co-occurrence, risk versus protective factors and the child's broader learning environment.

How can we best ensure that the multiple deficit approach to assessing and teaching children with literacy disorders eventually comes to influence education policy, so ensuring that it has the broadest possible impact? The government-commissioned Rose Report drew largely on the single deficit model of literacy disorder though it did make some brief references to issues of dimensionality and co-occurrence. What I believe we need is a revision and update of the Report to take into account recent research which has more strongly highlighted the importance of risk and protective factors and to then specify how this knowledge might inform school-based teaching provision, methodologies for early identification, assessment and intervention.

While multiple deficit models have greatly enhanced our understanding of literacy disorders and how they should be assessed and managed, there are still many questions yet to be answered and challenges to be addressed. Let us conclude by looking at a few of these. First, we have seen that while for dyslexic children, reading difficulties can usually be successfully remediated with programmes that systematically train phonological awareness and decoding skill, this is not the case for spelling. Indeed, many children – even those with mild to moderate dyslexia who may progress well in reading – continue to have long-term and often severe spelling problems. Teaching methodologies that take advantage of the greater orthographic regularity of larger sublexical units (like morphemes) may provide some answers; however, we still have a long way to go before we understand how best to teach spelling to dyslexic children. Second, there is the problem of the children with literacy disorders who Joe Torgesen refers to as 'treatment resisters'. These children appear to make very slow progress in response to what is often high-quality and appropriately targeted intervention. While we may reasonably surmise that treatment resisters are likely to be those children who have severe underlying deficits, additional co-occurring difficulties (which sometimes go unrecognized) and perhaps also fewer cognitive resources to draw on by way of compensation, we still need to address the issue of how best to teach them and to accommodate for their persisting difficulties. Maintaining intervention programmes beyond primary school and well into the secondary school years, closely monitoring the child's progress and making adjustments to teaching programmes as needed, teaching to identified 'strengths', and encouraging children to take maximum advantage of technological aids may provide some answers; clearly, however, such children, who often become increasingly disengaged from learning, remain a considerable challenge for parents and teachers. Finally, little research attention has been paid to personality-based protective factors inherent in the child which may improve educational outcome for children with literacy disorders. Importantly, these centre around temperament characteristics such as resilience, emotional stability, high frustration tolerance and ease of motivating, and perhaps also more cognitively related features like organizational ability. Children who have naturally high levels of these protective factors will likely make greater progress because they are motivated, persistent, well organized and committed. The challenge for teachers and parents though is how to best manage children who do not have these positive qualities and who are likely to 'give up at the first hurdle', disengage from learning and become highly avoidant. Such children are undoubtedly at risk for later mental health problems, which for some may be evident as internalized difficulties such as anxiety and depression and for others externalized problems such as aggressive and anti-social behaviours.

Literacy disorders are complex conditions for which a multiple deficit approach has answered many questions. With the continued commitment on the part of researchers, practitioner psychologists and speech and language therapists, teachers and parents, it is hoped that the remaining questions raised here will eventually be answered. The goal of all of us working with children who have literacy disorders is to make school-based learning a positive experience for them so that their educational outcomes are maximized and their self-esteem kept intact.

References

Addacus (2017) www.addacus.co.uk

Altman, G. (1997) *The Ascent of Babel.* Oxford: Oxford University Press.

American Psychiatric Association (2013) *Diagnostic and Statistical Manual of Mental Disorders (DSM) V.* Washington, DC: APA.

Ayres, J. (1972) *Sensory Integration and Learning Disorders.* Los Angeles, CA: Western Psychological Services.

Barnett, A., Henderson, S., Scheib, B. and Schulz, J. (2007) *Detailed Assessment of Speed of Handwriting.* London: Pearson Education.

Beck, I.L., McKeown, M.G. and Kucan, L. (2002) *Bringing Words to Life: Robust Vocabulary Instruction.* New York: Guilford Press.

Beery, K., Beery, N. and Buktenica, N. (2010) *Developmental Test of Visual-Motor-Integration, Sixth Edition (Beery VMI).* London: Pearson.

Bierman, K.L., Welsh, J.A., Heinrichs, B.S., Nix, R.L. and Mathis, E.T. (2015) 'Helping Head Start parents promote their children's kindergarten adjustment: The research-based developmentally informed parent program.' *Child Development 86,* 1877–1891.

Bishop, D. (2003) *Children's Communication Checklist, 2nd edition (CCC-2).* London: Pearson.

Bishop, D.V.M. (2006) 'Developmental cognitive genetics: How psychology can inform genetics and vice versa.' *Quarterly Journal of Experimental Psychology 59,* 1153–1168.

Bishop, D.V.M. (2017) 'The STEP Physical Literacy Programme: Have we been here before?' Accessed on 20 April 2020 at http://deevybee.blogspot.com/2017/07/the-step-physical-literacy-programme.html.

Bishop, D.V. and Adams, C. (1990) 'A prospective study of the relationship between specific language impairment, phonological disorders and reading retardation.' *Journal of Child Psychology and Psychiatry 31,* 1027–1050.

Bishop, D.V.M., North, T. and Donlan, C. (1996) 'Nonword repetition as a behavioural marker for inherited language impairment.' *Journal of Child Psychology and Psychiatry 37,* 391–403.

Bowey, J. (1995) 'Socioeconomic status differences in pre-school phonological sensitivity and first-grade reading achievement.' *Journal of Educational Psychology 41,* 476–478.

Bowyer-Crane, C., Fricke, S., Schaefer B., Mullard, G. and Hulme, C. (unpublished manuscript) 'Oral language intervention for children learning English as an additional language and monolingual children with language weaknesses.'

Bowyer-Crane, C., Snowling, M.J., Duff, F., Fieldsend, E. *et al.* (2008) 'Improving early language skills: Differential effects of an oral language intervention and a phonology with reading intervention with language delayed young children.' *Journal of Child Psychology and Psychiatry 49*, 422–432.

Bradley, L. (1981) 'The organisation of motor patterns for spelling: An effective remedial strategy for backward readers.' *Developmental Medicine and Child Neurology 23*, 83–91.

Bradley, L. and Bryant, P.E. (1983) 'Categorising sounds and learning to read: A causal connection.' *Nature 301*, 419–521.

Breeman, L.D, Jaekel, J. and Baumann, N. (2015) 'Preterm cognitive function into adulthood.' *Pediatrics 136*. doi:10.1542/peds.2015–0608.

Brooks, G. (2016) *What Works for Children and Young People with Literacy Difficulties? The Effectiveness of Intervention Schemes* (5th edn). Sheffield: Dyslexia-SpLD Trust. Accessed on 20 April 2020 at www.helenarkell.org.uk/documents/files/What-works-for-children-and-young-people-with-literacy-difficulties-5th-edition.pdf.

Burgoyne, K., Gardner, R., Whiteley, H., Snowling, M.J. and Hulme, C. (2018) 'Evaluation of a parent-delivered early language enrichment programme: Evidence from a randomised controlled trial.' *Journal of Child Psychology and Psychiatry 59*, 545–555.

Butterworth, B. (2003) *Dyscalculia Screener.* London: GL Assessment.

Byrne, B. (1998) *The Foundation of Literacy: The Child's Acquisition of the Alphabetic Principle.* Hove: Psychology Press.

Byrne, B. and Fielding-Barnsley, R. (1989) 'Phonemic awareness and letter knowledge in the child's acquisition of the alphabetic principle.' *Journal of Educational Psychology 81*, 313–321.

Cain, K., Oakhill, J. and Elbro, C. (2003) 'The ability to learn new word meanings from context by school-age children with and without language comprehension difficulties.' *Journal of Child Language 30*, 681–694.

Caravolas, M., Lervag, A., Mousikou, P., Efrin, C. *et al.* (2012) 'Common patterns of prediction of literacy development in different alphabetic orthographies.' *Psychological Science 23*, 678–686.

Carroll, J.M., Bowyer-Crane, C., Duff, F., Hulme, C. and Snowling, M.J. (2011) *Developing Language and Literacy.* Nuffield Foundation. Chichester: Wiley-Blackwell.

Cassar, M., Trieman, R., Moats, L., Pollo, T. and Kessler, B. (2005) 'How do the spellings of children with dyslexia compare with those of non-dyslexic children?' *Reading and Writing 18*, 27–49.

Catts, H.W., Adlof, S. and Weismer, S. (2006) 'Language deficits in poor comprehenders: A case for the Simple View of reading.' *Journal of Speech, Language and Hearing Research 49*, 278–293.

Chinn, S. (2009) *What to Do When You Can't Learn the Times Tables.* London: Egon Publishers.

Chinn, S. (2016) *The Trouble with Maths: A Practical Guide to Helping Learners with Numeracy Difficulties.* London: Taylor and Francis.

Clarke, P., Snowling, M., Truelove, E. and Hulme, C. (2010) 'Ameliorating children's reading comprehension difficulties: A randomised controlled trial.' *Psychological Science 21*, 1106–1116.

Clarke, P., Truelove, E., Hulme, C. and Snowling, M. (2014) *Developing Reading Comprehension.* Chichester: Wiley Blackwell.

Conners, K. (2008) *Conners 3rd Edition.* London: Pearson.

Conners, K. (2014) *Conners Continuous Auditory Test of Attention, CATA*. London: Pearson.

Conti-Ramsden, G., Botting, N. and Faragher, B. (2001) 'Psycholinguistic markers for Specific Language Impairment, SLI.' *Journal of Child Psychology and Psychiatry 42*, 741–748.

Cooper, M., Hammerton, G., Collishaw, S., Langley, K. *et al.* (2018) 'Investigating late-onset ADHD: A population cohort investigation.' *Journal of Child Psychology and Psychiatry 59*, 1105–1113.

Cunningham, A. and Stanovich, K. (1997) 'Early reading acquisition and its relation to reading experience and ability 10 years later.' *Developmental Psychology 33*, 934–935.

Daley, D., van der Oord, S., Ferrin, M., Danckaerts, M. *et al.* (2014) 'Behavioral interventions in attention-deficit/hyperactivity disorder: A meta-analysis of randomized controlled trials across multiple outcome domains'. *Journal of American Academy of Child and Adolescent Psychiatry 53*, 835–847.

DeFries, J.C., Alarcon, M. and Olson, R.K. (1997) 'Genetic Aetiologies of Reading and Spelling Deficits: Developmental Differences.' In C. Hulme and M. Snowling (eds) *Dyslexia: Biology, Cognition and Intervention*. London: Whurr Publishers.

Devine, T.G. (1981) *Teaching Study Skills: A Guide for Teachers*. Boston, MA: Allyn and Bacon.

Dilnot, J., Hamilton, L., Maughan, B. and Snowling, M. (2017) 'Child and environmental risk factors predicting readiness for learning in children at high risk of dyslexia.' *Development and Psychopathology 29*, 233–244.

Dowker, A. (2016) 'An independent evaluation of the effectiveness of Dynamo Maths.' www.dynamomaths.co.uk/evidence.

Dubicka B., Martin, J. and Frith, J. (2019) 'Screen time, social media and developing brains: A cause for good or corrupting young minds?' *Child and Adolescent Mental Health 24*, 203–204.

Duff, F., Reen, G., Plunkett, K. and Nation, K. (2015) 'Do infant vocabulary skills predict school-age language and literacy outcomes?' *Journal of Child Psychology and Psychiatry 56*, 848–856.

Dynamo Maths (2013) www.dynamomaths.co.uk

Elliott, C.D. and Smith, P. (2011) *British Abilities Scales III*. UK: GL Assessment.

Elliott, J. and Grigorenko, E. (2014) *The Dyslexia Debate*. New York: Cambridge University Press.

Feifer, S.G. (2016a) *Feifer Assessment of Reading (FAR)*. Oxford: Hogrefe.

Feifer, S.G. (2016b) *Feifer Assessment of Mathematics (FAM)*. Oxford: Hogrefe.

Frith, U. (1997) 'Brain, Mind and Behaviour in Dyslexia.' In C. Hulme and M. Snowling (eds) *Dyslexia: Biology, Cognition and Intervention*. London: Whurr Publishers.

Gathercole, S., Baddeley, A. and Willis, C. (1991) 'Differentiating phonological memory and awareness of rhyme: Reading and vocabulary development in children.' *British Journal of Psychology 82*, 387–406.

Gathercole, S. and Packiam-Alloway, T. (2008) *Working Memory and Learning: A Practical Guide for Teachers*. London: Sage.

Gayan J. and Olson R.K. (1999) 'Genetic and environmental influences on individual differences in IQ, phonological awareness, word recognition, phonemic and orthographic decoding'. Poster presented at the meeting of the Society for the Scientific Study of Reading. Montreal, Canada.

Gersten, R., Chard, D., Madhavi, J., Baker, S., Morphy, P. and Flojo, J. (2009) 'Mathematics instruction for students with learning disabilities: A meta-analysis of instructional components.' *Review of Educational Research 79*, 1202–1242.

Geva, E. and Wiener, J. (2015) *Psychological Assessment of Culturally and Linguistically Diverse Children and Adolescents: A Practitioners' Approach.* New York: Springer Verlag.

Gillingham, A.M. and Stillman, B.U. (1956) *Reading, Spelling and Oenmanship* (5th edn). New York: Sackett and Wilhelms.

Giola, G.A., Isquith, P.K. and Guy, S.C. (2015) *Brief Rating Inventory of Executive Function 2 (BRIEF2).* Oxford: Hogrefe.

Glutting, J., Adams, W. and Sheslow, D. (2000) *Wide Range Intelligence Test, WRIT.* Oxford: Pearson.

Golding, J., Pembrey, M., Jones, R. and ALSPAC Team (2002) 'ALSPAC – The Avon longitudinal study of parents and children.' *Paediatric and Perinatal Epidemiology 15*, 74–87.

Gooch, D., Hulme, C., Nash, P. and Snowling, M. (2014) 'Comorbidities in preschool children at family risk of dyslexia.' *Journal of Child Psychology and Psychiatry 55*, 237–246.

Gooch, D., Snowling, M. and Hulme, C. (2011) 'Time perception, phonological skills and executive function in children with dyslexia and/or ADHD symptoms.' *Journal of Child Psychology and Psychiatry 52*, 195–203.

Gough, P.B. and Tunmer. W.E. (1986) 'Decoding, reading and reading disability.' *Remedial and Special Education 7*, 6–10.

Goodman, R. (2007) 'The Strengths and Difficulties Questionnaire: A research note.' *Journal of Child Psychology and Psychiatry 31*, 581–586.

Goswami, U. (1990) 'A special link between rhyming skills and the use of orthographic analogies by beginning readers.' *Journal of Child Psychology and Psychiatry 31*, 301–311.

Goswami, U. and Bryant, P.E. (1990) *Phonological Skills and Learning to Read.* London: Erlbaum Associates.

Griffiths, Y.M. and Snowling, M.J. (2002) 'Predictors of exception word and nonword reading in dyslexic children: The severity hypothesis.' *Journal of Educational Psychology 94*, 34–43.

Grigorenko, E.L. (2001) 'Developmental dyslexia: An update on genes, brains and environment.' *Journal of Child Psychology and Psychiatry 42*, 91–125.

Harris, K.R., Graham, S., Mason, L. and Friedlander, B. (2008) *Powerful Writing Strategies for All Students.* Baltimore, MD: Paul Brooks Publishing.

Hatcher, P., Duff, F. and Hulme, C. (2014) *Sound Linkage.* Chichester: Wiley Blackwell.

Hatcher, P., Hulme, C. and Ellis, A.W. (1994) 'Ameliorating early reading failure by integrating the teaching of reading and phonological skills: The Phonological Linkage hypothesis.' *Child Development 65*, 41–57.

Hayiou-Thomas, M.E., Carroll, J.M., Leavett, R., Hulme, C. and Snowling, M.J. (2017) 'When does speech sound disorder matter for literacy? The role of disordered speech errors, co-occurring language impairment and family risk of dyslexia.' *Journal of Child Psychology and Psychiatry 58*, 197–205.

Heath, S.M., Hogben, J.H. and Clark, C.D. (1999) 'Auditory temporal processing in disabled readers with and without oral language delay.' *Journal of Child Psychology and Psychiatry 40*, 637–647.

Hecht, S.A., Burgess, S.R., Wagner, R.K. and Rashotte, C.A. (2000) 'Exploring social class differences in growth of reading skills from the beginning of kindergarten through fourth grade: The role of phonological awareness, rate of access and print knowledge.' *Reading and Writing: An Interdisciplinary Journal 12*, 99–127.

Hindson, B., Byrne, B., Fielding-Barnsley, R., Newman, R., Hine, D.W. and Shankweiler, D. (2005) 'Assessment and early instruction of preschool children at risk for reading disability.' *Journal of Educational Psychology 97*, 687–704.

Hoeft, F., Ueno, T., Reiss, A.L., Meyler, A. *et al.* (2007) 'Prediction of children's reading skills using behavioural, functional and structured neuroimaging measures.' *Behavioural Neuroscience 121*, 602–613.

Hoyt, C.S. (1990) 'Irlen lenses and reading difficulties.' *Journal of Learning Disabilities 23*, 624–626.

Hulme, C., Moll, K. and Brigstocke, S. (2016) *Test of Basic Arithmetic and Numeracy Skills.* Oxford: Oxford University Press.

Hulme, C. and Snowling, M. (1992) 'Deficits in output phonology: An explanation of reading failure?' *Cognitive Neuropsychology 9*, 47–72.

Hulme, C. and Snowling, M.J. (2009) *Developmental Disorders of Language, Learning and Cognition.* Chichester: Wiley Blackwell.

Jaekel, J., Wolke, D. and Bartmann, P. (2013) 'Poor attention rather than hyperactivity/impulsivity predicts academic achievement in very preterm and full-term adolescents.' *Psychological Medicine 43*, 183–196.

Jamieson, C. and Jamieson, J. (2006) *Manual for Testing and Teaching Spelling.* London: Wiley.

Jensen, P.S., Arnold, L.E., Swanson, J.M., Vitiello, B. *et al.* (2007) '3-year follow up of the NIMH MTA study.' *Journal of the American Academy of Child and Adolescent Psychiatry 46*, 989–1002.

Johnson, S., Hollis, C., Kochhar, P., Hennessy, E., Wolke, D. and Marlowe, N. (2010) 'Autistic spectrum disorders in extremely preterm children.' *The Journal of Pediatrics 156*, 525–531.

Johnson, S., Strauss, Gilmore, C., Jaekel, J., Marlowe, N. and Wolke, D. (2016) 'Learning disabilities among extremely preterm children without neurosensory impairment: Comorbidity, neuropsychological profiles and scholastic outcome.' *Early Human Development 103*, 69–75.

Johnson, S., Wolke, D., Hennessy, E. and Marlow, N. (2011) 'Educational outcomes in extremely preterm children: Neuropsychological correlates and predictors of attainment.' *Developmental Neuropsychology 36*, 74–95.

Krafnik, A., Flowers, D., Napoliello, E. and Eden, G. (2011) 'Gray matter volume changes following reading intervention in dyslexia children.' *NeuroImage 57*, 733–741.

Landerl, L., Fussenegger, B., Moll, K. and Willburger, E. (2009) 'Dyslexia and dyscalculia: Two learning disorders with different cognitive profiles.' *Journal of Experimental Child Psychology 103*, 309–324.

Landerl, K. and Moll, K. (2010) 'Co-morbidity of learning disorders: Prevalence and familial transmission.' *Journal of Child Psychology and Psychiatry 51*, 287–294.

Likierman, H. and Muter, V. (2006) *Prepare Your Child for School.* London: Vermilion Press.

Likierman, H. and Muter, V. (2008) *Top Tips for Starting School.* London: Vermilion Press.

Lonigan, C.J., Burgess, S.R. and Schatschneider, C. (2018) 'Examining the simple view of reading with elementary school children: Still simple after all these years.' *Remedial and Special Education 39*, 260–273.

Lonigan, C.J., Schatschneider, C. and Westberg, L. (2008) 'Impact of code-focused interventions on young children's early literacy skills.' In *Developing Early Literacy: In SREE Conference Abstract Template Report A-1 of the National Early Literacy Panel.* Washington, DC: National Institute for Literacy.

Madzwamuse, S.E., Baumann, N. and Jaekel, J. (2014) 'Neuro-cognitive performance of very preterm or very low birth weight adults at 26 years.' *Journal of Child Psychology and Psychiatry 56*, 857–864.

Manly, T., Anderson, V., Crawford, J. and Nimmo-Smith, I. (2016) *Test of Everyday Attention for Children 2 (TEA-Ch 2).* London: Pearson.

Marlow, N., Wolke, D., Bracewell, M. and Samara, M. (2005) 'Neurologic and developmental disability at six years of age after extremely preterm birth.' *The New England Journal of Medicine 352*, 9–19.

Martin, N., Piek, J.P. and Hay D. (2006) 'DCD and ADHD: A genetic study of their shared aetiology.' *Human Movement Science 25*, 110–124.

Maughan, B. (2013) 'Better by design: Why randomized controlled trials are the building blocks of evidence-based practice.' *Journal of Child Psychology and Psychiatry 54*, 1–5.

Maughan, B., Messer, J., Collishaw, S., Pickles, A. *et al.* (2009) 'Persistence of literacy problems: spelling in adolescence and at mid-life.' *Journal of Child Psychology and Psychiatry 50*, 839–901.

McArthur, G., Eve, P., Jones, K., Banales, E. *et al.* (2012) 'Phonics training for English-speaking poor readers.' Accessed on 21 April 2020 at www.ncbi. nlm.nih.gov/pmc/articles/PMC6517252

McGrath, L.M., Pennington, B.F., Shanahan, M.A., Santerre-Lemmon *et al.* (2011) 'A multiple deficit model of reading disability an attention deficit/hyperactivity disorder: Searching for shared cognitive deficits.' *Journal of Child Psychology and Psychiatry 52*, 547–557.

McPhillips, M., Hepper, P. and Mulhern, G. (2000) 'Effects of replicating primary-reflex movements on specific reading difficulties in children: A randomised double-blind controlled trial.' *Lancet 355*, 537–541.

Melby-Lervåg, M. and Hulme, C. (2013) 'Is working memory training effective? A meta-analytic review.' *Developmental Psychology 49*, 270–291.

Meyers, J.E. and Meyers, K.R. (1996) *Rey Complex Figure Test and Recognition Trial.* Oxford: Hogrefe.

Mody, M., Studert-Kennedy, M. and Brady, S. (1997) 'Speech perception deficits in poor readers: Auditory processing or phonological coding?' *Journal of Experimental Child Psychology 58*, 112–123.

Moll, K., Landerl, K., Snowling, M.J. and Schulte-Korne, G. (2019) 'Understanding comorbidity of learning disorder: Task dependent estimates of prevalence.' *Journal of Child Psychology and Psychiatry 60*, 286–294.

Moll, K., Snowling, M.J., Gobel, S.M. and Hulme, C. (2015) 'Early language and executive skills predict variations in number and arithmetic skills in children at family risk and typically developing controls.' *Learning and Instruction 38*, 53–62.

Moody, S. (2004) *Dyslexia: A Teenager's Guide.* London: Vermilion.

Muter, V. and Diethelm, K. (2001) 'The contribution of phonological skills and letter knowledge to early reading development in a multilingual population.' *Language Learning 51*, 187–219.

Muter, V. and Likierman, H. (2008) *Dyslexia: A Parent's Guide to Dyslexia, Dyspraxia and Other Learning Difficulties*. London: Vermilion Press.

Muter, V., Hulme, C., Snowling, M.J. and Stevenson, J. (2004) 'Phonemes, rimes, vocabulary and grammatical skills as foundations of early reading development: Evidence from a longitudinal study.' *Developmental Psychology 40*, 663–681.

Muter, V., Hulme, C, Snowling, M.J. and Taylor, S. (1998) 'Segmentation not rhyming predicts early progress in learning to read.' *Journal of Experimental Child Psychology 71*, 3–27.

Muter, V. and Snowling, M.J. (1998) 'Concurrent and longitudinal predictors of reading: The role of metalinguistic and short-term memory skills.' *Reading Research Quarterly 33*, 320–337.

Nash, H.M., Hulme, C., Gooch, D. and Snowling, M. (2013) 'Pre-school language profiles of children at family risk of dyslexia: Continuities with specific language impairment.' *Journal of Child Psychology and Psychiatry 54*, 958–968.

Nation, K., Adams, J.W., Bowyer-Crane, C. and Snowling, M. (1999) 'Working memory deficits in poor comprehenders reflect underlying language impairments.' *Journal of Experimental Child Psychology 73*, 139–158.

Nation, K., Clarke, P., Marshall, C. and Durand, M. (2004) 'Hidden language impairments in children: Parallels between poor reading comprehension and specific language impairment?' *Journal of Speech, Language and Hearing Research 47*, 199–211.

Nation, K., Cocksey, J., Taylor, J. and Bishop, D. (2010) 'A longitudinal investigation of early reading and language skills in children with poor reading comprehension.' *Journal of Child Psychology and Psychiatry 51*, 1031–1039.

Nation, K. and Snowling, M.J. (1998) 'Semantic processing and development of word recognition skills: Evidence from children with reading comprehension difficulties.' *Journal of Memory and Language 39*, 85–101.

Nation, K., Snowling, M. and Clarke, P. (2007) 'Dissecting the relationship between language skills and learning to read: Semantic and phonological contributions to new vocabulary learning in children with poor reading comprehension.' *Advances in Speech-Language Pathology 9*, 131–139.

Neale, M. (1997) *Neale Analysis of Reading Ability – Revised (NARA II)*. Windsor: NFER-Nelson.

Newbury, D.F., Paracchini, T.S., Scerri, L., Winchester, L. *et al.* (2011) 'Investigation of dyslexia and SLI risk variants in reading- and language-impaired subject.' *Behaviour Genetics 41*, 90–104.

Nicolson, R., Fawcett, A. and Dean, P. (2001) 'Developmental dyslexia: The cerebellar deficit hypothesis.' *Trends in Neurosciences 24*, 508–5011.

Numicon (2001) Oxford: Oxford University Press.

Nunes, T. and Bryant, P. (2009) *Children's Reading and Spelling: Beyond the First Steps*. Chichester: Wiley-Blackwell.

Oczkus, L. (2018) *Reciprocal Teaching at Work: Powerful Strategies and Lessons for Improving Reading Comprehension*, (3rd edn). Alexandria, VA: ASCD.

Olofsson, A. and Lundberg, L. (1985) 'Evaluation of long-term effects of phonemic awareness training in kindergarten.' *Scandinavian Journal of Psychology 26*, 21–34.

Paradise, J.L., Dollaghan, C.Q., Campbell, T.F., Feldman, H. *et al.* (2000) 'Language, speech sound production and cognition in three-year-old children in relation to otitis media in their first three years of life.' *Pediatrics 105*, 1119–1130.

Pennington, B. (2009) *Diagnosing Learning Disorders: A Neuropsychological Framework*. New York: Guilford Press.

Pinker, S. (1994) *The Language Instinct: The New Science of Language and Mind*. London: Penguin Press.

Polatajko, H.J. and Mandich, A.D. (2004) *Enabling Occupation in Children: The Cognitive Orientation to Daily Occupational Performance (CO-OP) Approach*. Ottawa: CAOT Publications.

Polatajko, H.J. and Cantin, N. (2010) 'Exploring the effectiveness of occupational therapy interventions, other than the sensory integration approach, with children and adolescents experiencing difficulty processing and integrating sensory information.' *American Journal of Occupational Therapy 64*, 415–429.

Poulsen, G., Wolke, D. and Kurinczuk, J. (2013) 'Gestational age and cognitive ability in early childhood: A population-based cohort study.' *Paediatric and Perinatal Epidemiology 27*, 371–379.

Price, G. and Ansari, D. (2013) 'Dyscalculia: characteristics, causes and treatments.' *Numeracy 6*, 1–16.

Rack, J., Snowling, M.J. and Olson, R. (1992) 'The nonword reading deficit in dyslexia: A review.' *Reading Research Quarterly 27*, 28–53.

Raine, A., Portnoy, J., Liu, J., Mahoomed, T. and Hibbeln, J.R. (2015) 'Reduction in behaviour problems with omega-3 supplementation in children aged 8–16 years: A randomized, double blind, placebo-controlled, parallel group trial.' *Journal of Child and Adolescent Psychiatry 56*, 509–520.

Ramus, F., Altarelli, I., Jednorog, K., Zhao, J. and Scotto di Covella, L. (2018) 'Neuroanatomy of developmental dyslexia: Pitfalls and promise.' *Neuroscience and Behavioural Reviews 84*, 434–452.

Ramus, F., Pidgeon E. and Frith, U. (2003) 'The relationship between motor control and phonology in dyslexic children.' *Journal of Child Psychology and Psychiatry 44*, 712–722.

Rasanen, P., Salminen, J. Wilson, A.J., Aunio, P. and Dehaene, S. (2009) 'Computer-assisted interventions for children with low numeracy skills.' *Cognitive Development 24*, 450–472.

Reynolds, D., Nicolson, R. and Hambly, H. (2003) 'Evaluation of an exercise-based treatment for children with reading difficulties.' *Dyslexia 9*, 48–71.

Ricketts, J., Sperring, R. and Nation, K. (2014) 'Educational attainment in poor comprehenders.' *Frontiers in Psychology 5*, 1–11.

Rose, J. (2009) *Identifying and Teaching Children and Young People with Dyslexia and Literacy Difficulties*. An independent report from Sir Jim Rose to the Secretary of State for Children, Schools and Families. Nottingham: DCSF.

Rubin, H. and Turner, A. (1989) 'Linguistic awareness skills in grade one children in a French immersion setting.' *Reading and Writing: An Interdisciplinary Journal 1*, 73–86.

Rucklidge, J.J., Eggleston, M.J.F., Johnstone, J.M., Darling, K. and Frampton, C.M. (2018) 'Vitamin-mineral treatment improves aggression and emotional regulation in children with ADHD: A fully blinded, randomized, placebo-controlled trial.' *Journal of Child Psychology and Psychiatry 59*, 232–246.

Samuels, S.J. (2000) 'Fluency.' In *National Reading Panel, Teaching Children to Read: An Evidence-Based Assessment of the Scientific Research Literature on Reading and its Implications for Reading Instruction, Reports of the Subgroups Sections 3.1–3.43*. Washington, DC: National Institute of Health.

Savage, R., Georgiou, G., Parrila, R. and Maiorino, K. (2018) 'Preventative reading interventions teaching direct mapping of graphemes in texts and set-for-variability aid at-risk learners.' *Scientific Study of Reading 22*, 225–247.

Saygin, Z.M., Norton, E.S., Osher, D.E., Beach, S. *et al.* (2013) 'Tracking the roots of reading ability: White matter volumes and integrity correlate with phonological awareness in prereading and early reading kindergarten children.' *Journal of Neuroscience 33*, 13251–13258.

Scarborough, H. and Dobrich, W. (1994) 'On the efficacy of reading to pre-schoolers.' *Developmental Review 14*, 245–302.

Scerri, T.S., Morris, A.P., Buckingham, L., Newbury, D. *et al.* (2011) 'DCDC2, KIAA0319 and CMIP are associated with reading-related traits.' *Biological Psychiatry 70*, 237–245.

Senechal, M., LeFevre, J., Thomas, E. and Daley, K. (1998) 'Differential effects of home literacy experiences on the development of oral and written language.' *Reading Research Quarterly 33*, 96–116.

Seymour, P.H.K. (2005) 'Early Reading Development in European Orthographies.' In M.J. Snowling and C. Hulme (eds) *The Science of Reading: A Handbook.* Oxford: Blackwell Publishing.

Silani, G., Frith, U., Demonet J-F., Fazio, F. *et al.* (2005) 'Brain abnormalities underlying altered activation in dyslexia: A voxel based morphometry study.' *Brain 128*, 2453–2461.

Simms, V., Gilmore, C., Cragg, L., Marlow, N. *et al.* (2013) 'Mathematics difficulties in extremely preterm children: Evidence of a specific deficit in basic mathematics processing.' *Pediatric Research 73*, 236–244.

Snowling, M.J. (2000) *Dyslexia.* Oxford: Blackwell.

Snowling, M.J. (2009) 'Changing concepts of dyslexia: Nature, treatment and co-morbidity.' *Journal of Child Psychology and Psychiatry.* Accessed on 21 April 2020 at https://onlinelibrary.wiley.com/doi/pdf/10.1111/j.1469-7610.2009.02197.x

Snowling, M.J., Duff, F.J., Nash, H.M. and Hulme, C. (2016) 'Language profiles and literacy outcomes of children with resolving, emerging or persisting language impairments.' *Journal of Child Psychology and Psychiatry 57*, 1360–1369.

Snowling, M.J., Gallagher, A. and Frith, U. (2003) 'Family risk of dyslexia is continuous: Individual differences in the precursors of reading skill.' *Child Development 74*, 358–373.

Snowling, M.J. and Melby-Lervåg, M. (2016) 'Oral language deficits in familial dyslexia: A meta-analysis and review.' *Psychological Bulletin 142*, 498–545.

Snowling, M.J., Muter, V. and Carroll, J. (2007) 'Children at family risk of dyslexia: A follow-up in early adolescence.' *Journal of Child Psychology and Psychiatry 48*, 609–618.

Snowling, M.J., Stothard, S., Clarke, P., Bowyer-Crane, C. *et al.* (2011) *York Assessment of Reading for Comprehension*, (2nd edn). London: GL Assessment.

Solan, H. (1990) 'An appraisal of the Irlen technique of correcting reading disorders using coloured overlays and tinted lenses.' *Journal of Learning Disabilities 23*, 621–623.

Sonuga-Barke, E. (2015) 'Diet and children's behaviour problems: Disentangling urban myth from clinical reality.' *Journal of Child Psychology and Psychiatry 56*, 497–499.

Spencer, M., Quinn, J.M. and Wagner, R.K. (2014) 'Specific reading comprehension disability: Major problem, myth or misnomer?' *Learning Disability: Research and Practice 29*, 3–9.

Spielman, A. (2018) Speech at the Pre-School Learning Alliance Annual Conference, 1 June 2018.

Stackhouse, J. (1982) 'An investigation of reading and spelling performance in speech disordered children.' *British Journal of Disorders of Communication 17*, 53–60.

Stainthorp, R., Powell, D. and Stuart, M. (2013) 'The relationship between rapid naming and word spelling in English.' *Journal of Research in Reading 36*, 371–388.

Stanovich, K.E. and Siegel, L.S. (1994) 'The phenotypic performance profile of reading disabled children: A regression-based test of the phonological-core variable difference model.' *Journal of Educational Psychology 86*, 24–53.

Stevenson, J., Buitelaar, J., Cortese, S., Ferrin, M. *et al.* (2014) 'Research Review: The role of diet in the treatment of attention-deficit/hyperactivity disorder: An appraisal of the evidence on efficacy and recommendations on the design of future studies.' *Journal of Child Psychology and Psychiatry 55*, 416–427.

Stevenson, J., Graham, P., Fredman,G. and McLoughlin, V. (1987) 'A twin study of genetic influences of reading and spelling ability and disability.' *Journal of Child Psychology and Psychiatry 28*, 229–247.

Storebø, O.J., Ramstad, E., Krogh, H.B., Nilausen, T. *et al.* (2015) 'Methylphenidate for children and adolescents with attention deficit hyperactivity disorder (ADHD).' *Cochrane Database of Systematic Reviews 25*. doi: 10.1002/14651858.CD009885.pub2

Stothard, S. and Hulme, C. (1995) 'A comparison of reading comprehension and decoding difficulties in children.' *Journal of Child Psychology and Psychiatry 36*, 399–408.

Strong, G., Torgesen, C., Torgesen, D. and Hulme, C. (2011) 'A systematic meta-analytic review of evidence of the effectiveness of the FastForWord Language Intervention Program.' *Journal of Child Psychology and Psychiatry 52*, 224–235.

Swan, D. and Goswami, U. (1997) 'Phonological awareness deficits in developmental dyslexia and the phonological representations hypothesis.' *Journal of Experimental Child Psychology 60*, 334–353.

Tallal, P. and Piercey, M. (1974) 'Developmental aphasia: Rate of auditory processing and selective impairment of consonant perception.' *Neuropsychologia 12*, 83–93.

Taylor, J. (2002) *Handwriting: A Teacher's Guide.* London: David Fulton Publishers.

Therrien, W. (2004) 'Fluency and comprehension gains as a result of repeated reading: A meta-analysis.' *Remedial and Special Education 25*, 252–261.

Thompson, P., Hulme, C., Nash, H, Gooch, D., Hayiou-Thomas, E. and Snowling, M.J. (2015) 'Developmental dyslexia; predicting individual risk.' *Journal of Child Psychology and Psychiatry 56*, 976–987.

Torgesen, J.K., Wagner, R.K. and Rashotte, C.A. (2012) *Test of Word Reading Efficiency, 2nd edition (TOWRE 2)*. Austin, TX: Pro-Ed.

Tunmer, W.E. (1989) 'The Role of Language-Related Factors in Reading Disability.' In D. Shankweiler and I.Y. Liberman (eds) *Phonology and Reading Disability: Solving the Reading Puzzle*. IARLDM. Ann Arbor, MI: University of Michigan Press.

Tunmer, W.E. and Chapman, J.W. (2012) 'The simple view of reading redux: Vocabulary knowledge and the independent components hypothesis.' *Journal of Learning Disabilities 45*, 453–466.

Uljarević, M., Katsos, N., Hudry, K. and Gibson, J. (2016) 'Practitioner review: Multilingualism and developmental disorders – an overview of recent research and discussion of clinical implications.' *Journal of Child Psychology and Psychiatry 57*, 1205–1217.

Van Ijzendoorn, M.H. and Bus, A.G. (1994) 'Meta-analytic confirmation of the nonword reading deficit in developmental dyslexia.' *Reading Research Quarterly 29*, 266–275.

Van Zuijen, T., Plakas, A., Maassen, B., Maurits, N. and van der Leij, A. (2013) 'Infant ERPs separate children at risk of dyslexia who become good readers from those who become poor readers.' *Developmental Science 16*, 554–563.

Wagner, R.K., Torgesen, J.K. and Rashotte, C.A. (1994) 'The development of reading-related phonological processing abilities: New evidence of bi-directional causality from a latent variable longitudinal study.' *Developmental Psychology 30*, 73–87.

Wagner, R.K., Torgesen, J.K., Rashotte, C.A., Hecht, S.A. *et al.* (1997) 'Changing relations between phonological processing abilities and word-level reading as children develop from beginning to skilled readers: A 5-year longitudinal study.' *Developmental Psychology 33*, 468–479.

Wagner, R.K., Torgesen, J.K., Rashotte, C.A. and Pearson, N. (2013) *Comprehensive Test of Phonological Processing 2 (CTOPP2)*. Austin, TXs: Pro-Ed.

Wechsler, D. (2014) *Wechsler Pre-School and Primary Scale of Intelligence, 4th edition (WPPSI IV)*. London: Pearson.

Wechsler, D. (2016) *Wechsler Intelligence Scale for Children, 5th edition (WISC V)*. London: Pearson.

Wechsler, D. (2017) *Wechsler Individual Achievement Test, 3rd edition (WIAT III)*. London: Pearson.

Wiig, E.H., Secord, W.A. and Semel, E. (2006) *Clinical Evaluation of Language Fundamentals, 4th edition (CELF 4)*. London: Pearson.

Wilkins, A., Evans, B., Brown, J., Busby. A. *et al.* (1994) 'Double-masked placebo-controlled trial of precision spectral filters in children who used coloured overlays.' *Ophthalmic and Physiological Orthoptics 14*, 365–370.

Wilkinson, G.S. and Robertson, G.J. (2017) *Wide Range Achievement Test 5 (WRAT 5)*. London: Pearson.

Wilson, A.J, Revkin, S.K., Cohen, D., Cohen, L. and Dehaene, S. (2006) 'An open trial assessment of "The Number Race", an adaptive computer game for remediation of dyscalculia.' *Behavioural and Brain Functions 2*, 1–16.

Wilson, P. (2005) 'Practitioner review: Approaches to assessment and treatment of children with DCD.' *Journal of Child Psychology and Psychiatry 46*, 806–823.

Wolf, M. and Bowers, P. (1999) 'The double deficit hypothesis for the developmental dyslexias.' *Journal of Educational Psychology 91*, 1–24.

Wolke, D. and Meyer. R. (1999) 'Cognitive status, language attainment, and prereading skills of 6-year-old very preterm children and their peers: The Bavarian Longitudinal Study.' *Developmental Medicine and Child Neurology 41*, 94–109.

Resources

A dozen books on literacy disorders I strongly recommend

Beck, I.L., McKeown, M.G. and Kucan, L. (2002) *Bringing Words to Life: Robust Vocabulary Instruction*. New York: Guilford Press.

Brooks, G. (2016) *What Works for Children and Young People with Literacy Difficulties? The Effectiveness of Intervention Schemes* (5th edn). Sheffield: Dyslexia-SpLD Trust. Accessed on 20 April 2020 at www.helenarkell.org.uk/documents/files/What-works-for-children-and-young-people-with-literacy-difficulties-5th-edition.pdf

Carroll, J.M., Bowyer-Crane, C., Duff, F. *et al.* (2011) *Developing Language and Literacy*. Nuffield Foundation. Chichester: Wiley-Blackwell.

Clarke, P., Truelove, E., Hulme, C. and Snowling, M.J. (2014) *Developing Reading Comprehension*. Chichester: Wiley Blackwell.

Gathercole, S. and Packiam-Alloway, T. (2008) *Working Memory and Learning: A Practical Guide for Teachers*. London: Sage Publishers.

Geva, E. and J. Wiener (2015) *Psychological Assessment of Culturally and Linguistically Diverse children and adolescents: A practitioners' approach*. New York: Springer Verlag.

Hulme, C. and Snowling, M. (2009) *Developmental Disorders of Language, Learning and Cognition*. Chichester: Wiley Blackwell.

Moody, S. (2004) *Dyslexia: A Teenager's Guide*. London: Vermilion Press.

Muter, V. and Likierman, H. (2008) *Dyslexia: A Parent's Guide to Dyslexia, Dyspraxia and Other Learning Difficulties*. London: Vermilion Press.

Nunes, T. and Bryant, P. (2009) *Children's Reading and Spelling: Beyond the First Steps*. Chichester: Wiley-Blackwell.

Pennington, B. (2009) *Diagnosing Learning Disorders: A Neuropsychological Framework*. New York: Guilford Press.

Snowling, M. (2019) *Dyslexia: A Very Short Introduction*. Oxford: Oxford University Press.

Support and resource organizations

British Dyslexia Association (www.bdadyslexia.org.uk) offers advice and support (through a telephone and email helpline) to individuals with dyslexia and their families and employers; it also offers specific services such as assessments and accredited courses.

AFASIC/Association for All Speech Impaired Children (www.afasic.org.uk) provides information, support and advice for individuals who have a speech and/or language disorder and their families; AFASIC has a telephone and email helpline, runs workshops and courses and provides links to access speech and language therapy services.

The Dyscalculia Information Centre (www.dyscalculia.me.uk) provides information to parents and teachers about dyscalculia and offers advice on teaching materials (includes an online shop), though this organization does not have the extensive resources of the other associations listed here.

National Attention Deficit Disorder Information and Support Service, ADDISS (www.addiss.co.uk) offers information, support and advice through their telephone and email helpline, bookstore and conferences and training courses for parents and professionals.

Connections in Mind (www.connectionsinmind.co.uk) provides coaching for independent learning for children and adolescents who have executive and attention problems that impact both academically and behaviourally. It provides a bespoke skill training service to the young person through face-to-face coaching, skype, email and text, and through parent support.

Dyspraxia Foundation (www.dyspraxiafoundation.org.uk) supports and advises individuals with dyspraxia/DCD and their families through their locally based events and workshops, as well as offering a telephone and email helpline resource.

Professional organizations

PATOSS/The professional association for teachers of students with specific learning difficulties (www.patoss-dyslexia.org) specializes in training and supporting teachers of individuals with specific learning difficulties through accredited training and continuing professional development courses: they also provide UK-wide lists of teachers and tutors for individuals and parents to contact.

British Psychological Society/BPS (www.bps.org.uk) is the professional association for chartered clinical and educational psychologists and also neuropsychologists. There is a directory of chartered psychologists which can help members of the public locate a chartered psychologist offering services in their area (note that the Health Care Professions Council HCPC is the regulator for practising psychologists in the UK).

Royal College of Speech and Language Therapists/RCSLT (www.rcslt. org.uk) is the professional body for speech and language therapists in the UK. The Association of Speech and Language Therapists in Independent Practice, ASLTIP (www.asltip.com) provides information and a contact point for members of the public searching for an independent (i.e. private) practising speech and language therapist.

Royal College of Occupational Therapists/RCOT (www.rcot.co.uk) is the professional body for occupational therapists in the UK; there is an online directory to enable members of the public to locate an occupational therapist in their area.

Chartered Society of Physiotherapists/CSP (www.csp.org.uk) is the professional body for chartered physiotherapists in the UK; the society provides information to the public about accessing NHS and private practising physiotherapists in their area.

Royal College of Psychiatrists/RCP (www.rcpsych.ac.uk) is the professional body for child psychiatrists in the UK. Referral to a child psychiatrist at NHS CAMHS (Child and Adolescent Mental Health Services) can be made through the child's and family's GP. The National Online Psychiatry Service (www.psychiatry-uk.com/psychiatry-for-children/) is an example of an online service to the public that can arrange private psychiatric consultation in their area.

Subject Index

Author Index